From S.M.T.
to Eastern Scottish

From S.M.T.
to Eastern Scottish

An 80th Anniversary Story

D. L. G. HUNTER

JOHN DONALD PUBLISHERS LTD.
EDINBURGH

ISBN 0 85976 159 2

Exclusive distribution in the United States of America and Canada by Humanities Press Inc., Atlantic Highlands, NJ 07716, USA.

Printed in Great Britain by Bell & Bain Ltd., Glasgow.

Foreword

Just over eighty years ago, when the first S.M.T. bus moved off from the Mound, few people would have guessed that history was being made. That first journey marked the birth of what has grown to become today's Scottish Bus Group, a truly national organisation with over 9,400 employees, 3,100 buses and an annual turnover of over £150 million.

David Hunter has traced the story of these eighty years in this welcome history of one of the major bus operators in Britain. It describes the buses and the bus routes, but it is also a story of the men whose drive and ambition created a business whose influence has spread far beyond Edinburgh and the Lothians.

Men like William Thomson and Sandy Bracken, who guided S.M.T. from the beginning; and men like the company's more recent general managers. In my own time in the Group, I have been fortunate to work with some of these men, and with distinguished busmen like James Amos, Morris Little and Roddy MacKenzie, all of whom feature in this book.

With the restructuring of Scottish Bus Group in 1985, the Eastern Scottish operating area was redefined to cover Edinburgh and the Lothians, in fact where it started all those years ago. Although the Borders area is now the responsibility of Lowland Scottish, Eastern remains one of the most influential S.B.G. companies, covering such an important part of Scotland. As we enter a new era of deregulated bus services, Eastern is facing up to new challenges and new opportunities of the 1990s and beyond.

I. S. Irwin,
Chairman, Scottish Bus Group.

Preface

As one of the earliest and most important bus companies in the country, the Scottish Motor Traction Co. Ltd. has long deserved to have its history put on record. The late James Amos, many years ago, urged the present writer to do so, and although more than willing, the opportunity was not then available. However, the company's activities in and around its Edinburgh base formed the subject of a chapter in the present writer's *Edinburgh's Transport*, published in 1964 and now out of print. This was not the whole story of course, and an attempt to cover all the company's activities has at last resulted in this book.

I clearly recollect the company's operations on the Queensferry Road from 1918 onwards, and indeed have an earlier recollection of riding into town from Corstorphine in one of the first Maudslay double-deckers in 1913; that curved door was so distinctive. Fortunately I started recording the rolling stock in detail about 1922, and these records have formed the basis of what has appeared here and elsewhere covering the twenties. Those who require fully detailed information on the vehicles may be referred to the fleet lists published by the P.S.V. Circle, though it should be cautioned that there are inaccuracies and omissions in their earlier period.

In common with many of the early bus companies, factual information has been hard to come by; even the company's minute books do not tell us all, and apart from timetables, there seem to be very few documents extant. Much newspaper research has, however, produced a fair picture of events and has shown some other sources sometimes to be inaccurate.

Many have assisted in the provision of information, mostly personal recollection, and of illustrations, and thanks are due to the following: Gavin Booth of the Scottish Transport Group who has considerably enhanced the post-second war rolling stock details and in other matters of the period too, as well as assisting with an adequate selection of illustrations; Robert Beveridge, Sandy Bracken, John Mack and Roderick MacKenzie of Scottish Omnibuses Ltd., and their forerunners; Alex Black (Galashiels), W. W. Black (Silverburn), H. Blake, J. K. D. Blair, Alan Brotchie, Robert Candlish, John Cummings, Alastair Douglas, Robert Grieves, Bill Guthrie, D. C. McMurtrie and T. Swinton Purves. Thanks are also due to Messrs Reid and McLaughlan of the (present) S.M.T. Co. Ltd., W. McGillivray and Mrs Pollock of the Traffic Commissioners Scottish Area office, and to the staffs of the following libraries: the British Newspaper Library at Colindale, the Library of the

Institution of Mechanical Engineers, Cambridge University Library, the public libraries at Birmingham and at Penicuik, and the Scottish Record Office at Edinburgh. Sources of information consulted have included the *Dalkeith Advertiser, Edinburgh Evening News, Edinburgh Evening Dispatch, Midlothian Journal, Musselburgh News, Portobello Advertiser, The Scotsman, Commercial Motor,* and *Motor Traction.*

It is unlikely that any work such as this will be entirely free from error, but it is hoped that this record can be accepted as substantially correct throughout.

The production of the book has been made possible by the interest and assistance of Ian Irwin, Chairman of the Scottish Bus Group, to whom I would record my indebtedness and thanks.

I must also thank John Tuckwell, Donald Morrison and Gordon Angus of John Donald Publishers Ltd. who have with enthusiasm smoothed the way to publication.

Contents

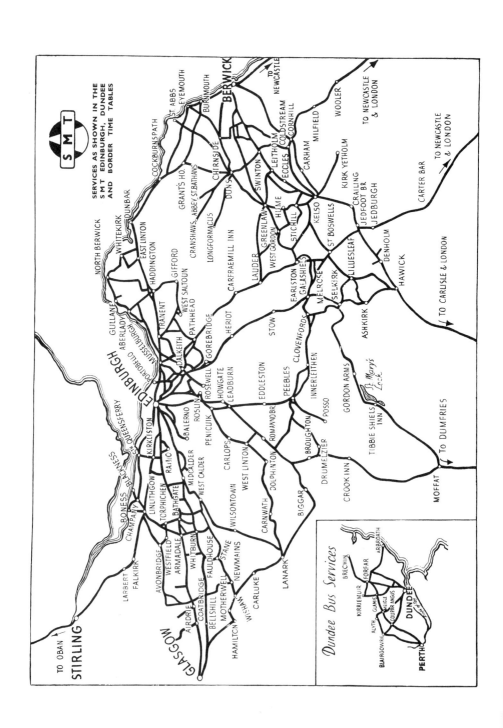

1

The Early Years and the Vehicles of the Period

The year was 1905. Horse buses were still in use in various parts of the country, but with the establishment of electric tramways in many of the larger centres of population, the former were being increasingly regarded as an inadequate means of transport. The motor bus was already on the scene and beginning to show promise as a better alternative, while in Edinburgh small motor wagonettes had been operating successfully between the Post Office and Haymarket since 1898, competing with the capital's ingenious and complex cable tramway system.

Against this background a group of men from Edinburgh and the Lothians proposed to form a company to be called the Scottish Motor Traction Company Limited which would provide public services to the countryside by motor bus. The company were also able to deal in motor vehicles of all kinds including motor boats, and 'to promote generally all methods of Motor Traction or Motor Haulage . . .'. This company was registered on 13 June 1905 with an authorised capital of £50,000, though for the time being only 30,000 £1 shares were offered, and about half of these taken up. The Chairman was the Master of Polwarth and the other directors were R. C. Cowan, J. A. Hood, F. B. Lea, A. J. Paterson and F. McDougal Williams.★ George Oliver, a partner in the accountants' firm of A. & A. Paterson & Oliver, 49 Queen Street, which was the company's registered office, was appointed secretary, and shortly afterwards William J. Thomson, later to become Lord Provost of Edinburgh, was appointed engineer and manager. Hailing from Caithness, he had been trained in the Arrol Johnson motor works and brought good experience with him.

The prospectus issued by the company stated: 'The Directors believe that the Motor Bus has now been so perfected that it is bound at no distant date to entirely supersede the Horse Bus, and they consider that there are many routes throughout Scotland on which it would be more profitable to

★ R. C. Cowan was a director of Alex. Cowan & Sons Ltd., papermakers, Penicuik; J. A. Hood was managing director of the Lothian Coal Company; F. B. Lea was managing director of the Airdrie & Coatbridge Tramways Company and director of the Greenock & Port Glasgow Tramways Company; A. J. Paterson was managing director of A. & A. Paterson & Oliver; and F. McDougal Williams was managing director of James Brown & Co. Ltd., papermakers, Penicuik.

1

run Motor Buses than to construct and maintain Tramways'. The routes over which it was proposed to establish the first services would be from Edinburgh to Barnton and Queensferry, Dalkeith and Eskbank, Loanhead and Lasswade, Slateford, Colinton and Juniper Green via Fountainbridge, Roslin, Glencorse and Penicuik via Morningside, Corstorphine and Kirkliston, but it is clear that a much wider field was envisaged for development. The promoters drew attention to the success of several similar ventures in England, quoting a report from their consulting engineers, Carmichael & Sherman of 14 Queen Street. With their help a specification for a vehicle to meet the requirements which were considered necessary had already been drawn up, and on 6, 7 and 9 June contracts had been entered into with three firms for the supply of vehicles which it was hoped would prove suitable. These requirements included a speed of 12 mph on level and 3 mph on a 1 in 6 gradient.

The tenders accepted were for five double-deck Durkopp buses from the Motor Car Emporium, London, at £885 each; five double-deck Maudslays, and two 16 hp Lifu steam-propelled buses from Morton of Wishaw. Delivery in August and September was called for with a penalty in default. Premises in Lauriston Street were bought for a garage to hold twenty vehicles.

The shareholders were told at a meeting on 1 November that twelve buses had been ordered, but none meeting the specification had yet been delivered. They also heard that two steam-propelled 'charabancs' had been operated around Bathgate to test the traffic potential. One route they ran was from Bathgate to Armadale. They had been registered in West Lothian by the S.M.T. Co. in September as SX32 and SX33. Although their experimental use was to continue for a few weeks more, they were then discarded on account of lack of power and difficulties with the boiler gases. A Belhaven and a Ducommon are said to have been tried also, perhaps in replacement of these, but they were not accepted either. The first Durkopp had also arrived on 7 October, but this failed in its hill-climbing performance, so the company repudiated its contract with the Motor Car Emporium, who thereupon raised an action which resulted in the company agreeing to accept the one Durkopp only at a reduced price of £810. It was disposed of as quickly as possible. So the company had perforce to await the delayed arrival of the Maudslays.

The first Maudslay was exhibited at the Motor Show in London in late November and was subsequently driven up from Coventry, arriving in Edinburgh on 24 December. Further trial on 26 December showed this machine to be so satisfactory that the company started the first public service between the Mound and Corstorphine on 1 January 1906, with this

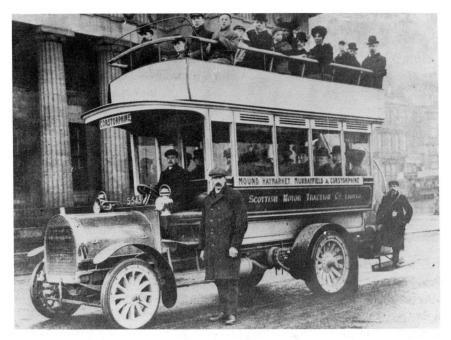

The start of it all: the company's first Maudslay bus about to start its first journey from the Mound, Edinburgh, to Corstorphine, 1 January 1906.   DLGH Collection.

one bus. An hourly service was provided, taking half an hour each way, and the fare was 3d. The press took little interest in the event, but of course Mr Thomson was there in person. The driver's name was Rollinson and the conductor was Benjamin Thomson, well known in later years as Inspector 'Wee Ben'. He has related how the Master of Polwarth insisted on getting the first ticket from him although he had been instructed not to take his fare.

The second Maudslay arrived early in March, and the other three plus a sixth one soon followed. The company used the Edinburgh licence number as their fleet number; these first six Maudslays were thus Nos. 52-57, with registration numbers S543-8. Possibly the Durkopp had been No. 51. The bodies, said to be by the Gloucester Carriage Company, were of orthodox pattern for the period, seating sixteen inside on longitudinal cane seats and eighteen on 'garden' seats upstairs. A curved hinged door was provided to the saloon. The engine was rated at 30/40 hp with chain drive to the artillery-type wheels. A 'sprag' brake could be dropped on the ground under the middle of the bus to prevent a run-back downhill should the vehicle stall. The colour scheme was green with cream panels, and the company's title was shown in full on the sides. Destination was shown on

A Maudslay charabanc at Carlops on the Carlops Circular Tour. Note the conductor, who would issue tickets to intermediate point to point passengers.   R. Grieves Collection

a small board hung from the driver's canopy, and on a route board below the side windows. Acetylene lighting was fitted.

With these further buses now delivered, two services were advertised to commence on the Queensferry Road on 21 April 1906, with a bus running from the Mound to South Queensferry at 10.00 am, 12.00, 2.00, 4.00 and 6.00 pm at a fare of 1/-. The other service, every 45 minutes from 9.45 am to 9.45 pm, turned off the Queensferry Road at Barnton and ran to the village of Cramond. The fare was 6d. and the 9.45 pm bus did not run on Sundays. It is believed however that a bus was running on the Cramond route for three or four weeks before the advertised date of 21 April. On 23 April the stance for the Corstorphine bus was changed to the Waverley Steps. A timetable and fares leaflet was issued regularly, and in June there was an earlier journey to Cramond at 8.15 am and three trips to Davidson's Mains only at 7.45, 8.40 and 9.30 am. These did not run on Sundays, but on Saturdays and Sundays the Cramond route now ran half-hourly till 10.15 pm. There was also a late trip to South Queensferry on Wednesdays at 10.30 pm for which 1/3 was charged. The Corstorphine service was also now half-hourly from 8.00 am to 10.00 pm and 10.30 pm on Saturdays, the Sunday service starting at 10.00 am.

Still more Maudslays were now on order, and the seventh bus arrived in the autumn of 1906. This and subsequent ones had rather wider straight-sided bodies with transverse seats in the saloon and a sliding door. They

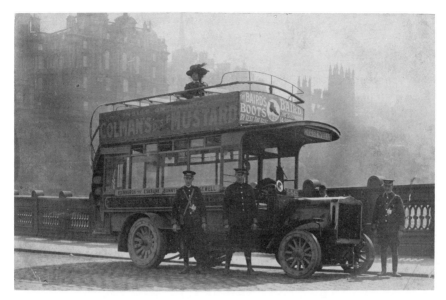

This Maudslay on the Rosewell route has a Stagg & Robson body and also a Thomson radiator.   Gavin Booth Collection

This view of the Fountainbridge, Edinburgh, garage was probably taken when it was opened in 1911. The charabanc nearest the camera on the right is a Rykneild and beyond it are two Rykneilds with double-deck bus bodies. First on the left is Maudslay charabanc No. 66 and behind it another Rykneild charabanc. Inspector John McDonald in the foreground on the right.   S.M.T. Co.

One of the first Lothians put into service, No. 91, with short low roof cab and radiator cowl. Note the spacing of the lettering and the garter-monogram.   DLGH Collection

seated eighteen inside and nineteen upstairs and are believed to have been by a different bodybuilder in London. For the last two of the initial fleet of thirteen, 32-seat 'toastrack' charabanc bodies with a wood roof and a windscreen behind the driver were also provided. A further three Maudslays arrived in 1909, bringing the total to sixteen. The numbers were:

58	bus	S549	1906	66	charabanc	S839	1907
59	bus	S550	1906	67	charabanc	S840	1907
60	bus	S551	1906	51	charabanc	S1378	1909
64	bus	S552?	1906	90	bus	S1379	1909
65	bus	S781	1907	99	charabanc	S1380	1909

There were also four or five Maudslay lorries, some of which seem to have carried bus bodies on occasion. S1391 was one of them. Two Maudslays were later fitted with a larger type of radiator designed by Mr Thomson. These were S543 and S545. S551 had a destination screen box mounted on stanchions on the front canopy.

The additional vehicles were used on a new service which commenced without advertisement on 29 September from Waverley Steps to Loanhead, with a few journeys terminating at Liberton. Then in October the Corstorphine service reverted to hourly for the winter and the fare was

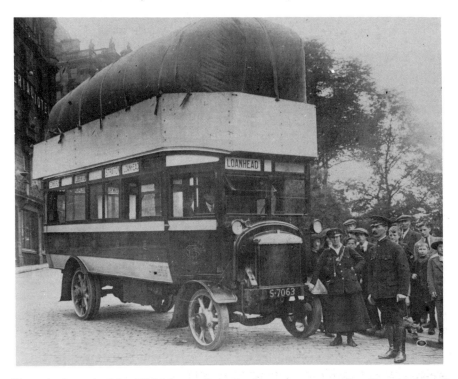

Towards the end of the 1914-18 war all the Lothians ran on gas. No. 66 at the foot of Waverley Bridge, Edinburgh, with Inspector McDonald and one of the few women conductresses.   DLGH Collection.

reduced to 2½d. The Queensferry and Cramond services were also much reduced with the latter being curtailed at Barnton. These two routes were suspended for the winter on 4 November, but later in the month there was a new service at twelve-minute intervals between Waverley Steps and Colinton Road. This was short-lived, ceasing after 5 January 1907: the road was said to be too rough.

Another new service was advertised to commence on 1 December 1906 to Dalkeith via Gilmerton and Eskbank with additional journeys to Gilmerton only, while the Corstorphine bus was extended right out to Uphall, though of course doing only four trips per day. The company's publicity, however, was very erratic, for the Dalkeith service had been shown in the timetable leaflet for October-November and in fact actually started on 21 October. More services were soon added. The first was to Penicuik which commenced on 22 December but was not advertised in the press. Next came routes to Bonnyrigg and also to Gorebridge, both running via Gilmerton, on 27 December, and to Pathhead via Gilmerton, Eskbank and Dalkeith, which commenced on 29 December. These last three routes were so advertised, though the Bonnyrigg route is reported to have actually started on the day before the advertised date.

A service to Kirkliston was started on 2 February 1907, and on 1 March it was extended to Winchburgh. This was not continued: the West Lothian County Council objected and it was dropped altogether after a few more weeks. Against this the other services were immediately popular and were soon augmented. The first tickets were printed by Pillans & Wilson, Edinburgh, and bore no stage names or numbers: 3d. ones were pink.

On 30 March 1907 the Queensferry route was restarted using a charabanc, but the Pathhead route was dropped after the same day. The Cramond route was also restarted for the summer on 4 May using a charabanc. From 3 August until the end of September a charabanc circular tour via Roslin and Penicuik to Carlops returning via Flotterstone was run twice daily, and for this the charabanc from the Cramond route appears to have been used. A Sundays only service to West Calder commenced on 6 October 1907 with three trips, while the Cramond service ceased, and the Queensferry service was run on Sundays only for another month before suspension for the winter.

One of the earliest accidents occurred on Saturday afternoon, 5 October 1907. The bus from Loanhead shed a wheel nearing the foot of Liberton Brae and, toppling over, scattered its complement of top-deck passengers. Five were detained in the Infirmary.

In March 1908 the timetable appeared in railway-like tabular form, the fares being given on the back. On Sundays slightly higher fares were charged and short-distance fares were not offered. From 1 March the Bonnyrigg route was extended to Rosewell, and an additional service run to Gorebridge via the Old Dalkeith Road (described as via Little France), Dalkeith and Eskbank. This replaced the service to Dalkeith via Gilmerton and Eskbank. The Queensferry service restarted on 9 April, and the Carlops tour on 8 June, though of course both were suspended again after the season. The service to Cramond was not revived.

A 25 hp Thornycroft bus with body by Liversedge was reported to be running on the Penicuik route in 1908. This seems to have been only on trial and there is no further record of it, although a small S.M.T. bus body with the number S974 was seen many years later, and this number fits the date.

By now the company had established its position on these routes to the surrounding country, mainly where the railway services were less convenient or more circuitous. The service frequencies were being gradually augmented. Passengers carried in one week in July 1908 were as follows: Queensferry 2400, Loanhead 3500, Penicuik 2700, Rosewell

A view of the driver's cab of a Lothian showing the pipe leading down from the gas bag. The engine is enclosed by the wooden casing. The rubber bulb horn is clearly seen. The bus body is one of the earliest pattern to which a new cab of standard size has been added.   DLGH Collection

3180, Gorebridge 5250, Uphall 3500, West Calder 350, Carlops 250. Ordinarily two vehicles were used for the Queensferry route, two for Loanhead and Penicuik, four for Gorebridge and Rosewell, and two or three for Uphall. With one more on the Carlops tour or West Calder this left one or two out of the then total of thirteen, to cover maintenance, breakdown or the occasional accident. Although there were mishaps from time to time, which were liable to be exaggerated in some quarters, no serious accident seems to have been recorded. Financially also the company was regarded as a success, a 5% dividend on the ordinary shares being paid.

The Queensferry and Carlops routes were again operated for the summer season of 1909, and in June 1909 a connecting service from Eskbank to Pathhead and Blackshiels was shown in the timetables. The West Calder Sunday service ceased after September, but from 5 February 1910 the route was partly covered by a new daily service to Mid Calder and Pumpherston, and the Sunday journeys to West Calder were restarted too on 6 March. In May 1910, and until October, two of the Blackshiels connections continued over Soutra hill (1200 ft.) to Lauder on Saturdays, Sundays and Mondays, and this was repeated during subsequent summers until about 1914, though latterly only on Sundays. The seasonal Queensferry and Carlops routes were again run in 1910. For the November 1910 timetable a reassessment of running times was made and nearly all were adjusted by a few minutes, some lengthened and some cut.

A parcels service had been set up early in 1908 with agents in the various towns and villages and with the Edinburgh & District Tramways Co.'s parcel service co-operating in the city. One of the minor problems was that, some of the surrounding towns being Royal Burghs, they continued to exercise their ancient rights to levy petty customs. These were, however, generally resolved by payment of a small annual sum, and after about 1930 the practice was dropped altogether. Private hire work was of course also undertaken from the beginning. Another activity that should be mentioned was a contract to carry the Post Office mails to and from various places, and in this connection three Albion vans in GPO red livery were run nightly to and from Glasgow via Bathgate, Coatbridge, Motherwell and Hamilton, from 1 December 1909. Later, larger Lacre and Star vans were used for the Post Office work. In some cases, however, the service buses were used, and from June 1911 the following interesting note appears in the timetable against the 5.45 am buses to Penicuik and to Rosewell: 'Passengers are only carried on the top of the 5.45 am bus to . . . the inside being reserved for mails'. It must have been a cold journey in winter if the rule was enforced. From October these two journeys are shown as starting from the GPO.

In 1910 four Ryknield 'R' type chassis were bought. Three double-deck bus bodies were also bought from Stagg & Robson of Selby. These were of that firm's stock design and differed from the Maudslay bodies mainly in having top-lights instead of slat ventilators above the windows. One of them was put on a Ryknield and S545 got one of the others. Another Ryknield got one of the earlier double-deck bodies and the other two Ryknields received charabanc bodies similar to the Maudslays. All the charabanc bodies are said to have been built by a Scottish firm. The numbers of the Ryknields were 61-63 and 87, S1687-90. They had a special form of shaft drive instead of chains and had the reputation of being quite fast but weak on hills.

In June 1911 new and larger garage and workshop premises were opened in East Fountainbridge for occupation by the buses, and the Lauriston Street garage was then mainly used for the mail vans. The Queensferry and Carlops routes ran for the season as usual. In November 1911 a Saturday and Sunday service was provided via Gilmerton and King's Gate to Dalkeith, Eskbank and Rosewell. In 1914 some journeys daily to both Rosewell and Gorebridge were made by this route, and by 1918 all buses via Gilmerton made this diversion through Dalkeith before reaching Eskbank.

On 1 May 1912 the Pumpherston route was extended to join the Uphall route, making a circular service both ways, at a round fare of 2/- from any point (2/3 on Sundays). Late services, outwards from the city up to 11.00 pm, were being provided on most routes, and at this time it was arranged for the returning buses to run direct to the garage via Nicolson Street and Lauriston Place from the south, or via Lothian Road from the west instead of going right in to the Waverley Steps. A change was made on 1 July 1912 when the starting point was moved from the latter to the top of the Waverley Bridge. A glazed frame remained fixed to the railings at the top of the Waverley Steps, however, until the mid-twenties, in which the company displayed their timetable sheets, later expanded to two sheets. The Queensferry and Carlops routes were again run for the season and their starting point remained at the Mound. Two new circular tours were run in August and September 1912. The first was an all-day trip on Mondays, Wednesdays and Fridays via Portobello, Haddington, Dunbar, North Berwick, Aberlady, Haddington and back to town via Newcraighall, with halts at Haddington, Dunbar and North Berwick. The town council were invited to an inaugural trip. The other ran twice a day on Tuesdays, Thursdays and Saturdays via Queensferry and Hopetoun to Linlithgow, returning via Winchburgh and Kirkliston. On both these tours, however, intermediate point-to-point fares were available. In November 1912 some return fares were offered on the Pumpherston and West Calder routes, and also to the Forth Bridge in the 1913 season. Earlier in 1912 tickets to the value of 10/- were offered at 12¼% discount. It may also be noted that children under twelve were allowed half-fare but were required to give up their seat to a full-fare passenger. Dogs were charged at one-third of the full fare.

On 11 December 1912 there was a strike of the bus crews over some dismissals. There was an attempt to run a few buses by some of the maintenance men, but then they came out too, and all services came virtually to a standstill. Earlier in the year the men had joined a trade union and they claimed the dismissed men, as active participants, were being victimised. There was much industrial unrest at the time. As Christmas approached the Post Office had to make alternative arrangements for the mails, for these runs had stopped too, but on Christmas Eve the men went back to work on undisclosed terms. It may be mentioned that the company ran a bonus scheme, and many employees were shareholders.

From February 1913 to about 1916 some of the Blackshiels connections were extended to Humbie, and from 2 March the Sunday service to West Calder was diverted to Whitburn instead. The 1913 summer services followed the same pattern as the previous years, the tours starting in June, and 'Special Evening Drives' to various destinations were run. A few Penicuik journeys were diverted through Loanhead. On 1 November 1913 some of the Uphall buses were extended to Bangour. The company's authorised capital was increased to £75,000 at this time.

Perhaps the most important event in 1913, however, was the appearance of a new bus, designed and built by the company's own staff. Although the company had been well satisfied with its Maudslays, a double-deck bus was not entirely suitable for the country routes and a more modern, single-deck vehicle was required. A great deal of thought had been given to this vehicle which was undoubtedly far ahead of its time. A novelty which did not become general practice elsewhere until many years later was the location of the driver alongside the engine, thus enabling a 32-seat saloon body to be accommodated on a vehicle only 23 ft. long, the same length as the old Maudslays and the maximum then allowed

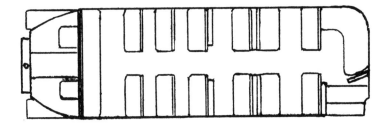

in Edinburgh. The saloon was partitioned into two parts and the off-side back corner was rounded, the seating being arranged as shown on the accompanying diagram. These features became a Registered Design (No. 616134) granted to W. J. Thomson and the Scottish Motor Traction Company Ltd. on 17 March 1913. There was a cut-away rear entrance with a short screen to the saloon in the little corner outside of which the conductor could stand on the top step. A short cab of the full width of the body but with a lower roof was provided for the driver and a sloping cowl covered the front part of the engine. Initially there was no radiator, but on trial this arrangement proved unsatisfactory and it is believed that this prototype bus, S3057, which appeared in April, did not enter service until it was modified following the use of the next few machines. The body of S3057 had been built by G. Hall & Co. of Pitt Street but the S.M.T. Co. had now acquired another workshop in Valleyfield Street and all further bodies for them were built there. In the next two (or three) of these the saloon partition was moved back one pair of seats and the disposition of the windows and top-lights reversed accordingly. The driver's cab was a little narrower than the saloon and slightly lengthened, while the sloping cowl was replaced by a flat-fronted cowl with a grille. Also the company's full title was now dropped from the sides of the vehicles and only the initials were used.* Following these, the next bodies had the driver's cab widened to match the saloon width again and the roof was raised to the same height as the rest of the body. There was no cowl and only a normal radiator stood in front of it. There were at least three of these bodies. On subsequent bodies the roof was of more elliptical shape and over the driver's cab had a gentle sweep down to the front. This became the standard form of construction. By 1917 the early bodies with low-roof driver's cabs had these removed and new cabs conforming to the standard construction built on to them. All the windows had removable top-lights of ground glass on which were painted the places on the route to which the bus was allocated, the termini also being shown on the two above the windscreen and on the back. After the war the ground glass and painted names were abandoned and paper bills stuck on inside, enabling buses to be changed about more readily. A clock was also then provided on the saloon bulkhead. The earlier bodies had sliding windows in the saloon, but these tended to rattle and were later made fixed, and an additional pillar was introduced dividing up the long window. Green leather cushion seats with spring backs were provided and the conductor's bell was a simple pull-cord. The buses were of course fitted with electric light. Later examples had a more highly curved roof. A 38 hp Minerva Silent Knight engine was

---

* It may be remarked that in everyday speech the use of 'S.M.T.' did not become usual until the early twenties: previously if an abbreviation was indulged in it was 'the Traction Company'.

fitted driving a four-speed chain-driven gearbox and worm-driven rear axle, but from 1915 a Tyler 35 hp engine had perforce to be used for the duration of the war. Solid tyres were of course fitted but the vehicle was well sprung. Thomson, Sandy Bracken and John West were those principally concerned in its design. The company aptly called their protégé the 'Lothian' but this name did not appear on the machines. The first of the new buses was licensed in June and was put on the Uphall route where it proved very successful, being decidedly faster, smoother and quieter than any of its contemporaries. No use was made of the near-side half of the driver's cab except sometimes to carry parcels. Since they nearly all lasted until 1929-30, the numerical details are rather complex and will be dealt with in the post-war rolling-stock in Chapter 5.

The full range of services applied again in the summer of 1914, the tours now starting on 1 July. In September the Loanhead route was extended to Lasswade, and an interesting variation was the running of the 1.00 pm outward journey via Captain's Road and thence direct via Edge. A new longer all-day tour to the Border country was run and called for a new charabanc, so a 31-seat charabanc body for the Lothian was produced. In the first one the radiator was sunk in flush with the front of the bodywork, but on subsequent ones this was altered to a projecting radiator, and the first one altered to this pattern also. The first one was also painted green when built, but afterwards pale yellow was adopted for the charabancs, with a waist bead picked out in brown. Several of the charabanc bodies built after the war had no waist beading and the side panels were formed into a rounded top over the frame. In June 1914 two 29-seat Albion charabancs were ordered also and one of these was No. 81, but on the outbreak of the war they were commandeered by the War Department. However, by September 1914, a sufficient number of Lothians had been produced to permit the withdrawal of all the Maudslays and twenty, refitted with platform lorry bodies, were offered for sale at £290 each and were soon snapped up. The Ryknields too were sold shortly afterwards.

The war had little immediate effect on the bus services and the Lothian charabancs enabled the summer tours to be continued until the first week of September 1916 when Defence Regulations banned them. However, for a short time early in 1915, the Bangour service was apparently provided on Saturdays and Sundays only, and from April some of the Penicuik buses were diverted through Roslin. With so many naval personnel accumulating at Queensferry that route became heavily loaded and the service was substantially increased to a half-hourly one, and continued through the winter too. As the vicinity of the Forth Bridge was under guard, the road between the top of the Hawes Brae and the east end of the town of Queensferry was closed and the buses proceeded via Dalmeny station and Hopetoun crossroads to enter the town from the west end. In July 1916 there was competition on the Queensferry route from the Edinburgh & District Motor Company, and over the weekend 22 to 24 July the S.M.T. Co. service was run as a circular route returning via Kirkliston as had been run by the Edinburgh & District Motor Company, but with the S.M.T. Co. service running in both directions round the circle. The Edinburgh & District Motor Company apparently ceased operation at that time and the S.M.T. Co. reverted to their ordinary service via Barnton from 25 July. The Mid Calder half of the Pumpherston circular route was withdrawn after August 1916.

In 1911 the S.M.T. Co. had started to develop their other motor vehicle interests and they were now doing a large trade in the supply, hiring and repair of commercial and private vehicles of all kinds, and held agencies for many makes. The company's own Lothian having proved so successful, it was now being offered on the market for both passenger and goods use, and to meet the demand a considerable extension of the Fountainbridge premises with full facilities for its production on a greater scale was undertaken in 1915. In 1915 a Lothian bus was supplied to the Auto Bus Car Co. Ltd. in Dunfermline and another to Perth Corporation, while a chassis specially arranged for normal control was supplied to McKirdy & McMillan at Rothesay for use as a charabanc. Orders were recorded for about a dozen Lothian lorries for firms in Scotland and England though, due to the war, some of the orders may not have been fulfilled and other makes of lorry supplied instead. Lothian lorries were, however, supplied to Jarvis Ltd. in London, John Wood & Son, Altrincham, James Brown & Sons, Penicuik, an unnamed farmer in Midlothian, and also the Edinburgh Fire Brigade who did not dispose of theirs for scrap until 1934. The S.M.T. Co. had a few Lothians among their own lorries also. The Fountainbridge works then had to undertake Government work, and in 1916 production of Lothian chassis was interrupted for a time. To augment their bus fleet the company converted their own Lothian lorries to buses and then sought to buy back Lothian lorries, offering lorries of other makes in exchange. About half a dozen were so acquired at this time and were provided with bus bodies.* After

* One of the last to come back was James Brown's the papermakers. In addition to delivering their paper it was also used for the distribution of foodstuffs under Government contract. Returning from one such trip to Peebles on 6 October 1919, when descending the hill into Penicuik, its driver suddenly collapsed and the vehicle plunged through the parapet of the Esk bridge and into the river far below. The wrecked lorry was duly recovered by S.M.T. and, after rebuilding and fitting a bus body, was re-registered as a new vehicle in their fleet. It is likely that this was SG2128.

the war the Lothian was not offered as a lorry, but a bus was supplied to the Great North of Scotland Railway Company and another four were supplied to Cousins Motor Service in Fife.

A total of 97 Lothians were built. The numbers of the 88 in the S.M.T. fleet will be found in the post-war rolling-stock Chapter 5, while details of the other nine which were owned by other operators are as follows:

Owner	Type	Regn. No.	Probable Chassis No.	Date
Edinburgh Fire Brigade	Lorry	S5678	T5.25	1915
Auto Bus Car Company Ltd.	Bus	SP2477	T5.31	1915
McKirdy & McMillan	N.C. Chassis	?	T5.39	1915
Perth Corporation	Bus	ES1970	T5.40	1916
G.N.S. Railway	Bus	SG704	T5.55	1920
Cousins Motor Service	Bus	SG1570	T5.64	1920
Cousins Motor Service	Bus	SG5716	T5.71	1922
Cousins Motor Service	Charabanc	SP7036	T5.72	1922
Cousins Motor Service	Bus?	SP9372	94	1924

Following abandonment of their first experimental bus service, Edinburgh Corporation sold three Tilling-Stevens petrol-electric buses, S4443-5, to the S.M.T. Co. in December 1914. These soon proved unable to cope with the hills encountered on most of the company's routes, and eventually two of them were fitted with charabanc bodies, possibly those from the two Albions. The remaining bus was used on the Broxburn route, but the chassis of this together with the two charabancs were sold early in 1918 to the Birmingham & Midland Motor Omnibus Company who used that make. Their bus bodies are believed to have been used temporarily on other S.M.T. vehicles for a short time: what appeared to be one of them was seen on a Thornycroft about 1923.

Jordan's service from Broxburn to Edinburgh was taken over in February 1917, and it was proposed to buy up the Edinburgh & District Motor Company too, but in April this was deferred on account of the already difficult petrol situation.

Soon petrol supplies became even more difficult and further steps had to be taken to maintain services. The answer was found by fitting up all the vehicles to run on coal gas. A shallow open box was built on the roof of the buses, and a similar box supported on stanchions, fixed over the charabancs, and into this box was lashed a large balloon which was charged with gas in Market Street, and also at the outer terminal in some cases. On the charabancs the gas was fed to the back of the engine casing by a tube of thin rubber, and this presented an attraction to schoolboys to try, unsuccessfully, to bring the vehicle to a halt by squeezing it. When returning with a diminished supply, the sagging gas-bag adopted a sort of wave motion from back to front as the vehicle ran through the breeze. There were occasional cases of gas-bags breaking loose altogether. The gas-bags were said to cost £50 each. Wear and tear was heavy and averaged 1¼d. per mile, and with gas at 2.17d. per mile, the total cost amounted to 3½d. per mile. The system served its purpose remarkably well with the fleet of about 40 vehicles and was indeed slightly cheaper than running on petrol at its then price. It was first used on the Lasswade route and next on the Penicuik route. It was alleged the buses ran better to Penicuik than back after refilling there. Petrol was still carried for starting and before stopping the engine. The gas-bags were discarded as soon as possible after the war but a few buses were still on gas in 1921, and some of the boxes remained for a time until there was an opportunity to remove them.

In 1917 a few more of the Penicuik journeys were diverted through Loanhead, including one which already went via Roslin, and the Whitburn route was suspended at the end of the year. The Pumpherston route was also suspended in May 1918 but restarted on 1 April 1919.

At the end of 1916 the only vehicles in the fleet which were not Lothians were the three ex-Edinburgh Corporation Tilling-Stevens, but over the next three years a number of other vehicles were added. Acquired from Jordan in February 1917 were three Halleys, one a 34-hp 30-seat bus with a platform entrance at the rear of the body by Steele of Wishaw, registered SX275. The others were a 40 hp bus of which no details have been found, and a small charabanc. SX134. It is doubtful if any of these were converted to run on gas. In early 1918 there was an Albion chain-driven bus with gas-bag on the Queensferry route, the origin of which is not known, but its body may have been one from the Tilling-Stevens. In the following summer what was presumably the same Albion appeared with a charabanc body, again carrying a gas-bag. Then in September 1918 the charabancs of the Edinburgh & District Motor Company were acquired. These included Commers and Albions. Roof boxes for gas-bags were partially built on some of them but the job was not completed. In 1919, after production of Lothians had restarted, the fleet is recorded as 45 Lothians and ten others which were Albion, Commer, Halley and Maudslay. The origin of the Maudslay is not known but it was a W.D. type with a charabanc body and wood roof. It was painted grey and ran on the Queensferry route. All of these ten 'others' had disappeared by 1920. Unfortunately neither S.M.T. numbers nor registration numbers can be given for any of them.

At this period, 1918-9, traffic was brisk, and the Queensferry route especially so. The last bus would stand at the Mound long before starting

A Lothian charabanc, No. 85, loading for the St Mary's Loch Tour at the Mound, Edinburgh.   F. C. Inglis

time completely packed — and no duplicate available. There was no limit and conductors did their best, sometimes squeezing half a dozen passengers onto the steps alone, and hanging on themselves outside of that! Fares would then be collected on alighting. In those days a full load was indicated by repeating the starting signal, i.e. four bells. The charabancs were used on the Queensferry route in the summer and they would be equally crammed with sailors sitting along both sides. The conductor collected his fares and punched tickets, hanging on the footboard outside while the vehicle careered along, and clambered along from row to row to do so, with a stride over the rear wheel arch. Today the whole procedure seems very precarious, although of course speeds were not so high and the roads were quieter. S.M.T. conductors as well as drivers normally wore leggings, and very few women were employed during the war. Uniforms had green piping. Williamson's ticket punches were used and the tickets were now printed by Williamson with all the stage names in 'fareboard' layout, both sides being used. The centre column on the front of the ticket was worded: 'The Scottish Motor Traction Co. Ltd. Available only on vehicle on which issued and to stage opposite punch hole.' The colours were: 1d. white; 1½d. mauve; 2d. blue; 3d. green; 4d. brown; 5d. yellow; 6d. brown; 7d. green; 8d. white with blue stripe; 9d. white with green stripe; 10d. white with blue stripe; 11d. white with yellow stripe; 1/- white with red stripe. Some higher values cannot now be recorded, but 1/8 was pale brown with red stripe, and 2/2 pale brown. No separate series was used for children etc., but three different sets were required for the lower values to cover the various

A Lothian charabanc on pneumatic tyres, No. 223, at St Andrew Square, Edinburgh. Travel Press & Publicity Co.

groups of routes, though occasionally a conductor would find himself having to use an inappropriate set. The special Sunday fares had been given up. Return tickets were now issued between the more important points and were surrendered for an Exchange Ticket of no face value, with a red number overprinted sideways, representing in pence half the value of the return ticket. Season tickets could also be obtained. Some one-way 1d., 1½d. and 2d. fares were also in vogue here and there, the uphill journey being a halfpenny dearer than downhill, or being offered inwards only within the city. These were printed right across the top of the ticket. There were no fixed stopping places though drivers were loth to stop on an up-grade, and regular travellers knew where the stage points were. The tickets were sometimes carried in a simple holder with two rows foot to foot and also back to back, giving sixteen positions; but often they were just made up into two or three bundles. The crews generally remained on the same route and became well known to their passengers. At Christmas time many a conductor decorated the inside of his bus with holly and coloured paper streamers. About 1927 some ticket colours were changed, the 8d. and 10d. tickets becoming brown though all the brown tickets were now of differing shades, while 7d. became grey and 9d. pale green. Timetables were now issued monthly, free, in a pocket-size booklet form arranged alphabetically, and although the display sheet was still issued to parcel agents etc. for some years, it was abandoned about 1929, by which time three or four sheets had been required to cover all the expanding services.

In 1919 the company produced an illustrated booklet with the title *Motor Transport for Business or Pleasure*. One of its pages, headed 'The Pioneers of the Motor Bus', may be quoted: 'When the Motor 'Bus was literally in its very infancy the great possibilities of this form of Public Transport were fully grasped by the Scottish Motor Traction Company. Today, the fleet of motor vehicles devoted to the service of the public in and around Edinburgh is the outcome of this enterprise, and in this direction the Capital is indeed well served. As the actual builders of these public vehicles we are able to produce a type of 'Bus which provides the maximum of comfort for a speedy journey under conditions of perfect safety. Wherefore we are recognised as the highest authority on all matters relating to passenger-carrying vehicles. Our experience, our expert knowledge of public requirements no less than our ability to meet them, are fully and freely at the disposal of municipalities, corporations, and private owners who are in search of the best type of Motor 'Bus or Charabanc for any kind of work. Enquiries relating to this subject are always welcome, and a visit to our Engineering and Coachbuilding Works in Edinburgh will explain, as no words can do, the pre-eminence of the Scottish Motor Traction company in the building of a Motor 'Bus.' The claim was well founded. The vehicle-selling activities had expanded too and the agencies listed in the booklet comprised Lanchester, Minerva, Crossley and De Dion Bouton cars, and Maudslay, Lacre, Star, Peerless, Seldon, Caledon, Thornycroft, Napier, Commer, and Vim commercial vehicles, together with Titan and Mogul tractors and the Yorkshire steam wagon.

The company's ordinary shares were now earning a dividend of 7½%, and in 1916 the authorised capital had been increased to £150,000. In 1920 it was increased to £250,000, and in 1926 was doubled to £500,000.

In July 1919 the Carlops, Dunbar and Melrose tours were restarted for the first season after the war, while on 3 October 1919 a service to Winchburgh was started. This had been shown in the timetables since June with a note that 'Due notice will be given when the above service will commence'. The highway authority still objected to the buses and appealed to the Ministry of Transport who eventually decreed that the company pay one penny per mile run towards the maintenance of the road. The Roads Act of 1920 of course cancelled this. The Queensferry route now ran every fifteen minutes in summer and every twenty minutes in winter.

The Whitburn route was restarted on 1 February 1920 on Sundays only, but a daily service was provided as far as Mid Calder, and a month or so later Whitburn was served daily too and the service increased. A half-hourly service of charabancs ran to Roslin via Lothianburn in the summer; this route commenced on 3 July 1920. Two new tours were added that summer, one to St Mary's Loch and Selkirk, the other via Stirling to Alloa from where the passengers sailed down the Forth to Queensferry in the company's motor yacht. Fares were increased by about 10% from September 1920.

The company's position was strengthened by an agreement concluded with Edinburgh Corporation on 12 May 1920 whereby the Corporation's activities were restricted to within the City boundaries and the S.M.T. Company agreed to provide efficient services on specified routes, including Gilmerton as a monopoly, and to charge a protective fare on tramway routes in the City. They also agreed to pay the Corporation one halfpenny per bus-mile within the City unless future legislation required the company to otherwise contribute towards road costs. The agreement was initally for seven years but continued in operation until 1954. A year afterwards, in 1921, the company threatened to interdict the Corporation for undertaking private hire work beyond the City. However, the Corporation desisted.

2

Expansion and Consolidation, 1920-1930

Until 1920 the company's bus services had been entirely based on Edinburgh, but now they established a foothold elsewhere — by buying from William Burke in July 1920 his contractor's business known as the Dundee & District Mechanical Transport Service. This was the beginning of expansion into areas well removed from Edinburgh, and it will be appreciated that the geographical area of the company's activities became so widespread that it would be impracticable to attempt to record every change or alteration of route which took place.

The Dundee & District Mechanical Transport Service had a small fleet of lorries including four J type Thornycrofts for which 'temporary' charabanc bodies were also available, and in September 1919 these were licenced by the Dundee magistrates for use on 'special occasions', the licence numbers being 1, 11, 14 and 18. The last was a 26-seater, the others 32. However, in July 1920 three new 30-seat charabanc bodies were on order from Reid of Carnoustie and these were fitted to Nos. 1, 14 and 18, while in August 1920 two more vehicles were licenced for 'special occasions' with licence numbers 13 and 29 and are thought to have been S.M.T. Thornycroft charabancs without lettering transferred to Dundee. No. 11 lapsed and may have been transferred to Edinburgh as No. 136, or it may have reverted to use only as a lorry. The garage was in Westfield Avenue, and William Burke remained as manager of the S.M.T.'s Dundee branch. In November 1920 a bus service to Forfar was started with licences Nos. 46-48 and three more vehicles in S.M.T. colours. This was followed in March 1921 by services to Inchture and to Blairgowrie via Alyth with a further four vehicles and licences Nos. 49, 50, 56 and 57. An additional vehicle, No. 58, was licenced for the Forfar route in May 1921, and in June the stance for the Forfar route was changed from the High Street in Dundee to North Lindsay Street, while the fare was increased from 2/- to 2/3. About this time the licences were transferred to the S.M.T. Company, though at least two of the new buses supplied from Edinburgh had been registered in Dundee. A licence for a service to Arbroath was refused but subsequently granted to operate on Sundays only.

In 1922 there was a route to Monikie and in 1923 another to Wellbank, both of which were later on extended to Forfar. A route to Kirriemuir via Glamis also started in 1923, and Blairgowrie was also served via Coupar

The first Thornycroft charabanc, No. 112, at the Mound, Edinburgh, on the frequent service to the Forth Bridge.   F. C. Inglis

Angus. There was, too, a service between Forfar and Kirriemuir but this was given up. Subsequent developments were the extension of the Forfar route to Brechin, the Inchture route to Perth and a service from Perth to Forfar via Coupar Angus and from Perth to Blairgowrie. The Arbroath service was eventually a daily one, but to Carnoustie only. Specific licence numbers applied to the various services but it seem unlikely that these were always followed as traffic developed. Further vehicles licenced in Dundee after 1923 are shown in the post-war rolling-stock in Chapter 5. Tours were also run from Dundee. A separate set of tickets was issued for the Dundee routes.

To return meantime to activities in Edinburgh: Lothians were still being built and it was the practice for bus and charabanc bodies to be exchanged each season in many cases. More vehicles were required quickly, however, and a large number of J type Thornycrofts, mostly charabancs, appeared. A bulk purchase of Thornycroft chassis from the Government Disposals Board was made by a syndicate which included the Maudslay Motor Co. and the S.M.T.Co., the latter acquiring 100 of them, of which about half became buses and charabancs in the company's fleet. It is no disparagement to say these did not compare favourably with the Lothians. At first they seemed unreliable, and a trip to Queensferry was liable to be punctuated by several involuntary stoppages while the driver did a little tinkering with the engine. In those days drivers did their own running repairs. However, these troubles were soon overcome and they did useful work. The Thornycroft buses ran the Whitburn route and were later much used in the Bathgate district.

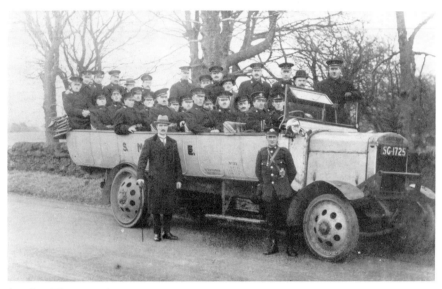

Another Thornycroft charabanc, No. 133, with a low-sided body, on a private hire. DLGH Collection

Vehicles were now being bought in large numbers so that it will be better to deal with the numerical details of the Thornycrofts and all subsequent additions to the fleet separately in Chapter 5.

At this period International Rugby matches were played at Inverleith, and on these occasions the S.M.T. ran a frequent service to the field from George Street, competing with the Corporation. Similarly charabancs were run to Musselburgh Races at a fare of 1/6. On 23 October 1920 the Bangour route was extended to Bathgate. New ground was broken on 4 December 1920 with a service from Waverley Bridge to Musselburgh and Tranent, running via Portobello High Street. From the beginning of February 1921 this was altered to run via Willowbrae Road and Milton Road. On Saturdays a frequent service was provided, and from 5 February some journeys on Saturdays and Sundays continued on to Haddington. The Haddington extension became daily from 2 May 1921, but reverted to Saturdays and Sundays only during the following winter.

On 8 January 1921 the Winchburgh route was extended to Linlithgow. Later, from 26 October 1922, through tickets were issued to Falkirk by the Scottish General Omnibus Company's service connecting at Linlithgow. The October 1921 timetable included a new alternative route to Penicuik via Lothianburn and also a new circular route both ways, via Gilmerton, Dalkeith, Wallyford, Musselburgh, and back to Edinburgh, but the district between Dalkeith and Musselburgh could not yet offer much traffic and this service was taken off again in February 1922, though

One of the two Thornycroft buses sent when new to Dundee for the Forfar route. It is seen after its return as Edinburgh No. 60 in the experimental grey livery and working from Bathgate depot. DLGH Collection

No. 221, one of the Thornycroft forward-control, 32-seat buses seen in Edinburgh at Corstorphine Road, Pinkhill. E. O. Catford

six journeys continued to be made via Musselburgh to Wallyford. In April these were reduced to Saturdays and Sundays only, and cancelled altogether in June. A route via Tranent to Ormiston commenced in December 1921. The starting point for these east-going services to Musselburgh, Tranent, Wallyford, Ormiston, and Haddington was transferred from the Waverley Bridge to the top of Waterloo Place on 1 April 1922. On 7 November 1921 the connecting service from Dalkeith to Blackshiels run by Adam Young of Eskbank was taken over with an increase of fares on the route giving rise to much local complaint. However, there was a general reduction of fares on 19 December 1921. Most of the services were then being gradually increased in frequency, and extra buses ran on Saturdays from Dalkeith to Gorebridge and Rosewell.

A new type of vehicle appeared in 1921, namely a fourteen-seat Fiat charabanc for longer day tours which were now started to the Trossachs and to Loch Earn. These were painted brown without lettering and hence were known as 'Brownies'; they ran on pneumatic tyres. A bus version was built in 1925 for use on some of the longer routes to be mentioned and also in the Bathgate district where competition developed. Details are given in Chapter 5. These were normally operated without a conductor.

When the Uphall route was extended to Bathgate, William Young & Sons, who operated in the area around that town, started a rival service between Bathgate and Edinburgh, Waterloo Place, and severe competition developed. Young's buses and charabancs were Commers painted dark green. Eventually the S.M.T. service was cut back to Uphall again and William Young ran a connecting service from Broxburn to Bathgate instead of running to Edinburgh. This change was made on 1 March 1922. Passengers changed at Broxburn on the outward journey, although, coming back, Uphall was the advertised changing point. This applied in the case of Pumpherston too from October, the Broxburn-Pumpherston service being extended to Mid Calder and West Calder, with connections from Edinburgh at Mid Calder. Through running to Bathgate was recommenced, however, with the acquisition on 1 January 1923 of William Young & Sons' services between Broxburn and Bathgate, and between Bathgate, Armadale and Linlithgow. William Young & Sons continued to operate their other routes in the Bathgate district until 1 April 1923, when these too were taken over by the S.M.T. Co. William Young & Sons' garage and fleet of eleven vehicles had been destroyed in a fierce fire in the early hours of 18 November 1922. New Commers were ordered but it is thought the company was unable to finance these, and their restricted activities until March 1923 may have been carried on with hired vehicles. A new garage was built by the S.M.T. Co. later in 1923,

A group of Fiat charabancs, 'Brownies', at St Andrew Square, Edinburgh, tours stance.
S.M.T. Co.

and five S.M.T. buses were sent there, so establishing another base for operations outside Edinburgh, but only eight years later these premises were given up in favour of a new garage on the Whitburn Road.

The routes from Bathgate were via Armadale to Linlithgow; to Blackburn, soon extended to Addiewell and West Calder; and to Whitburn, soon extended to Harthill. Another new route via Whitburn and Fauldhouse to Shotts followed soon afterwards. Yet another set of tickets was required for these routes.

Summer weekend traffic from Edinburgh to Queensferry was very heavy and the company were proud to advertise themselves as 'The company which can and does run a three minute service to the Forth Bridge'. It was an achievement, requiring about thirty vehicles, but the local passengers were not forgotten and some vehicles were regularly turned at Blackhall or Barnton to cater for them. There was no Telford Road then and the Blackhall turning point was at Forthview Terrace. When the touring charabancs returned in the early evening from their day's trips, they would be sent hurrying out to Queensferry to help bring in the crowds, usually without conductors. Drivers' hours were of course not so rigidly controlled in those days. In summer from 1921 the company's two new motor yachts, *Auld Reekie* and *Cramond Brig*, each carrying 120 passengers, provided pleasure cruises from Hawes Pier at the

One of the three International fourteen-seat buses used on the North Berwick route. DLGH Collection

Forth Bridge, as had also been available in the summer of 1914 with an earlier smaller vessel, *Electric Arc*.

The tours stance was removed from the Mound to St Andrew Square in 1922 and the S.M.T. Co. occupied the west side. A new route was started from Waverley Bridge via Slateford and Juniper Green to Balerno on 15 July 1922. Another from Waterloo Place to North Berwick via Longniddry, Aberlady and Gullane, at 9.30 and at two-hourly intervals till 5.30, started on 6 May 1923. This was run on Sundays only at first, and the first bus proceeded from Fountainbridge via Haymarket to Waterloo Place. It was a popular route and was augmented from 19 August, but did not become a daily service until 26 September 1925. A further new route leaving the Gorebridge route at Newtonloan proceeded to North Middleton and was started on 1 June 1923. A direct through service to West Calder commenced on 1 November 1923, but was later withdrawn. There was another general reduction in fares from 1 November 1923.

One of the few serious accidents in the company's earlier history occurred on 19 September 1924 when the steering gear failed, due to a metallurgical flaw, on a Lothian bus as it rounded the curve at Balerno railway station on its outward journey. Some of the railway passengers leaving the station were caught and two girls were killed and three other persons injured.

Production of the Lothian ceased after 1924. Manufacturers were now improving their designs, and equally suitable large vehicles were becoming available. The company, however, continued to build many of their bodies.

A small firm in Whitburn, James Scott, was taken over in 1924. In the summer of 1924 the Broxburn-West Calder route was temporarily cut at Mid Calder while the Almond bridge was closed for repair. In October 1924 the Bathgate-Linlithgow service was extended via Bridgeness and Grangepans to Bo'ness, and a circular route between Linlithgow and Bo'ness also started.

In January 1925 the Dean Motor Transport Company's service from Edinburgh to Bo'ness was taken over. This service started from a stance in George Street near Hanover Street and proceeded via Stockbridge to Blackhall and the Queensferry Road, but from 1 July the stance was changed to the Mound and the normal route by Queensferry Road was followed, by which time the Fiat buses had replaced the Dean Motor Transport's charabancs. Henderson's Central Motor Service of Bo'ness was bought up in March 1925. There were now small garages at Bo'ness and at Whitburn and garage premises were bought at Linlithgow in 1926. A service to Pencaitland via Tranent and Winton commenced on 4 February 1926.

At this time the legal speed of buses was still 12 mph, but the fourteen-seaters, weighing less than two tons, were allowed the then general 20 mph speed limit, so now most of the timetables were speeded up to an average to suit the 20 mph limit and a note added: 'As the above service is made out for small buses, the intermediate times, also arrival times at the destinations, may be somewhat later should large buses be run.' As the twelve mph speed limit had long become a dead letter, it made no difference in practice. Where small buses and large buses were running on the same road (e.g. Queensferry Road), the small bus was not supposed to pick up short-distance passengers if a large bus was following in sight.

An interesting public intimation in February 1926 was that the company's drivers were instructed not to dim their headlights for approaching traffic in the dark as it was believed to give rise to more danger than otherwise. This was of course before the days of dipping headlights.

The General Strike of 1926 resulted in the complete suspension of S.M.T. services from 4 May until 11 May, no attempt being made to run services with voluntary labour. Some of the independent operators attempted spasmodic journeys over some S.M.T. routes, however. An enquiry and booking office at 45 Princes Street, near the Waverley Bridge, was opened in June 1926. For a brief period in June 1926 a half-hourly service was run from the foot of Leith Walk to Queensferry via Ferry

Road. This was to drive off James Armstrong's charabanc from that route to Queensferry and ceased after he did.

The R.T. Motor Services route from Edinburgh to Peebles was taken over in June 1926, though the old stance in St David Street continued to be used for another two years. A variation of the North Berwick route, namely via Drem, commenced on 1 September 1926, but about 1929 this was altered to turn northwards at Ballencrieff crossroads to join the usual route at Aberlady. Meantime on 1 June 1927 a 'limited stop' service to North Berwick was tried, but was withdrawn again a few months later. Stops were made only at Musselburgh Town Hall, Longniddry, Aberlady and Gullane, and point-to-point passengers were not carried.

Expansion further afield was again afoot. The business of Brook & Amos Ltd., based in Galashiels, together with that of Adam Purves, also of Galashiels, was bought in April 1926, but for the time being the Brook & Amos name continued to be used for services in the Border country. The routes then in operation were from Galashiels to Walkerburn and Innerleithen, to Stow, to Selkirk and Hawick, to Jedburgh and to Kelso. There were also routes from Berwick to Coldingham and to Duns, and a journey on Saturdays and Sundays only from Galashiels to Berwick and back which became a daily service in June. A service was also provided between Hawick and Denholm. Tours were operated too, together with an extensive programme of excursions to all the shows and events in the Border towns throughout the season, and also on occasion to Edinburgh. Three- and six-day tours were offered for the Galashiels holiday week. There were small garages at Galashiels, Selkirk, Hawick, Denholm and Coldingham.

Harry Brook, who both earlier and subsequently operated buses in various parts of England, Scotland and Ireland, had joined forces with the Amos brothers at Galashiels to form Brook & Amos Ltd. on 25 September 1923. The company's capital was £9,000 and they originally owned eleven vehicles. The new firm took over Aikman of Galashiels shortly afterwards, and in September 1924 George Henderson & Co. Ltd., Coldingham, were also taken over, the capital thereafter being increased to £15,000. Gala Motor Transport Company with two vehicles were taken over just before Brook & Amos passed into S.M.T. hands, and Harry Brook departed for fresh ventures in south-west Scotland. James Amos soon came to Edinburgh to become the S.M.T. Co.'s traffic manager and later rose to succeed Sir William Thomson in 1948. Willie Amos remained at Galashiels to look after operations there.

The Brook & Amos subsidiary then went on to absorb most of the other local firms in the area including, on 12 October, the Selkirk Motor

William Johnston Thomson, the company's first engineer and manager and eventually chairman.   Gavin Booth Collection

Company who were competing on the Selkirk-Hawick route and who also served the Ettrick and Yarrow Valleys. Other firms absorbed at this period were Cairns & Welsh of Denholm whose route was to Hawick and Selkirk, Mitchell of Lilliesleaf who also ran to Hawick, and others whose businesses were private hiring: A. Mackay of Galashiels, Richardson of Innerleithen, A. & M. R. Little of Walkerburn, Wheelan of Hawick, J. H. Scott & Co. of Melrose, and Hamilton of Melrose.

The timetable for January 1927 included further services from Galashiels to Earlston, Berwick to Allanton, Duns to Cumledge Mill on Thursdays, Saturdays and Sundays, Hawick to Lilliesleaf on Mondays, Wednesdays and Saturdays, Hawick to Selkirk via Lilliesleaf and Midlem on Thursdays, and Hawick to Peebles on Sundays. The Coldingham route was extended to St Abbs. There was also a Sunday morning journey from Galashiels to Edinburgh via Stow, returning in the evening, on which pre-booking was necessary. There were now garages at Innerleithen, Jedburgh and Berwick. A new larger garage was built at Selkirk in 1927 and new small garages at Melrose and Earlston also.

Direct S.M.T. services from Edinburgh to Galashiels and Selkirk and

Maudlsay lightweight 32-seat bus with Vickers body, No. 494, on the Edinburgh-Glasgow route.   Gavin Booth Collection

from Edinburgh, Chambers Street, to Lauder, Earlston and Jedburgh were started on 1 August 1927, some journeys on the latter route running via Oxton. The Selkirk service was extended to Hawick on 12 October.

The Border Motor Transport Company who operated from Hawick to Jedburgh were bought up in September 1927, Ramsay with local routes around Peebles in October 1927, and John Turnbull of Kelso with routes to Edinburgh, to Berwick and to Jedburgh in December 1927.

At the beginning of 1928, with the absorption of these other firms, there were three routes between Kelso and Berwick, via Swinton, via Coldstream and via Cornhill, and also routes between Duns and Lauder, Duns and Coldstream, Coldstream to Wooler, Hawick to Jedburgh, Kelso to Jedburgh, Kelso to Hume, Peebles to Posso, Peebles to Moffat via Broughton, Biggar and Abington, and Peebles to Moffat via Tweedsmuir though the latter was soon dropped and instead the Moffat buses reached Biggar via Blyth Bridge, while those going only as far as Biggar continued to follow the route via Broughton. There were now of course garages at Peebles and Kelso. From 1928 all the Borders services were operated under the S.M.T. Company's name, though Brook & Amos Ltd. was not formally wound up until 1934.

In October 1926 a service through to Glasgow was established, with the acquisition of two firms, J. Tennant & Sons of Armadale, who ran a service between Bathgate and Coatbridge as well as local routes around Armadale, and Hendry's Motor Service with their route between Clarkston, Airdrie, Coatbridge and Glasgow. J. & D. Hendry were a

One of the last Maudslays, No. 57, of 1929, with S.M.T. body on a Galashiels-Melrose working.   DLGH Collection

subsidiary of Henry Lawson, who then absorbed Hendry's other routes. Midland Bus Services Ltd. of Airdrie also served this latter route (as also did Glasgow Corporation tramcars) and ran to Bathgate, but via Slamannan and Westfield. Midland Bus Services Ltd. declined to participate in joint operation of the Edinburgh-Glasgow service and preferred to develop independently their operations southwards and westwards of Airdrie and Glasgow, though they did agree to the S.M.T. Co. acquiring some new buses which they had on order and which the S.M.T. Co. needed for the Edinburgh-Glasgow service.

The through service between Edinburgh and Glasgow, every twenty minutes, commenced on 25 October. From 9 December an hourly 'limited stop' service officially taking two and a quarter hours was provided in addition to the ordinary service, the stopping places being Corstorphine Station Road, Broxburn, Uphall, Bathgate, Armadale, Airdrie, Coatbridge and Shettleston. Passengers were not set down at the first stop or picked up at the last one and local passengers were not carried between Broxburn and Uphall, Bathgate and Armadale, and Airdrie and Coatbridge. Later, stops at Blackridge, Caldercruix and Baillieston were added and the service ran half-hourly with the ordinary service also half-hourly leaving ten minutes afterwards, but in 1929 the 'limited stop' arrangement was abandoned and an ordinary service every fifteen minutes provided instead. The buses used on the 'limited stop' service carried a

One of the second, 1928, lot of Maudslay open coaches with Hoyal body, No. 626 on a private hire.   DLGH Collection

large inscribed board mounted on the top of the front of the roof on which a small light shone at night. Earlier, in 1920, the S.M.T. Company had opened sales premises in Reidvale Street in Glasgow, and now a few buses could be garaged there. There was now also a garage at Armadale but it was subsequently closed.

Allen & Kennedy of Broxburn were acquired in November 1926 but continued to run between Livingstone Station and Haymarket, Edinburgh as a subsidiary company under their old name for some time. There were also some Allen & Kennedy journeys from Broxburn to Pumpherston. Three S.M.T. buses ran carrying Allen & Kennedy's name in 1928 and 1929, and Allen & Kennedy tickets of S.M.T. pattern were issued. The service from Livingstone Station was extended to Waverley Bridge under the S.M.T. Company's name on 1 October 1929. From 1931 it ran on Saturdays only. A daily service was provided to Livingstone Station from Bathgate in 1933. There was of course now a small garage at Broxburn.

Another new route was to Ratho village, started in 1926 and proceeding via the Calder Road and Dalmahoy. In 1928 this service was altered to reach Ratho via the Glasgow Road and Ratho Station, but from 16 September 1930 it was again changed and ran from Chambers Street, routed via Gogar Station and Ratho Park to Ratho, from where it was extended down to the Glasgow Road at Ratho Station and continued to Pumpherston in place of the direct service there which had been

One of Brook & Amos' A.E.C. buses. Harry Brook is on the right.   R. Grieves Collection

transferred to the Chambers Street stance the previous year. By the next year the service was once more altered when the direct Pumpherston service from Chambers Street was restored, and the Ratho service terminated at Ratho Station, running from Waverley Bridge. The starting point of the Pumpherston service was removed to Waverley Bridge also three or four years afterwards. In subsequent years two journeys were run between St Andrew Square and Dalmahoy Gate via Glasgow Road, Gogar Station and Ratho Park in the summer.

Local routes around Bathgate had been developing too, new services being provided to Bents via Blackburn and Stoneyburn; to Seafield; to Westfield via Torphichen; to Armadale via Bathville; to Shotts via Armadale, Westcraigs and Harthill; also to Blackness on Sundays. Another new service was Linlithgow to Philpstoun. All these were in operation by 1928. On Wednesdays, Saturdays and Sundays, a few Broxburn to West Calder journeys were extended to Hardale Golf Club.

A rather alarming accident occured on 8 October 1927 when a fourteen-seater bus (SF2061) got out of control on the steep hill into Bo'ness and overturned, injuring eleven passengers.

From time to time there were complaints of overcrowding, and not only on S.M.T. buses, so in 1927 the Edinburgh magistrates ruled that the number of standing passengers should not exceed one third of the seating capacity of the bus.

In November 1927 certain Peebles journeys were diverted from Penicuik to run by Auchendinny and Howgate to Leadburn, and the route was also extended to Innerleithen and Walkerburn. Likewise some Blackshiels journeys were run via Edgehead. A few buses to and from

A group of Brook & Amos charabancs about to start on a Galashiels Co-op employees' outing. The leading one is A.E.C. No. 7 and the second one Daimler No. 19.   R. Grieves Collection.

Lasswade took the direct road either via Kirk Brae or via Captain's Road. A route to Gifford via Ormiston and Pencaitland was started on 1 February 1928, and the service continued on into Haddington to link these two places. A few of these buses made a diversion through West Saltoun. The Haddington route was extended to Dunbar on 1 March 1928 under an arrangement with Stark's Motor Service who operated from Dunbar. Berwick could be reached through the Border network but the Dunbar route was also extended there on 6 April 1928.

Newcastle was now the objective but was first reached by extension of the Jedburgh route via Carter Bar on 11 May 1928 with United Automobile Services Ltd. of Darlington participating in the operation of the service. George Deans' bus based at Lauder was bought in July 1927 to clear the way. Amos Proud of Choppington had been running a service from Newcastle to Edinburgh via Berwick since 8 August 1927, and when United Automobile Services Ltd. took over this firm the way was clear for a joint S.M.T. and United service on this route to commence on 1 October 1928. Four of the former Amos Proud buses taken over by United Automobile Services Ltd. were painted in S.M.T. colours for this service; they became S.M.T. property in April 1929. Meantime, on 1 August 1928, the S.M.T. services using the Waterloo Place stance had been

One of Brook & Amos' Leyland 24-seat 'convertibles' with its closed top fixed on. No. 33's crew appear to be in S.M.T. uniforms and the destination bills of S.M.T. type, so the photograph is probably about 1928.   S.O.L. Collection

transferred to the north side of St Andrew Square and proceeded via York Place and London Road. United Automobile Services' Amos Proud buses on the Newcastle via Berwick service, however, continued to use the Waterloo Place stance until 5 June 1929. Extension of the Edinburgh-Kelso route to Newcastle via Coldstream and Wooler had also been in view since early 1928 but action had been deferred, and this third route to Newcastle did not commence until summer 1929, again with United Automobile Services Ltd. participation. On these longer routes passengers might have more luggage with them so the buses used thereon were provided with a rack for luggage on the rear part of the roof, reached by a light ladder fixed on the near-side of the back.

From 5 October 1928 the Peebles route stance was transferred to Waverley Bridge and the Balerno service to the north-west corner of St Andrew Square, proceeding outwards via Princes Street and inwards via George Street. From the same date buses from the west reached Waverley Bridge via the Mound and Market Street. On 8 December 1928, the Whitburn route was extended through to Glasgow via Shotts and Hamilton.

Competition on the North Berwick route arose in the summer of 1928 when the Edinburgh Omnibus Company extended their 'White Line' buses on the Port Seton route to North Berwick with a return fare of 2/9.

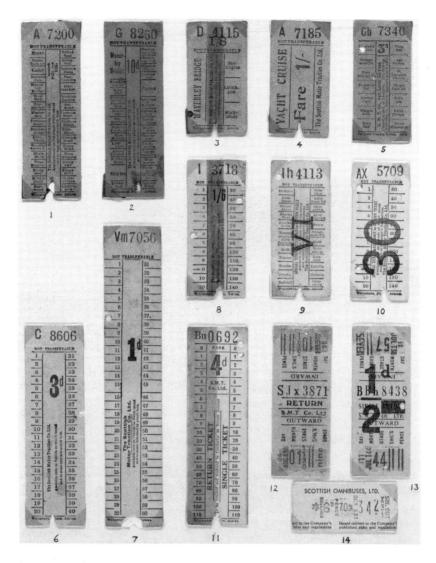

A selection of S.M.T. tickets from the author's collection. 1: 1920 period; 1½d. mauve fareboard type for Queensferry and Linlithgow routes; the stages for the Balerno and West Calder routes are printed on the back. See page 18. 2: 1920 period; 10d. brown fareboard type for Penicuik, Middleton, Gorebridge, Rosewell, Blackshiels and Haddington routes; none on back. 3: 1920 period; 1/8 pale brown with red stripe; Haddington, Linlithgow and Blackshiels. 4: 1/- blue ticket for the Yacht Cruise from Queensferry. See page 27. 5: 1932; 3d. pink fareboard type for Ayr Local Services. See page 51. 6: c. 1930; 3d. green, stage numbers 1 to 40. See page 44. 7: c. 1930; 1d. white, stage numbers 1 to 60. See page 44. 8: c. 1930; 1/6 green with red stripe, stage numbers to 140. See page 44. Punched twice for stage 46. 9: Exchange ticket: issued on the return journey in exchange for a return ticket. See page 19. A fareboard type example from the Dundee area. 10: Exchange ticket; with stage numbers 1 to 140. See page 19. Punched twice at 0 and 1, i.e. for stage 1. 11: c. 1932;

4d. blue and white Single/Return ticket, stage numbers 1 to 110. See page 53. Punched twice for single ticket to stage 1. 12: c. 1934; Setright insert type pink return ticket. See page 53. Issued for a 9d. return fare. Hours 5 to 24 and quarters are printed on the back; the two punched holes relate to the time of issue. 13: c. 1934; Setright insert type yellow ticket for fares including a halfpenny. See page 53. Issued for a 7½d. return fare. The other two punch holes relate to the time as printed on the back. 14: 1970s; Setright roll type white ticket. See page 119. Issued for a 6d. single fare.

An Albion, No. 96, with 28-seat front-entrance body, used for the Edinburgh-Glasgow limited-stop service.   Albion Motors

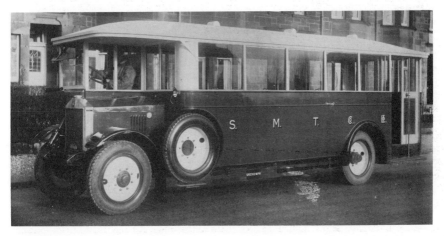

A novelty for S.M.T. at the time: one of two half-cab buses, Albions Nos. 544 or 545, obtained in 1926.   Albion Motors

Galashiels Market Square stance about 1928 showing, left to right, Maudslay coach of the first (1927) series, No. 620, Chevrolet charabanc Borders No. 73, Lothian bus on pneumatic tyres Borders No. 120, two more Maudslay coaches, and a Maudslay bus with Vickers body. In the background is one of Andrew Harper's Thornycroft buses from Peebles.   W. Lind Collection

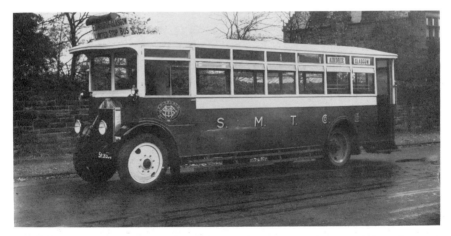

Forward-control Albions soon replaced the smaller ones on the Edinburgh-Glasgow limited-stop service, No. 638, seen here, being one of them, carrying the Edinburgh-Glasgow limited-stop headboard.   Albion Motors

Star fourteen-seat touring coach at St Andrew Square, Edinburgh, N7 in blue livery. DLGH.

Coast Line, their competitor on the Port Seton route, followed suit, extending their service to North Berwick also and offering a return fare of 2/6, S.M.T. joining them in this reduction with the return ticket available by either Coast Line or S.M.T. route. Of course White Line reduced their return fare to 2/6 and later to 2/-, S.M.T. and Coast Line cutting theirs too (to 2/3?), but on 29 June 1929 all three reverted to 2/6. By this time the Edinburgh Omnibus Company were in financial difficulty and their operations ceased entirely in January 1930. Coast Line then withdrew their North Berwick extension and S.M.T. restored the return fare to 2/9.

With so much expansion, additional garage and workshop accommodation was required and a large, new garage was built on a site at New Street with a new office building above. This was completed in November 1928. Buses entered down a slope from a point opposite Market Street, and the exit was direct from the garage floor level to a point lower down New Street. The touring coaches continued to be garaged at Fountainbridge, but in October 1936 an extension on two floors was added to the north end of the New Street garage, the lower floor being entered from Calton Road. The workshops were then also transferred to New Street, and Fountainbridge and Valleyfield Street were given up by the buses. The double-decker returned to the fleet on 1 January 1929 in the form of the Leyland Titan and these were used first on the Gorebridge and Balerno routes.

In February 1929 the company arranged to take a controlling interest in the business of W. Alexander & Sons Ltd., Falkirk, and also Midland Bus Services Ltd., Airdrie. Then on 15 August 1929 the company was itself reconstructed with a capital of £1,800,000, the L.M.S. and L.N.E Railway companies holding a half share between them, in accordance with their policy of investing in established road transport undertakings, arising from their new powers to engage in road transport services, granted by the Railway Road Powers Acts of 1928. This major financial development did not produce any evident change in the company's operations, and little or no integration between road and railway services except for interavailability of ordinary rail and bus tickets, which was introduced on many routes soon afterwards. A return bus ticket used for return by rail usually incurred a supplementary payment, however.

At this milestone let us take a look at the annual mileage run by the company's vehicles, to see how they have grown:

1906	161,200
1914	728,000
1918	1,040,000
1928	10,500,000

In 1928 the colours of the return tickets were:

5d.	yellow with green cross	2/6	green with pale green stripe
6d.	turquoise with white stripe	2/8	grey with turquoise stripe
8d.	white with turquoise stripe	2/9	blue with mauve stripe
9d.	pink with brown cross	2/10	purple with turquoise stripe
10d.	blue with mauve stripe	3/-	red with mauve stripe
11d.	white with red stripe	3/2	white with three vertical blue lines
1/-	pale purple with mauve stripe	3/4	white with two horizontal red bands
1/1	pink with white stripe	3/6	pink with blue stripe
1/2	purple with green stripe	4/-	white with three vertical red lines
1/3	green with mauve stripe	4/3	brown with white stripe
1/4	mauve with blue stripe	4/4	white with diagonal blue line
1/6	yellow with red stripe	4/6	white with brown stripe
1/8	green with turquoise stripe	4/8	white with bottom right half blue
1/9	grey with red stripe	5/-	white with red stripe
1/10	brown with red stripe	5/6	white with blue stripe
2/-	blue with white stripe	6/-	white with diagonal brown band
2/2	yellow with turquoise stripe	6/6	white with diagonal red band
2/3	white with diagonal red line	7/-	white with blue cross
2/4	pale green with green stripe	8/6	white with diagonal blue band

A new type of return ticket appeared in 1930 at the top of which was a small portion bearing the ticket number and value and the wording 'If this portion is detached this ticket is valid for CHILD only'. The colours of these tickets were:

3d.	white	2/6	grey with turquoise stripe
4d.	blue	2/7	blue with pink stripe
5d.	dull brown	2/8	yellow with white stripe
6d.	mauve	2/9	mauve with blue stripe
7d.	green	2/10	green with blue stripe
8d.	pale blue	2/11	yellow with purple stripe
9d.	yellow	3/-	green with deep green stripe
10d.	brown	3/1	deep brown with blue stripe
11d.	purple	3/2	yellow with green stripe
1/-	light red	3/3	white with red stripe
1/1	purple	3/4	brown with red stripe
1/3	grey	3/6	brown with red stripe
1/4	red	3/7	yellow with red stripe
1/5	dark brown	3/8	grey with brown stripe
1/6	pale blue	3/9	pale purple with mauve stripe
1/7	pale green with blue stripe	3/10	blue with mauve stripe
1/8	white with blue stripe	3/11	green with pale green stripe
1/9	grey with purple stripe	4/-	grey with blue stripe
1/10	grey-blue with pink stripe	4/1	deep brown with light brown stripe
1/11	blue with pale blue stripe	4/2	pale green with turquoise stripe
2/-	purple with blue stripe	4/4	blue with grey stripe
2/1	green with yellow stripe	4/5	purple with blue stripe
2/2	blue with white stripe	4/6	deep brown with blue stripe
2/3	green with mauve stripe	4/8	purple with pale green stripe
2/4	pale blue with white stripe	4/9	red with pink stripe
2/5	mauve with blue stripe	5/-	cerise with blue stripe

Some of the Star buses were later rebodied with eighteen-seat coach bodies built by Alexander Motors of Edinburgh. This is N35 in Galashiels depot.   DLGH

However, the practice of printing the stage names in 'fareboard' layout on the tickets had become impracticable on such a growing network and after 1930 tickets, both single and return, with stage numbers 1 to 40 (soon increased to 60), appeared instead. The wording in the centre column now became 'Available only on vehicle on which issued and to stage indicated by punch hole'. The colours of some of the single tickets were changed, 1½d. becoming blue, 4d. reverting to yellow, 6d. becoming mauve, 7d. pale green, 9d. red, 10d. purple, 11d. grey, and 1/- red, while there were additional values of 2½d. green, 3½d. mauve, 4½d. grey, 5½d. red, 6½d. pale green and 7½d. brown. Higher values were now:

1/1	brown	2/1	yellow with white stripe
1/2	pale green	2/2	grey with red stripe
1/3	grey	2/3	purple with red stripe
1/4	white with red stripe	2/4	pale blue with red stripe
1/5	blue with red stripe	2/5	brown with red stripe
1/6	green with red stripe	2/6	white with blue stripe
1/7	yellow with red stripe	2/7	green with blue stripe
1/8	pale green with red stripe	2/8	mauve with blue stripe
1/9	pink with red stripe	2/9	pink with blue stripe
1/10	mauve with red stripe	2/10	brown
1/11	pink with blue stripe	2/11	red
2/-	pale brown with red stripe	3/-	pale green

The 60-stage ticket was very long and cumbersome, however, and it was quickly replaced again by a shorter ticket with stages 1 to 9, 0 and 10, 20, 30, etc. up to 140, such tickets always being punched twice to produce the required stage numbers; 2d. tickets were now pink, 2½d. brown, and 5d. grey. There were also green 3½d. and 7½d. ones of differing shades. Known return tickets of this type were 3d. yellow with two diagonal black lines, 2/- blue with white stripe, and 4/- white with three vertical red lines. Tickets for higher-value fares were now written out and detached from books which retained a duplicate copy. There were three books with, respectively, singles on pale blue paper, returns pink, and exchange mauve. From 1 April 1929 the child's half-fare age was raised to 14 and dogs were charged at one-sixth instead of one-third fare. There were changes in passengers' luggage regulations too.

The Edinburgh to Hawick route was extended to Carlisle on 13 April 1929, and from 1 July a bus was run to Keswick, connecting there with an English company's service to Liverpool. There was also a service from Glasgow to Newcastle and Whitley Bay via Lanark, Biggar, Peebles, Galashiels, Jedburgh and Otterburn. The network of local services in the Border country was arranged to give connections between services at various points, though there were certain additional through-trips such as

Selkirk to Berwick via Galashiels and Duns on Saturdays and Sundays. There was a service from Duns to Grantshouse with connections to and from Edinburgh, and another from Chirnside to Coldingham and St Abbs. A bus ran on Saturday evenings from Galashiels to Yair Bridge. The timetable often noted late buses awaiting picturegoers, dancers, etc., reflecting a different pattern of life from today, while 'Waits on Pullman' referred to the overnight Edinburgh-St Pancras sleeping-car train calling at Galashiels around 10.30 pm and still so-called by the public though the Pullman cars had disappeared some 40 years before. Another small firm in the Borders, Fairbairn of Kelso, was acquired in July 1929.

Extension of the Linlithgow route onwards to Falkirk and Stirling raised a problem. Since 1926 several firms from these areas, including the Scottish General Omnibus Co. Ltd., who were running the connecting service from Linlithgow to Stirling, sought licences to run into Edinburgh but all were repeatedly refused. Conversely, Falkirk and Stirling refused to allow the S.M.T. Co. into their areas. James Penman of Bannockburn then started a service on 1 October 1928 between Bridge of Allan and Musselburgh. Only passengers already holding return tickets could be picked up in Edinburgh. However, after W. Alexander & Sons Ltd. became a subsidiary of the S.M.T. Co. in February 1929, a number of Alexander buses already licenced in Falkirk and Stirling were painted in S.M.T. Co. colours and took existing S.M.T. Edinburgh licence numbers. From 19 July 1929 these ran between Edinburgh and Stirling, bearing a label. 'On Hire to W. Alexander & Sons Ltd.'. Soon the Scottish General Omnibus Co. took over James Penman and on 1 January 1930 were themselves absorbed by W. Alexander & Sons Ltd. The Bridge of Allan-Musselburgh service then ceased. In April 1930 the Edinburgh-Stirling service was extended to Callander and to Crieff. After 1931 the services running through beyond Linlithgow were transferred to Alexander's auspices, though S.M.T. vehicles were sometimes used for duplication. For a period in the early part of 1930 the services on the Linlithgow road were diverted at the Drum Brae via Craigs Road to regain the main road near Turnhouse. The little extra traffic gathered was, however, not worth the inconvenience of following this narrow, hilly road. A service from Edinburgh to Oakbank was provided on Saturdays and Sundays only in 1929.

The last of the opposition on the Broxburn route was removed when West Lothian Motor Services running from Chambers Street to Pumpherston were taken over on 6 September 1929. Adjustments, upwards, of several fares in that area followed. A special return journey on Sundays for hospital visitors to East Fortune Sanitorium commenced on

The Leyland Titans appeared in 1929. These had open stairs. This one, formerly No. 696, is in New Street depot, Edinburgh, in blue livery with advertising slogan, as J22. DLGH

6 April 1930. White's service from Chambers Street to Balerno via Colinton was taken over on 20 February 1930, while a new circular service from Dalkeith via Newtongrange, Mossend and Dewartown was provided on Saturdays only in 1930. The Edinburgh-Walkerburn service was extended to Galashiels in September 1930.

A service from Edinburgh, Chambers Street, to Dumfries via Leadburn and Tweedsmuir, was started on 10 May 1930 jointly with the Caledonian Omnibus Co. Ltd. of Dumfries, while a summer-only service to Inverness started on 15 May, fare 17/6 single, 32/6 return. Other summer services to Blackpool, to Liverpool and to Manchester were run jointly with Ribble Motor Services of Preston from 18 June. The Liverpool service was continued throughout the year.

It was about this time that the still strong association between the staff social organisations of S.M.T. and the Yorkshire Traction Company Ltd. began, when an Edinburgh man in hospital in Barnsley was befriended by some Y.T.Co. busmen when visiting their own friends there. The Edinburgh man subsequently invited them to Edinburgh where they got to know S.M.T. busmen and their Claymore Club. Arising from this contact, annual dinners and football matches, alternately in Scotland and England, were arranged and have raised large sums of money for chosen charities, the home for blinded ex-servicemen at Linburn being a main beneficiary at the Scottish end.

A Leyland Lion, No. 87, at the Cathedral Street stance in Glasgow in 1929, on the Edinburgh-Glasgow route. The driver and conductor wear several licence badges from the various local authority areas through which they operated.   DLGH Collection

A 1930 Burlingham-bodied Leyland Tiger 27-seat coach, formerly No. 846, used on long-distance services, now H47, in Market Street, Edinburgh.   DLGH

E. Thomson, who had earlier sold his R.T. Motor Services to S.M.T. and who now operated as Thomson's Tours, had commenced in October 1928 a one-day service between Edinburgh and London, departing from 16 Princes Street at 8.00 a.m. The fare was £1.10/- single and £2.10/- return. He also ran in summer a two-day service by both east and west-coast routes with overnight stops at York and Chester respectively, and a selection of tours. Early in 1930, now facing competition from W. Scott & Co. of Edinburgh and other firms from south of the border, his fare had been reduced to £1 each way, and he was proposing an overnight service also, using double-deck sleeping coaches. These were not forthcoming, but an overnight service departing at 6.00 pm duly commenced on 16 April 1930 using ordinary coaches. The stance for his London services was now at 63 Princes Street, being just east of the Mound. However, on 11 April 1930, Thomson's business was acquired by the S.M.T. Co., though the London services continued to operate under the name of Thomson's Tours until 1 July when the S.M.T. Co. announced they had taken over the service and that their new luxurious coaches would be put on the service; these were the new Leyland Tiger coaches. Meantime, from 1 June, the fare had been restored to £1.10/- single and £2.10/- return. Thomson's Tours continued to be advertised as such until mid-August. E. Thomson, known to S.M.T. men as 'Jew' Thomson, became a hotelier. From 23 October the departure times became 2.00 pm and 10.00 pm, the former being from the Mound, but from the next summer all departures were from the Mound, at 7.00 am and 5.00 pm, being booked to take 16 hours 7 minutes with three short refreshment breaks. The day service now ran only in the summer period. In several subsequent years departure times and running times were amended slightly. In 1938 they had become 7.30 am and 5.30 pm from Edinburgh and 8.00 am and 7.30 pm from London, the night service taking 15 hours 19 minutes with only two refreshment stops. E. Thomson had not specified arrival times. It should be recorded that on 14 April 1930 one of Thomson's Tours' Daimler coaches, SC5237, on the southbound day service to London, crashed into a tree in the vicinity of Micklefield in Yorkshire. The vehicle was badly damaged, one passenger being killed and ten taken to Leeds Infirmary. It is possible that the arrangement to take over Thomson's Tours followed this disaster and was backdated to 11 April to cover liability for it: the licensing authority were not notified of the takeover until the end of the month.

The long-standing green and cream colour scheme of the company underwent a major change in the spring of 1930 when it gave place to blue. Waistbands painted cream, which had been dropped a year before, reappeared with it. After another nineteen years, green came back again in June 1949, but during the intervening years several variations in colour were applied to specific groups of vehicles. Details will be found in Chapter 5.

3

After the Road Traffic Act, 1930

In the early part of 1931, implementation of the 1930 Road Traffic Act no doubt helped to persuade some small operators that it would be better to sell out, and in May 1931 J. S. Dewar & Sons of Whitburn, J. Beuken & Sons of Fauldhouse, W. McDowal of Harthill, and J. Brodie of Harthill, were taken over. Dewar ran between Bathgate and Livingstone Station, and Brodie between Harthill and Bathgate. G. Forbes of Blackness, who ran from Blackness via Linlithgow to Standburn and Avonbridge, was acquired the following month. Then in August A. F. Masson of Linlithgow, whose routes were from Linlithgow to Broxburn via Kingscavil, Threemiletown, Ecclesmachen and Uphall, and from Linlithgow to Philpstoun, was taken over. Lamond Bros. of Winchburgh and T. Anderson of Winchburgh, both running between Winchburgh and Broxburn via Niddry, were taken over in February and April 1932 respectively. Also taken over in April 1932 were W. Rendall & Co. of Broxburn, who ran services from Broxburn to Queensferry via Winchburgh, Niddry and Kirkliston, and also via Newbridge, Lochend and Kirkliston, running also from Broxburn to Pumpherston and Oakbank. F. Nicol of Broxburn, who ran a Broxburn to Grangemouth service via Uphall, Threemiletown, Linlithgow and Bo'ness, was taken over in December 1932. W. McNair's service from Torphichen to Bathgate was acquired in August 1933.

On the other side of the city, Bowen's routes from Chambers Street to Elphinstone, via Newcraighall, Musselburgh and Smeaton, and from Chambers Street to Deantown via Millerhill, Monktonhall and Musselburgh, were taken over on 11 June 1931. This was followed on 24 February 1932 by Dunn's services between Musselburgh and Elphinstone, Tranent and Elphinstone, Dalkeith and Cousland, Dalkeith and Musselburgh, Dalkeith and Portobello, where the terminus was at Brighton Crescent, and a local service between Wallyford and Musselburgh. W. Sword of Dalkeith, who ran a service via Bonnyrigg, Lasswade, Loanhead and Roslin to Penicuik, was acquired at the same time. Some rationalisation of these services was quickly effected, the Dalkeith and Portobello service being linked through with the Dalkeith and Cousland service, the Dalkeith and Musselburgh service linked through with the Dalkeith and Penicuik service, and the Chambers Street

This fourteen-seat Dennis came from West Lothian Motor Services, and after working for a time at Galashiels as Borders No. 139 was sold to McNair of Torphichen, whose takeover in 1934 brought it back to the S.M.T. fleet as S1, seen here at Bathgate depot.   DLGH

and Elphinstone service linked through with the Tranent and Elphinstone service. The local Wallyford and Musselburgh service was extended via Newcraighall to Niddrie Mill, and the Chambers Street and Deantown service extended to Cousland, but soon the latter was terminated at Smeaton, except on Saturdays and Sundays, and later withdrawn altogether beyond Whitecraigs. A new garage was built at Dalkeith in 1932. Further afield, George Hudson & Sons, operating local routes northwards from Carlisle, were taken over on 1 January 1932.

There was also an interlude at Ayr where the company entered into an agreement with the town council to provide a service of buses in place of the Corporation trams. The Corporation were paid £20,000 with, in addition, payments of £2,500 per annum for ten years and £500 for eleven years. The replacement bus service, for which a fleet of locally registered Leyland Titan double-deckers was ordered, commenced on 1 January 1932, using some existing single-deckers pending delivery of the new vehicles. A set of tickets, 'S.M.T. Co. Ayr Local Services', with stage names in 'fareboard' layout, was provided. 1d. ones were white and 3d. ones pink, similar to those of Ayr Corporation. In some cases the word 'Ayr' was omitted. The bus services operated by Kilmarnock Corporation were also taken over on 1 January 1932, their nineteen buses — five

A Daimler coach, D3, ex-Thomson's Tours, with body by Cadogan of Perth, in Market Street, Edinburgh, on its way to New Street depot, Edinburgh.   DLGH

Albions and fourteen Thornycrofts — continuing to cover the local routes. Kilmarnock Corporation received a payment of £15,000 plus £1,000 per annum for 21 years.

Then, in June 1932, the Western S.M.T. Co. Ltd. was formed to absorb Midland Bus Services Ltd., the former Kilmarnock Corporation services, and also several firms, large and small, in the south-west part of Scotland, control of which had recently been acquired by the S.M.T. Co. Ltd. The Ayr local services with their vehicles were also thereafter operated by Western S.M.T. Co. Ltd. on behalf of the S.M.T. Co. Ltd., though the licences were not officially transferred to Western S.M.T. Co. Ltd. until 1963. Similarly, Central S.M.T. Co. Ltd. was also formed in June 1932 to absorb firms being taken over in and around Lanarkshire, including some companies owned by the L.M.S. Railway which had recently been transferred to S.M.T. Co. Ltd. control. The histories of Western S.M.T. Co. Ltd., Central S.M.T. Co. Ltd. and W. Alexander & Sons Ltd. are too extensive to incorporate in this history of their parent S.M.T. Co. Ltd.

A charge of one penny was now made for the pocket timetables, while a comprehensive volume covering all the group companies was also issued at 2d. A useful book of *Instructions to Drivers and Conductors of Public Service Vehicles* was issued to staff in 1932.

One of the first lot of A.E.C. Regal coaches of 1931 with 28-seat Cowieson bodies, B10 in New Street depot, Edinburgh.   DLGH

A further change in the ticket system was made about 1932 when a universal single/return ticket was adopted. These were issued for all values 1d. to 5/- with stage numbers 0 to 10 and 20, 30, etc., up to 110 down both sides. The left-hand half or, later, the left-hand column only, of the ticket was blue and punched twice in the now usual way for a return ticket, while the right-hand side was white and was used similarly for a single ticket. The centre column carried the fare at the top and underneath in two lines 'S.M.T. Co. Ltd.'. The remainder of the centre column was occupied by 'Return Ticket' and 'Single Ticket', printed lengthwise in large letters, and above the former, in the usual small print, it read: 'To be retained and tendered to Conductor on Return Journey'. The existing pattern of exchange tickets continued in use, as did also the book tickets for higher fares. These universal single/return tickets, however, were soon super-seded by the introduction of the 'Setright' ticket machine which, by the turn of its handle, printed the date, stage and fare on the outward or inward end of a basic ticket inserted into it. Three differently coloured tickets were used: singles were green, returns pink, and the third one was yellow overprinted in red with a large ½d. This latter was used for fares including a halfpenny, both single and return. Preprinted across the middle of the tickets was the serial number, 'S.M.T. Co. Ltd.' and the type of ticket according to its colour. Below this was 'Inwards' and above it 'Outwards', and then, in each case printed sideways, 'Day', 'Month', 'Stage,, 'Shilgs', and 'Pence'. Later these were replaced by the initials D, M, S, s and d. Each end of the ticket was blank to receive the information

The first S.M.T. bus with an oil engine was this A.E.C. Regal, B2, used on the North Berwick route.   DLGH

printed by the machine. On the return journey the opposite end of a return ticket was inserted in the machine for day, month and stage to be printed on it, no fare being shown in this case. On the yellow tickets a small punch hole was made in the word 'single' or 'return' as required. The Setright machine had three concentric knurled knobs on its left-hand side which were turned to give the day, the month and the stage number. On its right-hand side there was a knob which was turned to give the fare. The ticket was inserted in a slot on the face of the machine and the handle on its right-hand side was given a complete turn, being released to do so by a small lever beneath it which could be moved by the conductor's forefinger. So the old punch type of tickets disappeared after 1934.

The company was expanding its activities in many directions and in 1932 set up an Aviation Department to provide, at first, charter flights and joyrides with the intention of introducing regular air routes later on. Although there are said to have been as many as fourteen small aircraft, little was achieved in this field, and operations petered out at the end of 1934.

The company's trading and repairing of all kinds of vehicles, known as the Sales & Service Department, was much more successful and these activities had been gradually extended by acquiring businesses of this kind in many towns around the country.

The *S.M.T. Magazine* had been started in July 1928, at first partly as a staff magazine, but from January 1929 expanded into a popular journal promoting tourism. A subsidiary, Travel Press & Publicity Co., was formed about 1931-2 to continue the magazine which in 1935 combined

One of the 50 very comfortable, 32-seat A.E.C. Regal buses of 1932, B31, in New Street depot, Edinburgh.

with *Scottish Country Life* to become *Scotland's Magazine*. The Travel Press and Publicity Co. also undertook the publication of the group companies' timetables and all other such matters. In 1947 a *Gazetteer of Scotland*, with some indication of how to reach the various places by the group's bus services, was published. Regretfully *Scotland's Magazine* succumbed to changed economic circumstances in 1975. Another venture at this period was the acquisition of the Dryburgh Abbey Hotel, purchased from W. J. Thomson in 1934, which remained a useful asset to the company until 1983.

A rather circuitous route to Lanark commenced on 12 September 1932, running via Lothianburn, Penicuik, Carlops, West Linton, Dolphinton, Dunsyre and Carstairs, with a view to serving the district deprived of its railway service on the L.M.S. Dolphinton branch from Carstairs. In 1933 a summer service was run on Saturdays and Sundays from Gorebridge to Port Seton. The Glasgow and the Dunbar routes were also linked up in the summer so that passengers did not require to change in Edinburgh, but this arrangement was abandoned about 1937. A few Blackshiels journeys were again extended to Humbie. Local services in Peeblesshire were acquired from the Caledonian Omnibus Co. Ltd. in August 1933 in

A.E.C. Regals with 28-seat Burlingham bodies equipped with toilets were provided for the Edinburgh-London service in 1933, but were sometimes used for duplication on shorter routes, such as B79 seen here at the Mound, Edinburgh, for a Forth Bridge run. When the war came it was given a double-deck bus body and numbered BB8.

exchange for S.M.T.'s former Hudson local services from Carlisle.* Some of the Gorebridge buses were diverted to serve Easthouses instead of Eskbank on their way between Dalkeith and Newtongrange in 1933, and in April 1935 some of these Gorebridge journeys were extended to the new housing scheme at Birkenside. Afterwards the local Middleton service was provided as an extension of this route. In March 1935 some of the Lasswade buses were extended to Polton Road end. In May 1935 many of the Queensferry journeys were extended out to Hopetoun crossroads, where housing development was taking place on the western outskirts of the town, and two months later several journeys were diverted through Dalmeny village before descending the Hawes Brae. A direct service to the growing Wallyford village, and variation of the routes to Haddington by running a few journeys via Pencaitland and then direct to Haddington instead of via Gifford also came about this time.

The Road Traffic Act in April 1931 had precipitated the new numbering scheme for the vehicles which is detailed in Chapter 5. The Traffic Commissioners were also anxious that all bus services should be numbered. This was of course an undertaking of considerable magnitude. A scheme was, however, devised for routes radiating from Edinburgh,

*   These Peeblesshire routes had passed to the Caledonian Omnibus Co. Ltd. in 1932 when they took over the business of Andrew Harper of Peebles, who had steadfastly refused to sell to the S.M.T. His Edinburgh stance at Castle Terrace continued in use.

starting with No. 30 so as to avoid conflict with the numbers of the Corporation services. Services in the outlying areas used separate series of numbers with a prefix, Border area B; West Lothian etc. C; Dalkeith, Musselburgh, etc. D, though local routes from Broxburn and Linlithgow were numbered merely 1 to 25, and numbers do not seem to have been applied to the Dundee district routes. New vehicles were now usually equipped with roller-blind destination screens and a number screen, surmounted by a small panel lettered 'S.M.T.', on the front only, supplemented by the time-honoured paper bills on which the letters were now printed in blue instead of black. Existing vehicles continued to display these, and bore no service numbers. These service numbers were given in the timetables and displayed on the vehicles where so equipped from 1934. But the system was so complex and so many buses could not show the numbers that it is doubtful if they served any useful purpose to the public, and the same may be true today. The list was as follows:

1	Broxburn	— Hardale
2	Broxburn	— Oakbank
3	Broxburn	— Pumpherston
4	Broxburn	— Winchburgh
5	Broxburn	— South Queensferry via Winchburgh
6	Broxburn	— South Queensferry via Newbridge
7	Broxburn	— Bo'ness via Bridgend and Borrowstoun
8	Broxburn	— Bo'ness via Philpstoun and Borrowstoun
9	Broxburn	— Grangemouth via Bridgend and Borrowstoun
10	Broxburn	— Bo'ness via Philpstoun and Castleloan
11	Broxburn	— Threemiletown
12	Broxburn	— Linlithgow via Uphall and Bridgend
13	Linlithgow	— Bo'ness via Champany
14	Linlithgow	— Bo'ness via Borrowstoun and Castleloan
15	Linlithgow	— Bo'ness via Lochmill, Borrowstoun and Newton
16	Blackness	— Bo'ness
17	Linlithgow	— Avonbridge via Standburn
18	Linlithgow	— Standburn
19	Linlithgow	— Blackness via Champany
20	Blackness	— Avonbridge
21	Linlithgow	— Bathgate via Armadale
22	Linlithgow	— Philpstoun via Gateside
23	Linlithgow	— Winchburgh
24	Broxburn	— West Calder
25	Broxburn	— Mid Calder
30	St Andrew Square	— North Berwick direct
31	St Andrew Square	— North Berwick via Ballencrieff
32	St Andrew Square	— Haddington via East and West Saltoun
33	St Andrew Square	— Dunbar
34	St Andrew Square	— Pathhead via Ormiston

There were not many A.J.S. buses around. This one, E1, had been owned by Rendall's Blue Coach Service, Broxburn.   DLGH

A 30-seat double-entrance Albion, A102, which came from Hudson of Carlisle, is seen here at Kelso.   DLGH

One of Scott's Azure Blue Daimler coaches with 22-seat Hoyal bodies which became D15 DLGH.

35	St Andrew Square	— Ormiston
36	St Andrew Square	— Tranent direct
37	St Andrew Square	— East Fortune
38	St Andrew Square	— Pencaitland via Winton
39	St Andrew Square	— Haddington via East Saltoun
41	St Andrew Square	— Haddington direct
42	St Andrew Square	— Gifford via Ormiston and Pencaitland
43	St Andrew Square	— Pencaitland via Ormiston
44	St Andrew Square	— Cockburnspath
45	St Andrew Square	— Musselburgh Races
46	Chambers Street	— Elphinstone via Woolmet
47	St Andrew Square	— Haddington via Winton, Pencaitland and Samuelston
48	St Andrew Square	— Haddington via Ormiston, Pencaitland and Samuelston
50	Waverley Bridge	— Gorebridge via Little France
51	Waverley Bridge	— Rosewell via Little France
53	Waverley Bridge	— Pathhead via Little France and Edgehead
60	Chambers Street	— Tranent via Newcraighall and Elphinstone
61	Chambers Street	— Smeaton via Woolmet
62	Chambers Street	— Cousland via Millerhill
70	Waverley Bridge	— Gorebridge via Gilmerton and Eskbank
71	Waverley Bridge	— Rosewell via Gilmerton and Eskbank
72	Waverley Bridge	— Middleton via Gilmerton
73	Waverley Bridge	— Middleton via Little France
74	Waverley Bridge	— Blackshiels via Gilmerton and Edgehead
75	Waverley Bridge	— Bonnyrigg via Gilmerton
76	Waverley Bridge	— Gilmerton
77	Waverley Bridge	— Eskbank via Gilmerton
78	Waverley Bridge	— Pathhead via Gilmerton
79	Waverley Bridge	— Pathhead via Gilmerton and Edgehead

80	Waverley Bridge	— Newtongrange via Gilmerton
81	Waverley Bridge	— Edmonstone Road
82	Waverley Bridge	— Blackshiels via Gilmerton
83	Waverley Bridge	— Humbie via Gilmerton
84	Waverley Bridge	— Gorebridge via Gilmerton and Easthouses
85	Waverley Bridge	— Birkenside via Gilmerton
86	Waverley Bridge	— Birkenside via Little France
87	Waverley Bridge	— Dalkeith via Gilmerton
90	Waverley Bridge	— Lasswade via Liberton and Loanhead
91	Waverley Bridge	— Lasswade via Captain's Road
92	Waverley Bridge	— Penicuik via Liberton and Loanhead
93	Waverley Bridge	— Lasswade via Kirk Brae
94	Waverley Bridge	— Penicuik via Liberton and Roslin
95	Waverley Bridge	— Penicuik via Captain's Road
96	Waverley Bridge	— Penicuik via Liberton, Loanhead and Roslin
97	Waverley Bridge	— Penicuik via Liberton
98	Waverley Bridge	— Straiton via Liberton
99	Waverley Bridge	— West End Cottages via Liberton
100	Waverley Bridge	— Loanhead via Liberton
101	Waverley Bridge	— Roslin via Liberton and Loanhead
102	Waverley Bridge	— Roslin via Liberton
103	Waverley Bridge	— Polton Mill Road End via Liberton
104	Waverley Bridge	— Polton Mill Road End via Captain's Road
105	Waverley Bridge	— West End Cottages via Captain's Road
110	Waverley Bridge	— Ratho Station Road via Ratho
111	Waverley Bridge	— Ratho
112	Waverley Bridge	— Livingstone★
113	Waverley Bridge	— Bathgate direct
114	Waverley Bridge	— Uphall
115	Waverley Bridge	— Broxburn
116	Waverley Bridge	— Pumpherston via Ratho
117	Waverley Bridge	— Pumpherston direct
118	Waverley Bridge	— Armadale
119	Waverley Bridge	— Dalmahoy via Ratho
120	Waverley Bridge	— Kirkliston
121	Waverley Bridge	— Winchburgh
122	Waverley Bridge	— Linlithgow via Gorgie
130	Chambers Street	— Balerno via Colinton
131	St Andrew Square	— Balerno via Slateford
140	Waverley Bridge	— Oakbank
141	Waverley Bridge	— Mid Calder
142	Waverley Bridge	— Bathgate via Mid Calder and Uphall
143	Waverley Bridge	— Pumpherston via Mid Calder
150	Waverley Bridge	— Penicuik via Lothianburn
151	Waverley Bridge	— Roslin via Lothianburn

★   The 'e' at the end of 'Livingstone' was dropped in 1930 but frequently reappeared in timetables etc. during the following decade.

A 1933 Leyland Tiger with 34-seat Metropolitan-Cammell body, H101, at Dunbar depot.
DLGH

160	Mound	— South Queensferry
161	Mound	— Bo'ness direct
162	Mound	— Bo'ness via Miller's Pit
163	Mound	— Cramond Brig
230	St Andrew Square	— Newcastle via Grantshouse and Berwick
231	St Andrew Square	— Newcastle via Coldingham and Berwick
232	St Andrew Square	— Berwick via Coldingham
240	Mound	— London, one-day service
241	Mound	— London, two-day service, east coast
245	Mound	— London, two-day service, west coast
250	Waverley Bridge	— Glasgow via Shotts
251	Glasgow	— Newcastle
252	Glasgow	— Whitley Bay
260	Waverley Bridge	— Hawick via Little France
261	Waverley Bridge	— Carlisle via Little France
262	Waverley Bridge	— Galashiels via Little France
263	Waverley Bridge	— Selkirk via Little France
270	Chambers Street	— Newcastle via Little France and Jedburgh
271	Chambers Street	— Jedburgh via Little France
272	Chambers Street	— Kelso via Little France
273	Chambers Street	— Newcastle via Little France and Kelso
274	Chambers Street	— Kelso via Little France and Edgehead
275	Chambers Street	— Blackpool
276	Chambers Street	— Liverpool
277	Chambers Street	— Manchester
290	Waverley Bridge	— Galashiels via Howgate and Peebles
291	Waverley Bridge	— Galashiels via Penicuik and Peebles
292	Waverley Bridge	— Walkerburn via Howgate and Peebles

A 1934 Bedford with 20-seat Burlingham body, C27, at St Andrew Square, Edinburgh.
DLGH

The 1934 A.E.C. Regal buses had 34-seat Burlingham bodies. This is B104 in New Street
depot, Edinburgh.   DLGH

In 1934 Stark of Dunbar bought this A.E.C. 'Q' bus painted in S.M.T. livery for the Edinburgh-Dunbar route. DLGH

A 1935 A.E.C. Regal with 32-seat body by Alexander in the 'Coronation' livery of pale yellow and red with a blue roof; B147 in New Street depot, Edinburgh. DLGH

C44 was a 20-seat Bedford coach of 1935 with sliding-door entrance at the rear. It is seen at the Fountainbridge depot, Edinburgh.   DLGH

293	Waverley Bridge	— Peebles via Roslin and Penicuik
294	Waverley Bridge	— Walkerburn via Penicuik and Peebles
295	Waverley Bridge	— Peebles via Penicuik
296	Waverley Bridge	— Lanark
297	Chambers Street	— Dumfries
298	Waverley Bridge	— Peebles via Howgate
310	Waverley Bridge	— Glasgow via Bathgate
311	Glasgow	— Caldercruix
312	Glasgow	— Bathgate via Armadale
313	Glasgow	— Bathgate via Avonbridge
314	Glasgow	— Dunbar direct
321	Waverley Bridge	— Callander
322	Waverley Bridge	— Crieff
323	Waverley Bridge	— Stirling
324	Mound	— Inverness
B 1	Galashiels	— Kelso via Melrose and Maxton
B 2	Galashiels	— St Boswells via Melrose
B 3	Galashiels	— Kelso via Melrose and Clintmains
B 4	Galashiels	— Leaderfoot via Melrose
B 5	Galashiels	— Leaderfoot via Gattonside
B 6	Galashiels	— Jedburgh via Leaderfoot, St Boswells and Ancrum
B 7	Galashiels	— Melrose via Darnick
B 8	Galashiels	— Berwick via Melrose, Earlston, Greenlaw and Duns
B 9	Galashiels	— Earlston via Gattonside
B10	Galashiels	— St Boswells via Gattonside and Leaderfoot
B11	Galashiels	— Earlston via Melrose and Leaderfoot

V1 was a Leyland Cub from Graham of Hawick and is seen in Hawick depot.   DLGH

B13	Galashiels	— Selkirk via Lindean and Selkirk station
B14	Galashiels	— Hawick via Selkirk and Ashkirk
B15	Galashiels	— Selkirk via A7 main road
B16	Galashiels	— Peebles
B17	Galashiels	— Clovenfords
B18	Galashiels	— Walkerburn
B19	Galashiels	— Innerleithen
B20	Innerleithen	— Walkerburn
B21	Selkirk	— Hawick via Midlem and Hassendean
B22	Hawick	— Lilliesleaf via Hassendean
B23	Hawick	— Lilliesleaf via Ashkirk
B24	Hawick	— Newtown St Boswells via Hassendean
B25	Hawick	— Newtown St Boswells via Ashkirk
B26	Hawick	— Stobs via Linwood
B27	Hawick	— Thorterdykes
B28	Jedburgh	— Edgerston via Camptown
B30	Kelso	— Hume circular
B31	Kelso	— Berwick via Ladykirk, Horndean and Paxton
B32	Kelso	— Berwick via Coldstream, Swinton, Hutton and Paxton
B33	Kelso	— Berwick via Sprouston
B34	Kelso	— Berwick via Ednam, Leitholm and Swinton
B35	Kelso	— Duns via Ednam and Hassington
B36	Kelso	— Leitholm via Hassington
B37	Kelso	— Coldstream via Birgham
B38	Kelso	— Newcastle via Coldstream
B39	Kelso	— Hawick

Leyland Lioness bus O4, ex-Dick Bros., Dalkeith. DLGH

B40	Hawick	— Denholm
B41	Hawick	— Berwick via Jedburgh, Kelso and Wark
B42	Hawick	— Berwick via Jedburgh, Kelso and Birgham
B43	Kelso	— Hume via Ednam
B44	Kelso	— Sprouston and Carham circular
B45	Kelso	— Lauder via Westruther
B46	Kelso	— Earlston via Smailholm
B47	Kelso	— Jedburgh via Eckford
B48	Melrose	— Moffat
B49	Kelso	— Berwick via Leitholm, Whitsome and Allanton
B50	Berwick	— Dunbar
B51	Berwick	— St Abbs via Burnmouth and Eyemouth
B52	Berwick	— St Abbs via Ayton, Eyemouth and Coldingham
B53	Berwick	— Duns via Chirnside
B54	Berwick	— Chirnside via Foulden
B55	Chirnside	— St Abbs via Ayton and Coldingham
B56	Duns	— Grantshouse
B57	Duns	— Cumledge Mill
B58	Duns	— Swinton
B59	Berwick	— Chirnside via Hutton and Allanton
B60	Peebles	— Walkerburn via Traquair
B61	Peebles	— Innerleithen via Eshiels
B62	Peebles	— Dalatho
B63	Peebles	— Elliots Park
B64	Peebles	— Posso
B65	Galashiels	— West Gordon via Melrose and Earlston
B66	Galashiels	— Kelso via Maxton and Pirnie
B67	Galashiels	— Threepwood crossroads
B68	Melrose	— Threepwood crossroads
B69	Melrose	— Selkirk via Abbotsford
B70	Selkirk	— Moffat via St Mary's Loch

One of Dick Bros.' Daimlers, D23, in Dalkeith depot, still in its red and white livery but with S.M.T. diamond insignia.   DLGH

R2 was a Reo with 24-seat Eaton Coachworks body, from Dunn's fleet, seen at Dalkeith depot.   DLGH

C38 was an eleven-seat Chevrolet, ex-Bowen of Musselburgh. Nos. C1-8 were similar in appearance.   DLGH

This Lancia 20-seat bus from Lowson of Blairgowrie carried the number S1 and is seen at Muirhead, a short working from Dundee.

Among the buses transferred from the Western S.M.T. when their operations from Airdrie were taken over was this Leyland Tiger H119, seen at the Mound, Edinburgh, still with its Western headboard.   DLGH

C40	Bo'ness	— Dykehead via Bathgate and Whitburn
C41	Bathgate	— West Calder via Addiewell
C42	Bathgate	— Seafield
C43	Bathgate	— Bents via Blackburn and Stoneyburn
C44	West Calder	— Bents via Addiewell
C45	Bathgate	— Dykehead via Armadale and Harthill
C46	Bathgate	— Harthill via West Craigs
C47	Bathgate	— Eastfield via Armadale and West Craigs
C48	Bathgate	— Harthill via Durhamtoun
C49	Bathgate	— Whitburn via Durhamtoun
C50	Bathgate	— Livingston Station
C51	Bathgate	— Old Livingstone
C52	Bathgate	— circular via Armadale
C53	Bathgate	— Westfield via Torphichen
C54	Bathgate	— circular via Torphichen
C55	Bathgate	— Torphichen via Ballincrief
C60	West Calder	— Dykehead
C61	West Calder	— Fauldhouse
C62	West Calder	— Addiewell
C63	Bathgate	— Blackburn via Durhamtoun
C64	Bathgate	— Oakbank Cottages
C65	Bathgate	— Fauldhouse via Stoneyburn
C66	Bathgate	— Shotts via Whitburn and Fauldhouse
C67	Bathgate	— Fauldhouse via Whitburn
C68	Dykehead	— Bents via Fauldhouse

A Leyland Cheetah, T34, at the Mound, Edinburgh.   DLGH

C69	Fauldhouse	— Whitburn
C70	Bathgate	— circular via Standhill and Bathville
C71	Bathgate	— Bathville via Armadale
C72	Bathgate	— circular via Bathville and Blackridge
C75	Bathgate	— Bo'ness via Armadale, Linlithgow and Champany
C76	Bathgate	— Armadale
C77	Harthill	— West Craigs
C78	Airdrie	— Longriggend
D 1	Dalkeith	— Gorebridge via Eskbank
D 2	Dalkeith	— Rosewell
D 3	Dalkeith	— Rosewell via Lasswade
D 4	Dalkeith	— Pathhead
D 5	Dalkeith	— Blackshiels via Lowholm
D 6	Dalkeith	— Humbie via Edgehead
D11	Gorebridge	— Port Seton
D12	Wallyford	— Niddrie Mill
D13	Wallyford	— Musselburgh
D14	Wallyford	— Newcraighall
D15	Dalkeith	— circular via Newtongrange and Gowkshill
D16	Dalkeith	— Musselburgh
D17	Dalkeith	— Loanhead
D20	Dalkeith	— Portobello via Millerhill
D21	Cousland	— Portobello
D22	Dalkeith	— Cousland via Smeaton
D23	Elphinstone	— Musselburgh
D24	Penicuik	— Roslin
D25	Penicuik	— Musselburgh via Roslin and Dalkeith

It will be seen that provision was made for a good variety of possible short workings. Some, such as 122, were workers' buses. The lists can be taken as indicating all the services now being provided, with, in addition, the following in the Dundee area, where there had also been developments since 1923, including the acquisition of local operators, McCallum & Graham of Forfar, in 1925, some routes of Whyte Bros. of Blairgowrie in March 1928, and Gray of Kinrossie in May 1928:

Dundee, Commercial Street	— Carnoustie
Dundee, Court House Square	— Perth, Station Square
Dundee, North Lindsay Street	— Forfar direct
Dundee, North Lindsay Street	— Brechin via Forfar direct and Finavon
Dundee, North Lindsay Street	— Brechin via Forfar direct and Aberlemno
Dundee, North Lindsay Street	— Forfar via Baldovie and Wellbank
Dundee, North Lindsay Street	— Forfar via Murroes School and Wellbank
Dundee, North Lindsay Street	— Wellbank via Baldovie
Dundee, North Lindsay Street	— Wellbank via Murroes School
Dundee, North Lindsay Street	— Letham
Dundee, North Lindsay Street	— Forfar via Monikie (Sats. and Suns. only)
Dundee, North Lindsay Street	— Alyth
Dundee, North Lindsay Street	— Blairgowrie via Alyth
Dundee, North Lindsay Street	— Blairgowrie via Coupar Angus
Dundee, North Lindsay Street	— Muirhead
Dundee, Shore Terrace	— Ashlundie Hospital (Sats. and Suns. only)
Perth, Station Square	— Blairgowrie via Coupar Angus
Perth, Station Square	— Blairgowrie via Meikleour
Perth, Station Square	— Coupar Angus
Perth, Station Square	— Coupar Angus via Kinrossie
Perth, Station Square	— Forfar (Sats. and Suns. only)

Competition from County Motor Services Ltd. of Choppington, on the Newcastle to Edinburgh and Glasgow via Kelso route, was ended by the acquisition of that company by United Automobile Services Ltd. and the S.M.T. Company jointly in December 1932, and the S.M.T. Co. also took a small share in the acquisition by United Automobile Services Ltd. in August 1934 of Orange Bros. of Bedlington who had operated a London-Newcastle-Edinburgh-Glasgow route in the summer of 1930.

W. Scott & Co. Edinburgh, who ran long-distance tours and also services from Edinburgh to London and to Inverness, were acquired on 11 December 1932. Further small firms acquired at this period were W. Gardiner of Leitholm in July 1932, T. Bell of St Boswells in January 1934, W. Blackie of Eyemouth, running to Berwick in May 1934, J. Stenhouse of Yetholm, running to Kelso and to Wooler, on 1 November 1934, A. Graham of Hawick on 1 January 1935, Dick Bros. of Dalkeith with routes to Gorebridge and to Rosewell, on 1 April 1935, W. & J. Lowson of

A 1936 Leyland Tiger coach for the Edinburgh-London service, H141, loading at the Mound, Edinburgh. These very dark blue 22-seat coaches carried names from the Scott novels, this one being 'Lady of the Lake'. When the war came, they carried double-deck bus bodies, working local routes instead, and H141 became J63.   Gavin Booth Collection

Kirriemuir on 1 May 1935, and J. Browning & Sons of Whitburn, running to Bathgate via Armadale, on 1 August 1935. Some of these owned only one or two vehicles. In April and May 1935 nearly all the remaining tour operators in Edinburgh, namely Bowen, Herd, Sword, and Westwood & Smith, were taken over though the last-named continued under their old name until March 1936; only Cruikshank held out till October 1938.

Services operated by Western S.M.T. Co. Ltd. around Airdrie, the former Midland Bus Services Ltd. routes, to Newmains, Glasgow, Longriggend and Bathgate via Slamannan, were transferred to the S.M.T. Co. Ltd. together with their Airdrie garage and the vehicles engaged thereon, in July 1935, and the S.M.T. Co. premises in Glasgow were then no longer used by buses.

Congestion at the Waverley Bridge was now becoming acute. Buses arriving from the west proceeded via the Mound and Market Street, which was used as a 'park' for buses before proceeding to their stance. So arrangements were made for the starting point of all S.M.T. services to be concentrated in St Andrew Square. This took effect on 1 June 1936. The services to the east continued to use the north side of the Square, those to

A Daimler, D32, from the Westwood & Smith fleet with 32-seat Harrington body.
DLGH

the south took the south side, and those to the west the east side, except Balerno and the Queensferry road buses which were at the north-west corner. The south-west corner was used for tours and specials, though extended tours and the London service remained at the Mound until May 1937. Buses from south and west entered via St David Street, those leaving for the west proceeding via George Street and Castle Street. The Queensferry road buses used George Street and Charlotte Square in both directions. The stances were, of course, on the gardens side. The old uniform with leggings gave way to the cooler trousers in the summer of 1936. On 2 January 1937, the lone little outpost of the British Electric Traction group, the 'Coast Line' service of the Musselburgh & District Electric Light & Traction Co. Ltd., between Waterloo Place and Port Seton, was transferred to S.M.T. ownership. The starting point was also transferred to St Andrew Square in June, but the old route via King's Road and Baileyfield Road continued to be followed.

Early in 1937 negotiations over a wage claim did not go smoothly, and on 9 March all S.M.T. bus crews went on strike: they returned to work on 20 March, the buses having been off the road for eleven days.

The growing village of Gowkshill, up the hill from Newtongrange, was given a service in 1938. A Sunday journey was now run to East Fortune from Dalkeith also, and there were similar journeys from Dalkeith and from Newtongrange to Newbattle. The Balerno via Colinton route was also linked to the Port Seton route on Saturdays and Sundays, the buses proceeding right through and being further extended to the caravan site at Seton Dene. In the summer this service continued right through to North Berwick. Two special express journeys were run daily from Edinburgh to the Empire Exhibition in Glasgow, calling only at Broxburn and Bathgate.

A former Coast Line front-entrance Bristol, X1.   DLGH

Leyland Tiger H144 had also been a Coast Line bus.   DLGH

A Leyland Tiger 35-seat bus of 1936, H188, at St Andrew Square, Edinburgh. DLGH

There was a service from Bathgate to Hardale Golf Club and on Saturdays and Sundays in summer from Bo'ness to Blackness. Additional routes in the Borders were Galashiels to Bowden and Kelso to Kirk Yetholm. There were also now five short local town services in Galashiels, two in Selkirk, two in Hawick, and one in Berwick. A range of special services for mill-workers also ran in Galashiels, Selkirk and Hawick. There was a town service through Bathgate too, some buses on the Whitburn and Harthill services proceeding from and to Barrie Terrace. In the Dundee district there were now routes between Dundee and Kirriemuir, Kirriemuir and Forfar, and Forfar and Arbroath; also a bus on Saturday afternoons from Dundee to Auchterhouse Hospital. On the other hand the Dundee-Carnoustie and Dundee-Perth services had now been transferred to W. Alexander & Sons Ltd. W. & P. Robertson, who operated tours from Dundee, were taken over in February 1938, and a further part of Whyte Bros.' business in Blairgowrie on 10 August 1939.

So by the summer of 1939 we find the S.M.T. providing a very complete network all around Edinburgh, in West Lothian, part of Lanarkshire, and throughout the Borders, with certain routes in the Dundee district too. Almost every village was served. Basically the services to Balerno and to Port Seton ran every ten minutes, while Gilmerton was similar on average. Queensferry had a bus every fifteen minutes. Tranent and Penicuik's average interval was similar, while Broxburn and Dalkeith were served

A 1937 Leyland Tiger, H198, with 30-seat Duple body for the Edinburgh-London service, at the Mound, Edinburgh.   DLGH

Many of the 1929 Leyland Tigers received 29-seat Cowieson bus bodies in 1938, as H12, seen here in New Street depot, Edinburgh.   DLGH

One of the Leyland Titans supplied in 1938, J52. These had enclosed stairs and a plain, slightly bowed front.   DLGH

even more frequently. A half-hourly service was run to North Berwick and to Linlithgow. Fares were kept at a very reasonable level, and the following examples may be quoted: Barnton 3d., Juniper Green 3d., Gilmerton 4d. or 6d. return, Musselburgh 5d. or 8d. return. Kirkliston, Balerno, Loanhead and Dalkeith were 6d. with a return fare of 11d. in the case of the latter two. Queensferry, Port Seton and Tranent were 9d. and 1/4d. return. Broxburn and Penicuik were 10d., the former being 1/3d. return and the latter 1/6d. return. Linlithgow was 1/- and there was no reduced return fare offered. The inconsistency of the return fares seems to have arisen with the piecemeal expansion of services under varying conditions. Double-deck buses were normally used for Penicuik, Lasswade, Rosewell, Gorebridge, etc., and Balerno via Slateford routes. They were used on other routes on occasion too, but some places, e.g. Linlithgow, were barred to them by low bridges.

The range of tours had increased greatly by now; most of those already mentioned in the early twenties were now afternoon departures, as were others to such areas as the Lammermoors, the Meldons, the Moorfoots, and Moffat. All-day tours were now offered to the Scott Country, Bamburgh Castle, Dumfries, Loch Lomond, Loch Awe, Loch Tay, Loch Tummel, Gareloch, Glamis Castle, Gretna, Stranraer, Ayr, St Andrews, and Rothesay, sailing from Gourock. Many of these had been running since the late twenties. A comprehensive sightseeing tour of Edinburgh

B194 was an A.E.C. Ranger with 26-seat Park Royal body, ex-Robertson of Dundee. DLGH

was available both morning and afternoon, and there was also a range of more local tours in the surrounding countryside which ran largely according to demand, including in the evening. The longer tours were usually guaranteed to run no matter how few passengers booked. The company's motor yacht, *Auld Reekie*, now made daily sailings in summer from South Queensferry to the island of Inchcolm. Some tours were also operated from Galashiels and other important centres. In earlier days, the company had not thought there was much demand for extended tours covering several days and had entered that field only in 1931. But their popularity was growing too, and the range now included two-day tours to Oban, and to Braemar, and a four-day tour to Aberdeen and Inverness. On five-day trips there was a choice of the North-West Highlands, Skye, Mull or the 'Grand Highland', which included Wester Ross and Deeside. There was also a six-day tour to John O'Groats and a similar eight-day one including Deeside as well. England and Wales were included too with both four- and six-day tours to the Lake District, nine days to the Wye Valley, and thirteen-day tours to both Devon and Cornwall, and to the South Coast. The company's finances remained sound, with 10% being paid on the ordinary shares for several years past.

Then came the war. Outwardly there was little sign of any preparation by the S.M.T., but they were ready, and sufficient buses were

A Commer, W14, ex-Cruikshank, with 26-seat Waveney body.   DLGH

immediately fitted up with complete black-out curtains to keep services running, and the rest rapidly followed. This policy enabled the normal lighting to be used in the vehicles and was no doubt of advantage to the longer-distance passengers. On the other hand, passengers could not tell where they were and had to rely on the conductor or conductress, who was often equally 'lost', with the inevitable, unfortunate result on occasion. The older double-deckers with open platforms had to have a little screening fitted on the back. Headlights, of course, had to conform to regulations and the company intimated that the various running times were applicable to the hours of daylight only. Early in the war, some buses were taken for ambulance duties, and then some forty or so were requisitioned by the military authorities. The usual annual replacements were on order, however, and were duly received in 1940. Four double-deckers were lent to London later in the year.

At the end of the 1939 season the tours, summer services and long-distance services ceased, though the overnight London service was continued for a few months more but, except on Friday and Saturday nights, following a more westerly route. Special services such as that to East Fortune were no longer required and the linking of the Balerno and Port Seton routes ceased. Hardale Golf Club lost its service too. The route between Jedburgh and Newcastle was withdrawn, though a bus was run from Jedburgh as far as Edgerston on Tuesdays and Saturdays. On the

Leyland Tiger with 39-seat Alexander body, H255, supplied in 1940, seen in post-war green livery and with the S.M.T. diamond insignia flanked by aluminium strip.   DLGH

E18 was a wartime Guy double-decker with a Weymann body, seen in post-war green livery at St Andrew Square, Edinburgh.   DLGH

One of the dark grey Bedford wartime 'utility', 32-seat buses, C101, in St Andrew Square, Edinburgh. Note the wooden slat seats.   DLGH

other hand, a new service via Gullane was provided to West Fenton air station. One of these journeys ran via Port Seton. The caravan site at Seton Dene became a regular dormitory and two Port Seton journeys were extended there Mondays to Fridays. The accent was on essential traffic. Gradually the services had to be cut somewhat to meet the call of fuel rationing. The times of the last buses were brought forward in some cases, and Sunday services were more sparse. Duplication had to be virtually eliminated, and loadings were thus generally heavy. Nevertheless a remarkably good service was provided throughout the war.

Sixty Bedford utility buses were obtained, and the bodies for these, and many more besides, were built by S.M.T. at premises taken over at Marine Gardens, Portobello. The Ministry of Supply were also able to provide a number of double-deckers, and further double-deck bodies were obtained and fitted to former coaches. An early experiment was made, in March 1940, with a gas-producer fixed to the back of an AEC bus, No. B3, while later a number of AEC and Leyland vehicles were adapted for the standard producer-gas trailers and run on the fairly flat North Berwick route. A few buses on busy short-distance routes were fitted with longitudinal seats to give increased standing capacity in 1942.

Season tickets for adults were withdrawn about July 1941 but weekly

S6 was one of six Dennis Lancet IIs with 35-seat Strachan bodies supplied during the war. It is seen parked in Queen Street, Edinburgh, on Stark's Dunbar route and in green. DLGH

tickets available for one or, alternatively, for two daily return journeys, excluding Sundays, were made available at appropriate rates. The charge for dogs was increased to one-quarter fare. To assist in loadings at rush-hours some buses were run non-stop to outlying towns, such as Bathgate, in 1941. Then, in 1943, to discourage the long-distance traveller who had alternative rail service, some of the remaining long routes were cut, e.g. Edinburgh-Newcastle, cut at Berwick, so that there was no effective through service. However, a new service to be recorded was one on Saturdays and Sundays only to Kirknewton, which started in February 1943. The road through Turnhouse was closed because of the aerodrome and continued so for some time after the war, necessitating a diversion via Gogar for buses on the Linlithgow route.

When the war ended the vehicle black-out equipment was speedily removed, though the restoration of headlights to a satisfactory condition took much longer. There had been little change in the local routes being run, but some districts were growing rapidly and commanded a much increased service, e.g. Birkenside and Easthouses. An effort was made to provide improved services as soon as possible, but the effects of continued fuel rationing made this a slow process. Nevertheless the long-distance services were restarted on a restricted scale early in the summer of 1946. The routes to Newcastle were restored on 5 June, and on Saturdays and

Sundays there was a new route from Edinburgh to Berwick via Lauder, Greenlaw and Paxton, which started on 5 October. The suburban services to Gilmerton and nearby Danderhall were increasing with the growing population. Port Seton buses continued on to Seton Sands for the summer, while the Cousland-Portobello service was suspended during the winter. Some buses on the Millerhill route proceeded via Danderhall, and from 5 October the Kirknewton route was continued on to Mid Calder. There were two buses on Saturdays to Glenkinchie road-end in East Lothian. Various useful school or workers' services, usually once inward in the morning and outward in the evening, appeared in the timetables such as Cousland to St Andrew Square, Wallyford to St Andrew Square via Inveresk, Danderhall to Dalkeith via Millerhill. Other workers' journeys were run direct to and from such places as the North British Rubber Works and other factories in Edinburgh and Leith, being operated to Dalkeith, Linlithgow, Bathgate, etc. Not all of them were advertised, however. There were new services from Duns to Abbey St Bathans started on 11 February 1946, to Cranshaws and to Longformacus, both started on 21 May, and to Heughead, started on 10 October. A service from Hawick to Ancrum commenced on 4 June 1947.

Some local routes around Airdrie operated by W. Irvine of Glenmavis had been taken over on 1 May 1940, and Campbell Bros., who operated a few vehicles from Whitburn, were taken over on 8 July 1945. W. H. Boyd of Bo'ness, with tour licences, was also acquired in 1945. Additional services included Airdrie to Greengairs via Rigghead and also via Whiterigg, Airdrie to Meikle Drumgray, Airdrie to Glenmavis, extended to New Monkland on Sundays, and Coatbridge to Gartcosh and Mount Helen, later extended to Muirhead on 15 December 1947. These services were not numbered. A town service was started in Bo'ness in 1947, and on 15 May 1948 a service three days a week from Bathgate to Forth.

Another acquisition in December 1947 was the Dalkeith-Bonnyrigg-Cockpen-Newtongrange-Easthouses-Dalkeith circular service, and the Wednesdays, Saturdays and Sundays service from Dalkeith to Carrington and Toxside, hitherto run by R. Cockburn & Sons of Eskbank. Local services in Musselburgh grew, including new ones to Stoneybank, to Ashgrove, to Edenhall Hospital, and to Preston, i.e. near Prestonpans station — the latter extended to and from St Andrew Square via King's Road on Sunday evenings, still with its Dalkeith area service number D92. From May 1949 a service was provided on Saturdays from Dalkeith to Rosslynlee Hospital.

A list of the numbers allocated to new services and alterations since 1934 should now be given:

A post-war A.E.C. Regal with 35-seat Duple body, B268, at St Andrew Square, Edinburgh.   DLGH

26	Broxburn	— Loganlea
27	Linlithgow	— Blackness via Philpstoun
28	Broxburn	— Grangemouth via Philpstoun and Linlithgow
40	St Andrew Square	— West Fenton via King's Road and Port Seton
43	St Andrew Square	— Glenkinchie road end
49	St Andrew Square	— Wallyford via Willowbrae
50	St Andrew Square	— Birkenside via Little France
52	St Andrew Square	— Humbie via Little France and Edgehead
54	St Andrew Square	— Pathhead via Little France
55	St Andrew Square	— Blackshiels via Little France and Edgehead
56	St Andrew Square	— Humbie via Little France
57	St Andrew Square	— Eskbank via Little France
58	St Andrew Square	— Gilmerton (previously 76)
68	St Andrew Square	— Bonnyrigg via Gilmerton (previously 75)
69	St Andrew Square	— Gorebridge via Gilmerton and Gowkshill
75	St Andrew Square	— Middleton via Little France and Easthouses
80	St Andrew Square	— Birkenside via Gilmerton and Gowkshill
82	St Andrew Square	— Blackshiels via Little France
84	St Andrew Square	— Birkenside via Gilmerton and Easthouses
86	St Andrew Square	— Middleton via Gilmerton and Easthouses
88	St Andrew Square	— Dalkeith via Little France
89	St Andrew Square	— Birkenside via Gilmerton, Easthouses and Gowkshill
117	Glasgow	— Airdrie
118	Glasgow	— Longriggend
119	Glasgow	— Clarkston
123	St Andrew Square	— Linlithgow

Many of the pre-war A.E.C. Regals were rebodied in 1947-8, mostly with Alexander bodies, but some, such as B28, seen here at Duns, received bodies by Burlingham, while others received Croft bodies.   DLGH

124	St Andrew Square	— Linlithgow Bridge
135	St Andrew Square	— North Berwick via King's Road and Port Seton
142	St Andrew Square	— Bathgate via Livingston Station
144	St Andrew Square	— Kirknewton
164	St Andrew Square	— Hopetoun crossroads
165	St Andrew Square	— Hopetoun crossroads via Dalmeny
166	St Andrew Square	— South Queensferry via Dalmeny
167	St Andrew Square	— Bo'ness via Mannerston
170	St Andrew Square	— Musselburgh via King's Road
171	St Andrew Square	— Seton Dene via King's Road
172	St Andrew Square	— Port Seton via King's Road
190	Glasgow	— Bathgate via Slamannan
191	Glasgow	— Coatdyke via Lightburn
279	St Andrew Square	— Berwick via Lauder, Greenlaw and Paxton
B00	Hawick	— Jedburgh via Denholm
B27	Hawick Town services	
B50	Duns	— Abbey St Bathans
B66	Duns	— Longformacus
B69	Duns	— Cranshaws
B71	Selkirk Town services	
B72	Galashiels	— St Boswells via Leaderfoot
B73	Galashiels	— Bowden

Pre-war Leyland Tigers were also rebodied with Alexander or Burlingham 35-seat bodies. H66 is one of the latter on the Elder Street approach to the St Andrew Square bus station, Edinburgh.   DLGH

B74	Bowden	— Newtown station
B80	Kelso	— Kirk Yetholm
B81	Duns	— Heughead
B86	Galashiels	— Yair Bridge
B87	Hawick	— Cogsmill
B88	Hawick	— Ancrum
B89	Kelso	— Earlston via Mellerstain
C34	Bathgate	— Forth
C56	Bathgate	— Hardale Golf Club
C57	Bathgate	— Bo'ness
C79	Bathgate	— Armadale via Bathville
C80	Airdrie, Gartlea	— Newmains
C81	Airdrie, Gartlea	— Chapelhall
C82	Airdrie, Gartlea	— O'wood
C90	Bathgate, Barrie Terrace	—Whitburn via Durhamtoun
C91	Bathgate, Barrie Terrace	— Harthill via Durhamtoun
C98	Bo'ness town service circular	

Several other C numbers were allocated which seem to have applied to works or other special journeys. There was also an unnumbered town service in Bathgate from North Bridge Street to Easton, which commenced on 21 July 1947.

D10	Dalkeith	— Newtongrange via Newbattle
D18	Dalkeith	— East Fortune
D26	Cousland	— Portobello via Dalkeith
D27	Dalkeith	— Penicuik
D92	Musselburgh	— Preston
D94	Dalkeith	— Gowkshill
D95	Dalkeith	— Cockpen circular
D96	Dalkeith	— Toxside
D99	Dalkeith	— Rosslynlee

It is noteworthy that the company had managed to keep its same scale of fares despite the war. About the only increase was a halfpenny on the fare to Juniper Green. On the other hand, there were one or two instances of small reductions.

The company had turned over much of its resources to war work, and had equipped a large building at Portobello, part of the old Marine Gardens, where military and other vehicles were assembled. After the war this was turned into a modern bodybuilding works for the company's needs, being opened as such in July 1948.

With such large-scale activities, the company's vehicles inevitably met with accidents from time to time, but while some of these were no doubt alarming, very few resulted in serious casualties to passengers. Two in the Edinburgh area may be mentioned. After a sidelong collision on the Glasgow road near Ingliston on 6 June 1934, a west-going bus crashed into a tree and one passenger was killed while twenty-four others and the crew were injured.

On 20 June 1941, a bus from Port Seton, travelling westwards at speed up Portobello Road, got out of control and crashed head-on into a tramcar, killing five bus passengers and injuring thirty-three.

A subsidiary company, S.M.T. Insurance Co. Ltd., was formed in 1945 to handle the insurance risk of all the group companies' public vehicles.

4

Scottish Omnibuses Ltd.

Another major change in the company's constitution was now impending. Early in 1948 the new British Transport Commission were offered the opportunity of investigating the company's finances with a view to a voluntary sale of the bus and coach operations. The result was the approval at a special general meeting of the company on 8 April 1949 of the sale of the company's bus undertaking, including the subsidiary operating companies and the insurance company, to the British Transport Commission with effect from 1 April 1948. The authorised capital of the S.M.T. Co. Ltd. had, in 1938, been increased to £2,750,000, and the company owned nearly all the stock or share capital of both Western S.M.T. Co. Ltd. and Central S.M.T. Co. Ltd., although there were minor complexities regarding certain of the subsidiary companies still legally functioning under these companies' ownership. The company also held a majority of the ordinary shares of W. Alexander & Sons Ltd. The finances of the preceding year were duly sorted out and a new company, Scottish Omnibuses Ltd., was registered on 8 April 1949. The Scottish Motor Traction Co. Ltd. then devoted itself to its other interests, vehicle agencies, sales, repairs, etc., at the many S.M.T. Sales & Service Co. Ltd. depots throughout Scotland and the Borders area. Western S.M.T., Central S.M.T. and W. Alexander & Sons Ltd. — except for the coach-building activities of the latter which were not included in the sale — continued as subsidiaries of Scottish Omnibuses Ltd. in the ownership of the British Transport Commission. By agreement the fleet name 'S.M.T.' was continued on the buses and coaches of Scottish Omnibuses for a period of years. Later, the Highland Transport Co. Ltd., partly owned by the British Transport Commission through its former L.M.S. railway shareholding, was fully acquired by a new company, Highland Omnibuses Ltd., formed in 1951 to bring it into the group too. As this is primarily a history of the bus operations, it is now Scottish Omnibuses Ltd. that concerns us here.

Sir William Thomson, as he had now become, retired at this time, whereupon Mr James Amos, who had come along with Brook & Amos in 1926 and was latterly manager of the S.M.T. Co.'s bus department, became chairman of the new company. Mr Robert Beveridge, who had been with the company since 1914, was appointed general manager.

A post-war Bedford, C183, with 25-seat Duple style body, at Waverley Bridge, Edinburgh.   DLGH

'Sandy' Bracken, another of the small staff from the earliest days and long since chief engineer, retired in 1948. There was little or no sign of the change of ownership, and the new company continued to operate as of old. The change to the green livery in June 1949, already mentioned, is said to have been quite coincidental. However, the old ABC type of pocket timetables disappeared in favour of one rather larger book in tabular form in 1951, issued twice a year by British Transport Advertising from their office in Castle Terrace.

A note on some of these long-serving personalities may not be out of place. William Thomson was an able man but seems to have been of a stubborn disposition, not always easy to get on with. He had his failings and, with perhaps a hint of arrogance, many found him less than endearing. During the 1914-18 war he told a board meeting he was too busy to prepare a report for them. Robert Beveridge, on the other hand, was a quiet and likeable gentleman. Sandy Bracken was a hard worker with perhaps a touch of the rough diamond in him, but he had a kind heart and was always ready to help anyone. Although of a slightly later period, James Amos should be included among them. He was of a kind nature and retained the country interests of his early life. At the same time the bus industry was his lifework and he worked hard for it, expecting the same of his staff.

The Caledonian Omnibus Co. Ltd., also nationalised, was disbanded

Several post-war Bedfords were soon rebodied with 24-seat Burlingham 'Seagull' bodies, such as C175, seen here leaving St Andrew Square, Edinburgh.   DLGH

and its services were taken over by Scottish Omnibuses Ltd. and Western S.M.T. from 1 January 1950, though the old name was not relinquished until June when S.M.T. took over operation of the Edinburgh-Dumfries service entirely. An internal rationalisation was the transfer at the end of 1949 of all the S.M.T. services in the Dundee area to W. Alexander & Sons Ltd., who were the predominant group company in the territory, together with the Westfield Avenue garage and all the vehicles concerned.

The first post-war fares increase took effect on 4 December 1950, and there have been further increases in most years since. With fuel rationing finished and traffic booming at summer weekends, Scottish Omnibuses found they could use many more vehicles than they had available, despite considerable additions to the fleet. Use was made of other vehicles from the group or allied companies where opportunity offered, but in addition, in July 1951 and for several summers following, a few dozen buses, both single and double-deck, were hired from Edinburgh Corporation on Saturday afternoons and used on a wide variety of S.M.T. services. A new Rule Book was issued to the staff of all the group companies in May 1951, while a well-produced monthly staff magazine, *The Scottish Omnibus*, made its debut in February 1955.

In 1951 the services to East Fortune had been restored and a service run from North Berwick to West Fenton. There was a new service from Edinburgh to Riccarton House and another on Saturdays only to

The post-war double-deckers were A.E.C. Regals. The third batch supplied in 1950 had Burlingham bodies, of which BB87, seen in Market Street, Edinburgh, is one. DLGH

Hopetoun House. The Linlithgow-Blackness service was now combined with a Linlithgow-Avonbridge service. Peebles to Posso was extended to Langhaugh and services ran from Peebles to West Linton and to Glen Lodge. An interesting extension of route commenced on 10 September 1951, arising from the withdrawal of the passenger train service from Polton, when it was agreed to run five journeys, including some from Dalkeith, down the very steep hill into the little village, so that in the absence of trains a walk to Polton road-end was avoided. On 18 August 1952, the long-distance services were transferred to a new stance at the east end of Queen Street, thus easing the position at St Andrew Square, which was becoming chaotic on summer Saturdays. The Dumfries service was also transferred there from Castle Terrace on 4 May 1953, and in April 1954 the Queen Street stances were equipped with stance poles of the latest type being used by the Corporation.

Competition on the Edinburgh-London night service developed in 1951 when Northern Roadways, a Glasgow-based firm engaged mainly on contract work, secured licences to run an overnight service using coaches with a toilet compartment and a hostess to distribute free snacks. They also ran similar overnight services from Glasgow to London in competition with the Western S.M.T. service, and from Glasgow to Birmingham and Glasgow to Bournemouth. Eventually, after much objection, argument and appeal in the Traffic Courts, Northern

Underfloor engines arrived in 1951 with new A.E.C. Regal IV coaches with 30-seat Alexander bodies equipped with toilets for the Edinburgh-London service. B441 is at St Andrew Square, Edinburgh. DLGH

Roadways' licences were withdrawn and their Edinburgh-London service ceased on 6 April 1956. Faced with this competition, S.M.T. had reintroduced coaches with toilets on their service too. S.M.T. took over the Glasgow-Bournemouth service southwards on Fridays and northwards on Saturdays in summer only and through return passengers only were carried. The Glasgow-Birmingham service was taken over by Midland Red, Ribble and North Western with S.M.T. also having an interest. Soon this service ran in summer only too and then disappeared from the S.M.T. timetable.

An hourly express service between Edinburgh and Glasgow was started on 24 November 1951. There was one pick-up point at Edinburgh Zoo westbound and at Baillieston eastbound, these points being used to set down in the opposite direction. A flat fare of 4/- single, 6/5d. return was charged. The zoo picking-up/setting-down point was changed to Corstorphine Station Road in 1957. An overnight journey with limited stops was introduced on three nights a week in summer on the Edinburgh-Inverness route in 1952, and also an overnight journey in summer to Scarborough. Other new services in 1952 were Edinburgh to Lennoxlove House in summer only, a local service in Penicuik, Glasgow to Drumpark via Lightburn, and the extension of the Selkirk-Ettrickbridge service to Ettrick Post Office on Saturdays only. There was also a temporary service

B478 was one of a later lot without toilet facilities and seating 38. It is carrying an Institute of Transport party at Hopetoun House, South Queensferry.   DLGH

from Edinburgh to Turnhouse. On 12 February 1953 a new service was started from Edinburgh to Alloa via Linlithgow and Bo'ness, and on 10 August another from Glasgow to Chapelhall Industrial Estate. A town service in Linlithgow started on 2 February 1953, and Airdrie to Thrashbush on 5 October. There were increased overnight services to London in summer 1954, and the through service in summer to Manchester was restarted. The service to Riccarton House ceased in 1954 and the Dalkeith-Toxside service ran only as far as Rosebery in the winter of 1954-5. A local service from Dalkeith to Mayfield commenced on 8 March 1954, and there were through journeys from Edinburgh to Mayfield the following year. A circular service from Haddington to Yester appeared in the timetables from 1955, though it seems to have been run in 1954 too.

A new agreement was concluded with Edinburgh Corporation on 1 July 1954 covering the respective spheres of operation and fares. As a result of this, and the withdrawal of the Portobello and Musselburgh tramway service, the S.M.T. service from St Andrew Square to Port Seton and its variations (Nos. 170-1-2) were diverted to follow the old tramway route through Portobello and Joppa, together with a new service to Galt Road, Musselburgh, from 14 November 1954. The latter was extended to Wallyford on 6 February 1955. The local journeys to Gilmerton and other points within the city boundary to which the company hitherto ran 'duplicates' at busy periods ceased as the Corporation services were augmented. A gyratory system for all traffic was put into operation temporarily in St Andrew Square in the spring of 1956 in connection with the roadway repairs in Princes Street, and this necessitated the stances being changed to the 'buildings' sides around the Square for the time being. A service from Glasgow to Broomhouse started on 1 June 1955, and the service to Lennoxlove House was withdrawn after that summer. A service, outwards on Fridays, returning on Sundays, from Edinburgh to Oban, operated in the summers of 1955 and 1956, after which it lapsed until 1965 when it was provided on summer Saturdays only. A town service in Jedburgh commenced on 16 January 1956 and some Birkenside buses were diverted through Mayfield from 1 October 1956. In the Borders a new service, started in 1957, ran on Tuesdays and Fridays from Selkirk to Ettrickbridge via Bowhill.

Early in 1956 Mr Roderick MacKenzie was appointed general manager in succession to Mr Beveridge, then due to retire.

A long-standing grievance of the travelling public was the lack of a bus station, for St Andrew Square provided no shelter whatever for waiting passengers. The company had decided before the war that this amenity would be provided and started purchase of their chosen site. Of course the war halted all progress with the project, and afterwards resumption was delayed by difficulties with planning permission for a reasonably long period. Eventually, however, the scheme reached fruition with the official opening on 5 April 1957 of the station at Clyde Street with its four platforms with shelters and other amenities. It cost over £250,000 and could handle 120 buses per hour. Even so congestion could arise in the summer peak periods. An exhibition of coaches was held on 5 and 6 April, and normal traffic began to use it on 7 April, with a gyratory traffic system round St Andrew Square, St Andrew Street and St David Street. Buses entered the station via York Place and Elder Street, except those from the south which proceeded from the Post Office via East Register Street until that street was closed in May 1970 with the St James Square development, after which they had to use Leith Street, York Place and Elder Street. All buses depart into St Andrew Square. The site is eminently suitable, in contrast to the town planners' proposals at that time for two or more bus stations at points as far removed from one another and from the main railway station as Shrubhill and Morrison Street.

On 13 January 1958 Lowland Motorways Ltd. were acquired. Their services in the area eastwards of Glasgow were based on a garage in Shettleston Road and were:

Parkhead Cross	— Cardowan
Parkhead Cross	— Garthamlock
Parkhead, London Road	— Barlanark via Barrachnie
Shettleston	— Barlanark via Gartocher Road
Shettleston	— Cranhill
Shettleston	— Wellhouse
Carntyne	— Mount Vernon
Barrachnie Cross	— Hillingdon, works service
Garthamlock	— Cathcart, works service
Parkhead	— Gartloch Hospital, visiting service

New services in the area were subsequently added: Parkhead-Provanhall on 5 October 1958 and Baillieston-Easterhouse on 4 May 1959.

A larger garage nearer to Glasgow than that at Airdrie, the former Clarkston garage of Midland Bus Services Ltd., was now clearly necessary, and a site at Baillieston was chosen for the new building which was opened on 14 November 1960. A new bus station was opened at Kelso on 16 May 1960.

A Saturday journey from and to Dunbar was diverted via Traprain from 10 December 1960. A service from Edinburgh direct to Prestwick Airport, designated 'The Transatlantic Express', and on which new coaches bearing names were at first used, commenced on 15 May 1961. There were other new services in 1961 from Broxburn to Roman Camp and to Crossgreen, and also from Galashiels to Dingleton Hospital, while following the raising of the speed limit the London service times were cut to around fourteen hours from 5 February 1962.

Early in 1961 the S.M.T. insignia, so well known for so long, had begun to disappear from the vehicles in favour of the company's title of Scottish Omnibuses, but on 9 May of the same year a structural reorganisation of the companies in the group took effect and 'Scottish Omnibuses' was felt to be insufficiently descriptive: so, after a time, the fleet name became merely 'Scottish', which was of course no better. During 1963 and 1964 there were several experiments with different liveries, mainly with a lighter green in various forms, and the S.M.T. diamond insignia appeared again for a time. 'Eastern Scottish' was thereupon chosen for the fleet name, being applied from about the end of 1964, while in 1965 the rather darker, so-called Lothian green was adopted for bus livery, with coaches remaining predominantly cream.

Rebuilding and extension of the Musselburgh garage, which had been acquired with Bowen's business in 1935, was completed on 27 April 1962, and the company also built a large new works on a site at the old Marine Gardens at the Portobello end of Seafield Road. All the engineering and body workshops were transferred there from the New Street premises

Some of the post-war A.E.C. Regals were lengthened and rebuilt with full fronts in 1953. B340 is one of these parked in Queen Street, Edinburgh.   DLGH

which then became a depot garage only, accommodating 290 buses. The new Marine Works cost £85,000 and were opened on 24 May 1962.

On the demise of the British Transport Commission at the end of 1962, control of the group passed to the state-owned Transport Holding Company. During the period of B.T.C. control the Travel Press & Publicity Company had become dormant, but now it was revived and registered as the Travel Press & Publicity Co. Ltd. to handle its functions as before.

Baxter's Bus Service, Airdrie, was an important acquisition on 17 December 1962, adding a network of local services around Airdrie and Coatbridge. Although repainting of Baxter's vehicles in Scottish Omnibuses colours was started, it soon ceased as it was realised that the public did not relish uniformity and that goodwill would be better preserved by retaining Baxter vehicles on Baxter's routes. Baxter's garage in Victoria Road continued in use too. When new buses were transferred there in subsequent years they were usually repainted with Baxter's name and dark blue colour.

Stark's Motor Services Ltd. at Dunbar, in which the S.M.T. Company had long had an interest, and whose buses on the Edinburgh-Dunbar route had always been painted and lettered in S.M.T. livery, were fully

B429, a 1954 A.E.C. Monocoach, 45-seat Park Royal body, leaving St Andrew Square, Edinburgh. DLGH

absorbed on 1 January 1964. Local routes were from Dunbar to North Berwick, to East Fortune, to Spott, to Oldhamstocks, and from North Berwick to Haddington via Athelstaneford and also via Drem. There was also a Dunbar town service in summer and some tours.

What was aptly referred to as 'the end of an era' was the retiral in October 1963 of the group's chairman, James Amos, whose name had become almost a legend in Scottish road transport circles. His successor was W. M. Little, Edinburgh Corporation's Transport Manager.

The drastic reduction in railway services which took place in the 1960s had little effect on the provision of bus services in the company's field, as the area was already well covered by bus services, though, of course, many people missed the quicker and generally more comfortable journey by train. An express bus started from Dunbar at 7.40 am and picked up only at West Barns and East Linton, arriving at St Andrew Square at 8.40 am. There was a return journey at 12.15 pm on Saturdays and two journeys, 4.15 pm and 5.40 pm, on Mondays to Fridays, but from September 1971 only the latter outward journey was operated and there was no inward journey on Saturdays either. This service ceased altogether in the summer of 1974. Some of the local services from Peebles were given up about 1964.

The opening on 4 September 1964 of the Forth Road Bridge had an

The first Bristol coach, A1, in St Andrew Square, Edinburgh, 1954.   DLGH

immediate impact on Eastern Scottish services in that direction. From the following day a half-hourly service was provided between St Andrew Square and Dunfermline, alternate buses proceeding through South Queensferry on their way to and from the bridge, the others reaching it direct. Another service was provided every hour between St Andrew Square and Leven, half-hourly as far as Kirkcaldy on Saturdays. W. Alexander & Sons (Fife) Ltd. worked these new services jointly with Eastern Scottish. Railway fares to and from Fife were cut to counter the new competition. From the same date the Alloa service was operated via South Queensferry and Bo'ness instead of Linlithgow and Bo'ness. An interesting point was the adaptation of a bus, B302, to convey cyclists and their machines, free, across the bridge until the cycle paths were completed on 23 January 1965.

The numbers applied to the various new services since 1950 should now be given together with changes which had been applied to some other services, viz.:

1	Broxburn	— West Calder
5	Broxburn town service	
16	McNair Street	— Cranhill (Glasgow area)
18	Linlithgow	— Whitecross
24	Broxburn	— Kirknewton
46	Edinburgh	— Tranent via Woolmet

The 32-seat lightweight bus designed and built by S.M.T. in 1955. S1 at the St Andrew Square bus station, Edinburgh.   DLGH

The Bristol Lodekka was a 60-seat double-decker. This one was originally AA3 in 1956 but was sold to Highland Omnibuses Ltd. in 1963 and returned to Eastern Scottish in 1972 as AA576.   A. J. Douglas

49	Edinburgh	— Wallyford
50	Edinburgh	— Newtongrange via Danderhall and Eskbank
57	Edinburgh	— Ormiston via Danderhall and Gowkshill
59	Edinburgh	— Easthouses via Gilmerton
61	Edinburgh	— Whitecraigs via Millerhill
62	Edinburgh	— Dalkeith via Niddrie Mill, Millerhill and Whitecraigs
63	Edinburgh	— Dalkeith via Danderhall, Millerhill and Whitecraigs
64	Edinburgh	— Easthouses via Danderhall
69	Edinburgh	— Middleton via Gilmerton and Gowkshill
70	Edinburgh	— Newtongrange via Gilmerton and Easthouses
75	Edinburgh	— Newtongrange via Danderhall and Easthouses
77	Edinburgh	— Arniston via Danderhall, Easthouses and Gowkshill
83	Edinburgh	— Birkenside via Gilmerton and Mayfield
93	Edinburgh	— Polton village via Kirk Brae
96A	Edinburgh	— Penicuik via Loanhead
117	Edinburgh	— Pumpherston
120	Glasgow	— Chapelhall via Shawhead
122	Haddington	— Yester circular
125	Glasgow	— Clarkston via Lightburn
126	Glasgow	— Caldercruix via Plains
127	Glasgow	— Coatdyke
144	Edinburgh	— Mid Calder via Kirknewton
145	Edinburgh	— Kirknewton
150A	Edinburgh	— Penicuik via Lothianburn and Auchendinny
168	Edinburgh	— Bo'ness via Mannerston
169	Edinburgh	— Hopetoun House
174	Edinburgh	— Ashburnham Road via Dalmeny
175	Edinburgh	— Craigiehall
176	Edinburgh	— Wallyford via Galt Road
177	Dreghorn	— Craigiehall
180	Edinburgh	— Rosyth Dockyard
192	Glasgow	— Broomhouse via Lightburn
194	Glasgow	— Easterhouse
195	Baillieston	— Easterhouse
248	Glasgow	— Whitburn via Bellshill
249	Edinburgh	— Glasgow via Bellshill
253	Edinburgh	— Scarborough
254	Glasgow	— Scarborough
256	Glasgow	— Bournemouth
268	Edinburgh	— Liverpool, night service
269	Edinburgh	— Kelso via Westruther and Gordon
300	Edinburgh	— Prestwick
303	Edinburgh	— Ingliston Highland Show
304	Edinburgh	— Heads of Ayr
309	Edinburgh	— Glasgow Express
325	Edinburgh	— Alloa
381	Edinburgh	— Dunfermline direct
382	Edinburgh	— Dunfermline via South Queensferry

383	Edinburgh	— Leven
B18	Peebles	— Walkerburn
B21	Selkirk	— Lilliesleaf
B23	Hawick	— Ashkirk
B25	Hawick	— Jedburgh
B26	Galashiels	— Hawick
B29	St Abbs	— Duns
B45	Kelso	— Westruther
B47	Kelso	— Newtown St Boswells via Maxton
B49	Kelso	— Duns via Fogorig
B58	St Abbs	— Coldingham
B60	Peebles	— Innerleithen via Traquair
B62	Innerleithen	— Glen Lodge
B64	Peebles	— Langhaugh
B65	Galashiels town service	
B70	Selkirk	— Dumfries
B72	Galashiels	— Clintmains
B73	Peebles	— West Linton
B75	Galashiels	— St Boswells via Bowden
B76	Kelso	— Berwick via Coldstream, Swinton, Ladykirk and Hutton
B77	Kelso	— Swinton via Eccles
B78	Galashiels	— Bowden
B79	Kelso	— Duns via Eccles
B81	Duns	— Heughead or Ayton
B82	Selkirk	— Ettrick Post Office
B83	Selkirk	— Gordon Arms
B84	Hawick	— Ashkirk via Lilliesleaf
B85	Hawick	— Wells Sawmill via Denholm
B90	Duns	— Berwick via Paxton
B91	Kelso	— Ancrum via Roxburgh
B92	Hawick	— Minto
B93	Kelso	— Westruther
B94	Kelso	— Peel Hospital via Jedburgh
B95	Kelso	— Peel Hospital via Earlston
B96	Peebles	— Peel Hospital
C20	Airdrie	— Tannochside
C21	Airdrie	— Tollcross
C24	Airdrie	— Gartcosh or Muirhead
C25	Airdrie	— Greengairs via Rigghead
C26	Airdrie	— Greengairs via Whiterigg
C27	Airdrie	— Glenmavis
C29	Airdrie	— Whinhill
C30	Broxburn Academy	— Pumpherston
C33	Broxburn	— Bo'ness via Bridgend
C35	West Calder	— Dykehead via Oakbank Cottages
C36	Bo'ness	— Bangour Hospital
C37	Linlithgow town service	

A Leyland PD2/20 of 1957, HH548, loading at St Andrew Square, Edinburgh.   S.O.L.

A 70-seat front-entrance Bristol Lodekka of 1962, AA887, on an Edinburgh-Birkenside run.   A. J. Douglas

C39	Airdrie	— Whitburn
C41	Bathgate	— Edinburgh via Loganlea and Mid Calder
C58	Bathgate	— Avonbridge
C59	Bathgate	— Woodend Colliery
C62	Polbeth	— Stoneyburn
C73	Bathgate	— Whitburn via Armadale
C74	Bathgate	— Dixon's Pit
C90	Bathgate	— Shotts via Standhill
C91	Bathgate town service	
C92	Dykehead	— Fauldhouse
C94	Bathgate	— Polbeth via Stoneyburn
C95	Bathgate	— Fauldhouse via Standhill
C96	Bathgate	— Whitburn via Standhill
C97	Bathgate	— Harthill via Standhill
D 1	Dalkeith	— Birkenside
D 3	Dalkeith	— Musselburgh via Whitecraigs
D12	Wallyford	— Stoneybank
D17	Dalkeith	— Roslin
D19	Dalkeith	— Whitecraigs
D21	Musselburgh	— Monktonhall Colliery
D23	Musselburgh	— Tranent
D28	Musselburgh	— Woolmet via Newcraighall
D30	Dalkeith	— Polton village
D31	Dalkeith	— Mayfield
D57	Bathgate	— Dales via Armadale
D90	Musselburgh	— Newcraighall
D93	Tranent	— Wallyford
D94	Dalkeith	— Birkenside via Gowkshill
D96	Dalkeith	— Rosebery and Firside

The numbers applied to a few of the new services duplicated the numbers of certain existing services, viz.:

13	Edinburgh	— Dumfries via Thornhill
13B	Edinburgh	— Tweedsmuir via Biggar and Broughton
13C	Edinburgh	— Biggar via Blyth Bridge
15	Parkhead	— Provanhill
17	Parkhead	— Cardowan
18	Parkhead	— Easterhouse
21	Parkhead	— Garthamlock
22	Parkhead	— Barlanark
28	Edinburgh	— Tweedsmuir via West Linton and Broughton
51	Broxburn	— Roman Camp
D27	Musselburgh	— Woolmet via Newcraighall

It should be noted too that the following numbers no longer appeared in the list: 27, 39, 40, 44, 58, 68, 74, 76, 78, 79, 92, 95, 105, 116, 135, 152,

A 36ft.-long A.E.C. Reliance with 38-seat Alexander Y type body, with wide windows, B910, leaving St Andrew Square bus station, Edinburgh.   A. J. Douglas

274, 293, 313, 314, B00, B1, B31, B41, B42, B43, B48, B55, B67, B68, C51, C56, C70, C72, C77, C79, D10, D11, D18, D26.

However, a new arrangement of numbering was applied to all Eastern Scottish routes from 4 January 1965, and these were henceforth clearly shown in the timetables which later in the year were issued in a new and more comprehensive '24-hour clock' format. Routes from Edinburgh were numbered between 1 and 135, though not all numbers were used:

1	Edinburgh	— London, express
2	Edinburgh	— London, 2-day service
3	Edinburgh	— London, 3-day service
4	Edinburgh	— London, 4-day service
5	Edinburgh	— Inverness
6	Edinburgh	— Prestwick
7	Edinburgh	— Heads of Ayr
8	Edinburgh	— Oban
9	Edinburgh	— Aberdeen
15	Edinburgh	— Glasgow Express
16	Edinburgh	— Glasgow via Bathgate
17	Edinburgh	— Pumpherston
18	Edinburgh	— Livingston Station
27	Edinburgh	— Glasgow via Shotts

C7, a Bedford VAS with 24-seat Duple body, in the grounds of the company's Dryburgh Abbey Hotel.   Gavin Booth

28	Edinburgh	— Oakbank
29	Edinburgh	— Mid Calder via Kirknewton
30	Edinburgh	— Kirknewton R.A.F. Station
35	Edinburgh	— Glasgow via Chapelhall
36	Edinburgh	— Glasgow via Bellshill
37	Edinburgh	— Ratho Station Road via Ratho Park
38	Edinburgh	— Stirling
39	Edinburgh	— Callander
40	Edinburgh	— Crieff
42	Edinburgh	— Alloa
43	Edinburgh	— Bo'ness direct
44	Edinburgh	— Bo'ness via Miller's Pit
45	Edinburgh	— South Queensferry via Dalmeny
46	Edinburgh	— Hopetoun House
52	Edinburgh	— Balerno direct
53	Edinburgh	— Balerno via Colinton
55	Edinburgh	— Dunfermline direct
56	Edinburgh	— Dunfermline via South Queensferry
57	Edinburgh	— Kirkcaldy or Leven
61	Edinburgh	— Lanark via West Linton
62	Edinburgh	— Galashiels via Penicuik
63	Edinburgh	— Galashiels via Auchendinny
66	Galashiels	— Peel Hospital
67	Peebles	— Peel Hospital
68	Galashiels	— Yair Bridge
70	Edinburgh	— Penicuik via Loanhead and Roslin
71	Edinburgh	— Penicuik direct
72	Edinburgh	— Penicuik via Lothianburn
73	Edinburgh	— Penicuik via Lothianburn and Auchendinny
74	Edinburgh	— Polton Mill Road end via Straiton

BB963 was an A.E.C. Renown with 74-seat Park Royal body, seen in Edinburgh on a journey to Penicuik.   A. J. Douglas

75	Edinburgh	— Polton Mill Road end via Captain's Road
76	Edinburgh	— Polton village via Liberton Inn
78	Edinburgh	— Rosewell via Gilmerton
79	Edinburgh	— Rosewell via Danderhall
80	Edinburgh	— Danderhall
81	Dalkeith	— Rosslynlee Hospital
83	Edinburgh	— Middleton via Gilmerton
84	Edinburgh	— Middleton via Gilmerton and Gowkshill
85	Edinburgh	— Birkenside via Danderhall and Gowkshill
86	Edinburgh	— Birkenside via Gilmerton and Mayfield
87	Edinburgh	— Birkenside via Gilmerton and Gowkshill
88	Edinburgh	— Birkenside via Gilmerton and Easthouses
89	Edinburgh	— Birkenside via Gilmerton, Easthouses and Gowkshill
90	Edinburgh	— Arniston via Danderhall, Easthouses and Gowkshill
91	Edinburgh	— Mayfield via Danderhall
95	Edinburgh	— Carlisle
96	Galashiels	— Selkirk via Lindean
97	Galashiels	— Hawick
98	Edinburgh	— Berwick via Lauder, Greenlaw and Paxton
99	Edinburgh	— Dumfries via Moffat
100	Edinburgh	— Dumfries via Biggar
101	Edinburgh	— Biggar via West Linton and Blyth Bridge
102	Edinburgh	— Tweedsmuir via West Linton
103	Edinburgh	— Tweedsmuir via Leadburn

James Amos in characteristic pose. He came with the Borders firm and rose to become chairman of Scottish Omnibuses Ltd., retiring in 1963. His life was buses.   S.O.L.

106	Edinburgh	— Dunbar direct
107	Edinburgh	— Dunbar, express
108	Edinburgh	— Dunbar via Traprain
109	Edinburgh	— Musselburgh
112	Edinburgh	— Haddington via Gifford
113	Edinburgh	— Glenkinchie Road end via Ormiston
114	Edinburgh	— Pencaitland via Winton
115	Haddington	— Yester
117	Edinburgh	— Haddington via Winton and Samuelston
118	Edinburgh	— Haddington via Ormiston and Samuelston
120	Edinburgh	— East Fortune Hospital
121	Edinburgh	— Pathhead via Ormiston
122	Edinburgh	— Ormiston via Tranent
124	Edinburgh	— North Berwick direct
125	Edinburgh	— North Berwick via Ballencrieff
126	North Berwick	— Drem
129	Edinburgh	— Seton Sands
130	Edinburgh	— Wallyford via Portobello
131	Edinburgh	— Tranent via Newcraighall and Smeaton
132	Edinburgh	— Dalkeith via Niddrie and Whitecraigs
134	Edinburgh	— Tranent via Niddrie and Smeaton
135	Musselburgh	— Tranent via Cousland
140	Broxburn	— Loganlea
142	Broxburn	— Oakbank

145	Broxburn	— South Queensferry
147	Broxburn	— Grangemouth via Bridgend road end
148	Broxburn	— Grangemouth via Philpstoun
149	Broxburn	— Grangemouth via Bridgend
150	Broxburn	— Bo'ness via Bridgend road end
151	Broxburn	— Bo'ness via Philpstoun
152	Linlithgow	— Philpstoun
153	Bo'ness	— Bangour Hospital
155	Broxburn	— Winchburgh
156	Broxburn	— Roman Camp
157	Broxburn	— Crossgreen
160	Bathgate town service, Ramsay Crescent	
161	Bathgate town service, Easton	
162	Bathgate town service, Glenmavis Drive	
163	Bathgate town service, Belvedere	
164	Bathgate town service, Falside	
165	Bathgate town service, Boghall	
168	Bathgate	— Bents
169	Bents	— Bangour Hospital
171	Bathgate	— East Calder via Polbeth
172	Bathgate	— Polbeth via Stoneyburn
173	Polbeth	— Bangour Hospital
175	Bathgate	— Seafield
176	Bathgate	— Oakbank
178	Bathgate	— Shotts via Armadale
184	Polbeth	— Shotts via Loganlea
185	Polbeth	— Shotts via Oakbank Cottages
186	Harburn	— Shotts via Loganlea
187	Harburn	— Shotts via Oakbank Cottages
190	Bo'ness	— Shotts via Whitburn
191	Bathgate	— Shotts via Whitburn
193	Bathgate	— Harthill
194	Bathgate	— Harthill via Standhill
200	Bathgate	— Livingston Station
203	Bathgate	— Whitburn via Armadale
206	Bathgate	— Forth
210	Glasgow	— Bournemouth
211	Glasgow	— Easterhouse
213	Glasgow	— Bathgate via Slamannan
215	Glasgow	— Longriggend
216	Glasgow	— Caldercruix
217	Glasgow	— Clarkston
218	Glasgow	— Clarkston via Lightburn
219	Glasgow	— Coatdyke
220	Glasgow	— Broomhouse
221	Glasgow	— Drumpark
222	Baillieston	— Easterhouse
227	Parkhead	— Provanhall
228	Shettleston	— Cranhill

229	Parkhead	— Cardowan
230	Parkhead	— Easterhouse
231	Parkhead	— Gartloch
232	Parkhead	— Garthamlock
233	Parkhead	— Barlanark
240	Airdrie	— O'wood
241	Airdrie	— Newmains and Law Hospital
242	Airdrie	— Greengairs via Wattstown
243	Airdrie	— Greengairs via Darngavil
245	Airdrie	— Muirhead
246	Airdrie	— Gartcosh
250	Gartlea	— Whinhall
251	Gartleahill	— Rawyards
252	Airdrie	— Thrashbush
253	Gartleahill	— Thrashbush
254	Gartlea	— Thrashbush
255	Gartlea	— Victoria Crescent
258	Airdrie	— Glenmavis
260	Glasgow	— Chapelhall
263	Airdrie	— Whitburn
312	Blackness	— Avonbridge
314	Bo'ness town service	
320	Dalkeith	— Polton village
321	Musselburgh	— Penicuik
324	Dalkeith	— Cousland
325	Dalkeith	— Millerhill
326	Dalkeith	— Portobello
328	Dalkeith	— Cockpen circular
329	Dalkeith	— Toxside or Rosebery
332	Musselburgh	— Newcraighall
337	Wallyford	— Stoneybank
341	Musselburgh	— Preston
350	Galashiels	— Earlston via Melrose
351	Galashiels	— Earlston via Gattonside
352	Galashiels	— Kelso via Melrose
353	Galashiels	— St Boswells via Gattonside
354	Galashiels	— St Boswells via Bowden
355	Galashiels	— Jedburgh via Leaderfoot and Ancrum
356	Galashiels	— Dingleton Hospital
357	Kelso	— St Boswells via Maxton
358	Galashiels	— St Boswells via Bogly Burn
360	Galashiels	— Berwick
361	Berwick	— Duns via Ayton
362	Berwick	— Chirnside via Allanton
366	Galashiels town service, Meigle Street	
367	Galashiels town service, Balmoral Road	
369	Galashiels town service, Halliburton Place	
370	Galashiels mill service, Buckholm Mill via Bank Street	
371	Galashiels mill service, Buckholm Mill via Channel Street	

A351, a 1970 Bristol REMH6G with Alexander M type body, in the distinctive yellow and black livery for the Edinburgh-London service.   A. J. Douglas

408	Hawick mill service, Tower Knowe-Mansfield	
409	Hawick mill service, Glebe Hill-High School	
410	Hawick mill service, Tower Knowe-Weensland Park	
411	Hawick mill service, Mansfield-Braemar Factory	
412	Hawick mill service, Burnfoot-Braemar Factory	
413	Hawick mill service, Burnfoot-High School	
414	Hawick mill service, Burnfoot-High Street	
415	Hawick mill service, High School-Weensland Park	
420	Hawick	— Kelso
421	Hawick	— Minto
422	Hawick	— Ancrum
423	Hawick	— Wells
424	Galashiels	— Ancrum
427	Hawick	— Peel Hospital
430	Duns	— Bankend
431	Duns	— Cranshaws
432	Duns	— Longformacus
433	Duns	— Heughead
435	Duns	— Grantshouse
436	Berwick	— St Abbs via Ayton
437	Berwick	— St Abbs via Burnmouth
438	Berwick	— Coldingham
439	Highfield	— Spittal

AA283, one of the Bristol VRT double-deckers which went to England in exchange for
FLF6Gs.   A. J. Douglas

372   Galashiels mill service, Buckholm Mill via Kirkbrae
373   Galashiels mill service, Netherdale via Low Road
374   Galashiels mill service, Netherdale via Tweed Road
380   Selkirk town service, Bridge Street
381   Selkirk town service, Raeburn Lane
383   Selkirk mill service, Heather Mill-Episcopal Church
384   Selkirk mill service, Whinfield Mill-Episcopal Church
385   Selkirk mill service, Heather Mill-Market Square
386   Selkirk mill service, St Mary's Square-Episcopal Church
387   Selkirk mill service, Philiphaugh Mill-Market Square
390   Selkirk   — Dumfries
391   Selkirk   — Ettrickbridge End
394   Hawick   — Lilliesleaf
395   Hawick   — Lilliesleaf via Old Belses
396   Hawick   — Newtown St Boswells
397   Selkirk   — Lilliesleaf
400   Hawick   — Burnfoot direct
401   Hawick   — Burnfoot via Ramsay Road
402   Hawick town service, Weensland Park
403   Hawick town service, Silverbuthall
404   Hawick town service, Lynwood
406   Hawick mill service, Thorterdykes-Braemar Factory
407   Hawick mill service, Duke Street-Braemar Factory

A Daimler Fleetline double-decker with 75 seats, DD713, carrying overall advertising.
A. J. Douglas

442	Duns	— Kelso via Swinton
443	Duns	— St Abbs
444	Kelso	— Berwick via Eccles and Whitsome
445	Kelso	— Berwick via Eccles and Allanton
448	Kelso	— Berwick via Coldstream and Whitsome
449	Kelso	— Berwick via Coldstream and Paxton
450	Kelso	— Berwick via Coldstream and Ladykirk
452	Kelso	— Berwick via Cornhill
453	Kelso	— Sprouston circular
455	Kelso	— Kirk Yetholm
456	Kelso	— Hume circular
457	Kelso	— Earlston via Mellerstain
458	Kelso	— Duns via Fogorig
459	Kelso	— Westruther
460	Kelso	— Peel Hospital via Jedburgh
461	Kelso	— Peel Hospital via Earlston
463	Jedburgh town service, Hindhousefield	
470	Peebles town service, Elliot's Park	
471	Peebles town service, Kingsmeadows	
473	Peebles	— Langhaugh
474	Peebles	— West Linton
480	Dunbar	— North Berwick
481	North Berwick	— Haddington via Athelstaneford
483	North Berwick	— Haddington via Drem

A Leyland National 52-seat bus, N865, at work in the Glasgow area.   A. J. Douglas

484	Dunbar	— Drem
485	Dunbar	— Oldhamstocks
486	Dunbar	— Spott
487	Dunbar town service, summer only	
500	Edinburgh	— Manchester
501	Edinburgh	— Liverpool
502	Edinburgh	— Liverpool, night service
503	Edinburgh	— Blackpool
504	Edinburgh	— Berwick via Heughead
505	Edinburgh	— Newcastle via Berwick
506	Edinburgh	— Newcastle via Coldingham
507	Edinburgh	— Newcastle via Berwick, limited stop
508	Edinburgh	— Newcastle via Jedburgh
509	Edinburgh	— Jedburgh
510	Edinburgh	— Newcastle via Kelso
511	Edinburgh	— Kelso
513	Edinburgh	— Humbie
514	Edinburgh	— Humbie via Edgehead
515	Glasgow	— Whitley Bay
516	Edinburgh	— Scarborough
517	Glasgow	— Scarborough

Service 507 stopped only at Dunbar, Berwick, Belford, Alnwick and Morpeth.

A new Saturdays only service jointly with Alexander's of Fife from Edinburgh to Glenrothes via the Forth Road Bridge commenced on 20 February 1965 numbered 58, and the summer Edinburgh-Inverness service took the new shorter route over the Forth Road Bridge from 1965. A workers' service, 16A, from Uphall to the North British Rubber Mills in Edinburgh, commenced later that year. The time-honoured stance in Galashiels Market Square was moved to Stirling Street in July 1965. At Dalkeith a new bus station and depot on the site of the former railway station was opened on 11 September 1966. Some services were withdrawn in 1965, viz: 98 Edinburgh-Berwick via Lauder, Greenlaw and Paxton; 473 Peebles-Langhaugh, Peebles-Glen Lodge, and Selkirk-Ettrickbridge via Bowhill.

From 1 October 1967 services 17 and 200 were replaced by a new 200 which operated from Edinburgh to Bathgate via Pumpherston, Livingston New Town, Village and Station. Other additions at this period were:

25	Edinburgh	— Armadale, limited stop workers' service
60	Edinburgh	— St Andrews
61A	Edinburgh	— Lanark via Currie (one early morning trip only)
70A	Penicuik town service	
86A	Edinburgh	— Birkenside via Danderhall and Mayfield
87A	Edinburgh	— Birkenside via Danderhall and Gowkshill
97	Melrose	— Hawick via Lilliesleaf and Hassendean
310	Linlithgow town service	
327	Dalkeith town service	

A long-distance service numbered 11, Edinburgh to Portree, summer Saturdays only, commenced on 3 May 1969, running via the Forth Road Bridge, Perth, Dalwhinnie, Spean Bridge and Kyleakin ferry. In 1971 it was extended to Uig.

The widespread adoption of the occupational five-day week, the extension of car ownership and the changing pattern of evening entertainment were now affecting all bus services, and on many routes the frequency of service was being reduced, especially in the evenings and on Sundays. A few services in the Borders were being operated without conductors in 1969, and some Baxter services even earlier, but one-man operation was slow to spread. A start was made at Dalkeith depot on 4 May 1970 with services 131, 513 and 514, and the Edinburgh depot followed with services 61, 61A, 100, 101, 102, 103, 112, 113, 114, 117, 118, 121 and 123 on 30 August. Nevertheless, retrenchment in rural areas was becoming necessary and service 206 was withdrawn on 5 July 1970, while service 142 had been diverted from Oakbank to Kirknewton in 1969. Services from Dunbar to Spott and 483 between North Berwick and Haddington were withdrawn in 1971 and service 484 curtailed at East Fortune. The Penicuik town service became No. 320.

Delays in delivery of new buses at times led to shortage of vehicles, and in the summer of 1969 in particular, buses from other of the group companies, and also from Edinburgh Corporation, were hired to help augment Eastern Scottish services.

Meanwhile, a major change in the higher management structure took effect on 1 January 1969 with the formation of the Scottish Transport Group which, with responsibility to the Scottish Office, took over the Scottish interests of the nationalised Transport Holding Company. The Scottish Transport Group thus covered mainly the Scottish Bus Group Companies and their subsidiaries, together with the former railway and MacBrayne steamer services to the Scottish islands and on the Clyde coast, and functioned under the chairmanship of Col. P. M. Thomas. W. M. Little became its depute chairman and managing director and remained chairman of the Scottish Bus Group. The management organisation of the latter was at the same time considerably altered, among the ensuing changes being the transfer of R. MacKenzie, Eastern Scottish general manager, to become an executive director of the Scottish Bus Group. His successor at New Street was J. W. Tweedie, but after exactly a year he also became an executive director of the Scottish Bus Group, whereupon Ian R. Kydd became general manager of Eastern Scottish. The Scottish Transport Group headquarters were set up in Carron House in George Street, Edinburgh, in October 1969.

Eastern Scottish services to and from the city had so far not been much affected by staff troubles, although there was a strike over wages which lasted from 2 till 27 March in 1970. On the other hand, fares of course escalated. Increases were authorised to take effect on 3 March 1952, 3 November 1952, 5 April 1954, 9 May 1955, 5 March 1956, 13 May 1957, 23 September 1957, 5 January 1959, 10 October 1960, 14 August 1961, 30 July 1962, 5 August 1963, 18 May 1964, 17 April 1966, 19 November 1967, 2 February 1969, 26 October 1969, 21 June 1970, 21 February 1971, and 24 June 1973. At the 1967 increase the minimum fare became 4d., while decimalisation in 1971 brought a minimum of 2p.

The one-way traffic arrangements in St Andrew Square, North St David Street and North St Andrew Street had entailed a vast unproductive mileage each year for Eastern Scottish services to the east and, eventually, it was agreed that from 15 December 1970 traffic could use North St Andrew Street in the northward direction so that buses could leave the bus station and proceed direct by North St Andrew Street to York Place. A new bus station was opened in Airdrie on 18 May 1971. The small garage at Selkirk was closed.

In 1972 the company threatened widespread withdrawal of many rural services, especially in the Borders, unless the local authorities concerned helped them to meet the operating deficits which, despite savings by the gradual spread of one-man operation, were becoming unbearable. In some districts there was considerable reluctance to face the issue and eventually, although some services were reprieved, Nos. 357, 362, 394, 421, 443, 444 and 450 ceased from 15 October 1972 while others were reduced in frequency. Service 115 had already been withdrawn and 101, 102 and 103 followed from the end of that year. In some cases a minimal service run by a local operator with local authority support was provided instead, and some other routes were partly covered by the Post Office's new 'Postbus' services.

On the other hand, long-distance coach services were flourishing and new ones were started such as Edinburgh-Paignton, numbered 12, summer only, in 1973, and Edinburgh-Hull for connection to the North Sea ferries, started on 21 April 1975, numbered 388. There were, however, some new bus services too, viz: a Saturdays only service, 206, from Bathgate to Breich, started in 1973, though it survived only till 29 December 1974. Another new route from Edinburgh to Bathgate direct via Livingston, 201, started on 27 May 1974. Another new service, 53A, ran during term-time from Edinburgh to the new Heriot-Watt University at Riccarton, just outside the western city boundary. Housing development above Balerno resulted in the extension of that route from its original terminus at the foot of the village, up the hill through the village, and took place in June 1973. Services had to be reduced and tours and private hires suspended during a two-week fuel delivery strike at the end of May 1974.

The list of service numbers in 1974 included some changes and a considerable number of workers' services. The alterations and additions were:

10	Edinburgh	— Bournemouth
12	Edinburgh	— Torquay
14	Glasgow	— Livingston express
16A	Uphall	— Fountainbridge
18A	Broxburn	— Livingston Station via Crossgreen
19	Edinburgh	— Pumpherston via Mid Calder
20	Edinburgh	— Bathgate B.M.C. Factory
20A	Pumpherston	— Bathgate B.M.C. Factory
21	Edinburgh	— Bathgate T.C.C. Factory
22	Glasgow	— Bathgate B.M.C. Factory
23	Blackridge	— Bathgate T.C.C. Factory
24	Clarkston	— Woodend Colliery
31	Fauldhouse	— Sighthill via West Calder
31A	Fauldhouse	— Broxburn G.W.C. Factory
31B	Harthill	— Broxburn G.W.C. Factory

31C	Edinburgh	—	Broxburn G.W.C. Factory
32	Fauldhouse	—	Sighthill via Blackburn
47	Edinburgh	—	Craigiehall
48	Dreghorn	—	Craigiehall
49	Edinburgh	—	Rosyth Dockyard
50	Edinburgh	—	Rosyth Dockyard via Sighthill
53A	Edinburgh	—	Riccarton
54	Edinburgh	—	Ingliston Horse Show
65	Innerleithen	—	Glen Lodge
72A	Edinburgh	—	Penicuik via Lothianburn and Bush House
72B	Edinburgh	—	Penicuik via Lothianburn and East Howgate
73A	Edinburgh	—	Penicuik via Lothianburn, Auchendinny and Bush House
73B	Edinburgh	—	Penicuik via Lothianburn, Auchendinny and E. Howgate
78A	Edinburgh	—	Rosewell via Gilmerton and Polton Bank
79A	Edinburgh	—	Rosewell via Danderhall and Polton Bank
85A	Edinburgh	—	Thornybank Trading Estate
91A	Edinburgh	—	Mayfield via Darcy Road
109	Edinburgh	—	Wallyford via Inveresk
110	Edinburgh	—	Musselburgh Races
111	Dalkeith	—	Haddington Ranco Factory
127	North Berwick	—	Drem via Gullane
135	Musselburgh	—	Tranent via Cousland
142	Broxburn	—	East Calder
143	Broxburn	—	Kirknewton
180	Bathgate	—	Armadale circle
181	Bathgate	—	Armadale circle
195	Fauldhouse	—	Bathgate B.M.C. Factory
196	Fauldhouse	—	Dixon's Pit
200	Edinburgh	—	Bathgate via Craigshill
201	Edinburgh	—	Bathgate via Carmondean
207	Bathgate	—	Dunfermline
224	Clarkston	—	Coatbridge via Victoria Place
233	Clarkston	—	Barlanark
234	Barrachnie	—	Hillingdon
235	Easterhouse	—	Hillingdon
236	Easterhouse	—	Renfrew
237	Rutherglen	—	Cathcart
247	Coatbridge	—	Sun Foundry
256	Rawyards	—	Health Centre
258	Airdrie	—	New Monkland
259	Clarkston	—	Hillingdon
261	Garrowhill	—	Hamilton
270	Coatbridge town service		
273	Coatbridge town service		
276	Coatbridge town service		
279	Coatbridge town service		
282	Coatbridge town service		
285	Coatbridge town service		
288	Coatbridge town service		

S685, a Seddon Pennine VII with Alexander T type body.   A. J. Douglas

291   Coatbridge town service
294   Coatbridge town service
297   Coatbridge town service
322   Dalkeith   — Monktonhall Colliery
334   Musselburgh   — Dalkeith Colliery via Ashgrove
335   Musselburgh   — Dalkeith Colliery via Levenhall
339   Musselburgh   — Edenhall
342   Musselburgh   — Thornybank Trading Estate
365   Galashiels town service, Netherdale
368   Galashiels town service, Balnakiel
388   Edinburgh   — Hull
390   Selkirk   — Gordon Arms
430   Duns   — Abbey St Bathans
441   Kelso town service, Lempitlaw
464   Jedburgh town service, Starret Factory
482   East Fortune   — Haddington
484   Dunbar   — East Fortune
520   Glasgow   — Whitley Bay Express

Service numbers 4, 28, 30, 68, 97, 101, 102, 103, 115, 176, 206, 243, 357, 362, 371, 383, 386, 387, 394, 395, 397, 421, 422, 423, 424, 442, 443, 450, 453, 454, 456, 461, 483, and 486 had disappeared.

Fares increases now occurred with such rapid frequency, viz. on 14

A Volvo Ailsa with Alexander 81-seat body, VV156, on its way into Edinburgh bus station.   A. J. Douglas

April 1974 and again on 4 August 1974, that an arrangement to apply increases concurrently with the national 'threshold' wage awards was sought, but the Government's wages threshold scheme lapsed at the end of October so, instead, a third increase in fares in 1974 was allowed from 27 October with a pledge that there would be no further increase for six months, despite which a fourth increase within a year took effect on 16 March 1975. The minimum fare now became 6p. The Setright ticket machines, into which a partially preprinted ticket was inserted, were replaced in the early seventies by the type which, by the same method of operation, printed and projected a one-inch wide white ticket from a roll carried in the machine.

A rather unusual strike at the Bathgate depot had some effect on Edinburgh services. This was in protest at the continued use on rush-hour duties of two buses, A625 and A627, which the staff complained were 'too old'. This strike lasted from September to November 1974, by which time industrial trouble was brewing over the forthcoming national wage negotiations. Strike action on this issue took place at various depots, apparently according to their militancy, and it finally petered out only just before the end of the year.

The reorganisation of local government which took effect in Scotland on

16 May 1975 laid upon the new Regional Councils overall responsibilities for transport matters including highways, planning and public transport facilities, in all of which they were increasingly subject to detailed control by central government. The new regime had no immediate effect on Eastern Scottish bus services, the regions mainly concerned being Lothian and Borders, though Strathclyde and Central regions were involved also. However, it should be recorded that with their demise imminent, Edinburgh Corporation proposed to sell their transport undertaking to the Scottish Bus Group. But this did not happen, and the former Edinburgh Corporation Transport Department passed into the hands of the new Lothian Regional Council who then ran it as Lothian Region Transport.

It was several years before any steps towards integration of services or fares materialised. In regard to the latter there was soon public complaint. The boundaries of Edinburgh District Council — in effect the successor, with much reduced powers, to the Corporation — were extended to include such places as Balerno and Queensferry, which continued to be served only by Eastern Scottish, whose unassisted fare scale to such places was much higher than that of Lothian Region Transport to, for example, Juniper Green, just over two miles short of Balerno. Ratepayers in Balerno found themselves paying higher 'Edinburgh District' rates without benefiting from lower fares on what was seen as the Edinburgh transport service controlled by Lothian Region. Later in the year a working party representing the Convention of Scottish Local Authorities, the Scottish Office and the Scottish Bus Group was set up to consider local authority/ S.B.G. relations which it was evident were not running smoothly, and the S.B.G. appointed a planning officer to liaise with the regions. Eventually, in 1981, Lothian Regional Council agreed to subsidise the Eastern Scottish fares to places within Edinburgh District to equalise them with the Lothian Region Transport fare scale, but the move was thwarted by the Scottish Office with whom the region were out of harmony. So the justifiable complaints from Balerno etc. perforce continued. They had been aggravated, particularly in 1977-8, by allegations of unreliable Eastern Scottish service, though in due course these died down.

Reverting to 1975, it may be mentioned that Mr W. M. Little retired from the chairmanship of the S.B.G. on 31 March 1975, being succeeded by the Group's secretary, Ian S. Irwin, and Mr R. MacKenzie retired from the S.B.G. in June 1976. From the beginning of June 1975, the Edinburgh-Glasgow express service used the newly opened Monklands motorway into Glasgow, but since British Rail introduced their much-improved Edinburgh-Glasgow service in 1971 patronage of this Eastern Scottish service 15 had slumped, despite cut-price fares; so from 15

December 1975 it was diverted to proceed through various parts of Livingston New Town providing express service thence to both Glasgow and Edinburgh, but not effectively between Edinburgh and Glasgow. The Edinburgh-Dunbar 107 express service had declined too and the last journey ran on 4 July. 'Piped' music and taped advertisements on the upper deck of fifty buses from Edinburgh, Musselburgh and Dalkeith depots began on 29 September, bringing in additional revenue from the promoters, 'Sounds in Motion'.

A new livery of white with blue roof and skirt was applied to the motorway coaches on the London service in 1976: they carried a new fleet name, 'Scottish', in large blue letters together with a logotype based on the St Andrew's Cross. Later, in 1978, this lettering was applied to all vehicles, but with 'Eastern' in lowercase letters ahead of it. 7 March 1976 saw an increase in fares ranging from 1p more on 8p and 10p fares upwards. The Edinburgh-London fare was now £6. A new service, 376 to Leicester, with Barton Transport participation, was now in operation. One-man operation of some buses spread to Linlithgow, Peebles and Dunbar depots.

In mid-1976 Borders Regional Council complained about the £390,000 subsidy being sought by Eastern Scottish for services in the region and made public a number of suggestions reckoned to save £100,000, including more one-man operation, reduced frequencies on some services, elimination of limited-stop journeys and various other alterations. Arising from all this, all Borders services, except a few from Berwick, became one-man operated from 25 July and a revised timetable came into operation on 2 August. Some 62/63 Edinburgh-Galashiels via Peebles journeys terminated at Peebles. Service 448 Kelso-Coldstream-Berwick terminated at Coldstream; 452 Kelso-Sprouston-Cornhill terminated at Sprouston; 396 Hawick-St Boswells was extended to Leaderfoot, and services 390, 435 and 458 were withdrawn, but new weekday services were 434 Duns-Eyemouth, and a schooldays and Saturdays Duns-Kelso via Coldstream. Services 365 and 369 were withdrawn on Sundays. Some services elsewhere were also withdrawn, 156 in the mornings, 314 in the evenings and 310 entirely; 42 Edinburgh-Alloa terminated at Bo'ness, and service 60 Edinburgh-St Andrews was diverted in summer via Anstruther holiday camp.

Services around Livingston were altered from 29 September, involving 27, 35, 143 and 201. with new service 198 Centre to Craigshall via Almond Road, and circular 199 via Knightsridge, Howden and Ladywell: these did not run on Sundays. Further withdrawals soon followed, viz. 145, 236 and 312, with reduced frequencies on several other routes. These no doubt helped to contain at existing level for 1977 the subsidies sought from Lothian and Strathclyde. Glasgow services transferred to a new Buchanan Street bus station on 17 December 1976. New services early in 1977 were 459 Kelso-Greenlaw-Duns, and from Livingston Centre to Dedridge 196, and to Deans 197, while 144 was diverted via Livingston Centre and 207 was withdrawn. The Dixon's Pit service was renumbered 33. From 21 February services 227 and 232 were replaced by a circular 227 Parkhead-Garthamlock anti-clockwise and 232 clockwise, also 212 limited stop Glasgow-Easterhouse. Fares increased again on 6 March 1977, the fare to London now becoming £7.

In the summer of 1977 the blue livery of the buses used on the former Baxter services in the Airdrie area was finally abandoned and several alterations in these services were made. Elsewhere, 337 was withdrawn and 321 extended from Musselburgh to Wallyford, while some journeys to Birkenside made a minor diversion in Gorebridge. In the Borders the Post Bus Service took over the Wednesday Kelso-Peel Hospital service 460, though Eastern Scottish still provided the Sunday journey. Three 'Solomatic' ticket machines were tried experimentally but did not find favour. Service 216 was extended to Longriggend, 171 was extended to Oakbank road end, and the Carlisle terminus extended to the railway station. A new service, 256 from Rawyards to Airdrie Health Centre, commenced on 29 August. Service 61 was withdrawn, and a stop at Biggar was included in the overnight motorway service to London. Services 220, 221 and 222 became weekdays only, 215 peak hours only, 217 was extended to Longriggend and 218 at peak hours to Caldercruix, all from 31 October. The Haddington terminus for some Edinburgh journeys was changed to Dunbar Road and the Broxburn terminus of 155 changed to East Mains Industrial Estate. Some local services in Hawick were also revised. Reflecting a changing social pattern, services at Christmas and also at New Year were very much reduced this year, early and late journeys being cancelled and some routes not operated at all.

In 1978 an additional stop was made on Sundays by the Edinburgh-Glasgow service 15 at Ingliston, and the motorway services to London, to Bournemouth, and to Torquay now called at Livingston. From 8 May, service 233 was replaced by a circular service 233-4 Shettleston, Barlanark, Barrachnie, weekdays only. An application for a fares increase was heard by the Traffic Commissioners on 22 and 23 February 1978 and showed that Eastern Scottish's public image had slumped badly, with much public complaint of unreliable service, shortage of buses, too many old ones and frequent breakdowns. So the fares increase did not take immediate effect. The Edinburgh-London fare went up to £8. However,

Another Seddon Pennine VII, S960, with Plaxton body, on a local journey in Musselburgh.   A. J. Douglas

One of the first lot of Border Couriers; 13-seat Bedford-Reebur, C5.   A. J. Douglas

a new monthly ticket allowing unlimited journeys between specified points in Lothian Region was introduced experimentally on 11 June. Buses with drivers were hired from Lothian Region Transport for a special service to the Royal Highland Show at Ingliston, Eastern Scottish providing conductors. The general manager, Ian Kydd, retired in poor health to be succeeded on 1 September by John Edmond. The fleetname, in a new style common to all the Scottish Bus Group companies, was adopted at this time, viz. 'Eastern' in large lowercase letters and 'Scottish' in smaller blue capitals with a saltire between and carried in a forward position. A new service, 61, from St Andrew Square via Gorgie, Calder Road and Riccarton to Currie, operated jointly with Lothian Region Transport, commenced on 25 September.

Other changes in services in the 1978 timetable, and not so far mentioned, included some route/number variations, but also a few new services:

19	Edinburgh	— Bathgate via Knightsridge
85	Edinburgh	— Middleton via Danderhall and Gowkshill
88	Edinburgh	— Newtongrange via Gilmerton and Easthouses
90	Edinburgh	— Birkenside via Danderhall, Easthouses and Mayfield
101	Edinburgh	— Dumfries via Penicuik
141	Broxburn	— Pumpherston via Crossgreen
144	East Calder	— Bangour
146	Linlithgow	— Bo'ness via Crawfield Road
312	Blackness	— Linlithgow-Manuel
322	Penicuik	— Wallyford via Stoneybank and Musselburgh
330	Glasgow	— Scarborough
331	Glasgow	— Whitley Bay
332	Glasgow	— Edinburgh-Hull
359	Galashiels	— Melrose via Tweedbank
449	Kelso	— Coldstream
452	Kelso	— Sprouston
457	Kelso	— Duns via Stichill
462	Berwick town service	
482	North Berwick	— Haddington via Athelstaneford Mains
486	Dunbar	— West Barns (summer only)
497	Berwick town service	
933	Edinburgh	— Southport (summer Saturdays only)
983	Edinburgh	— Morecambe (summer Saturdays only)

Services 500-3 were renumbered respectively 831, 884, 881 and 981, and 507 became X50. The following services had been withdrawn: 24, 39, 40, 46, 61A, 65, 67, 73B, 86A, 184-7, 325, 332 (Musselburgh-Newcraighall), 354-5, 390, 430-3 and 445.

A new bus station and depot for sixty vehicles, depot code N, was

A Leyland Tiger, H318, with Plaxton Paramount body, seen on a private hire in Hamilton. A. J. Douglas

officially opened at Livingston on 2 March 1979, followed by an 'open day' on the next day and for normal services on 5 March. The Broxburn depot was then closed and closure of the former Baxter's Victoria depot at Airdrie followed on 18 March. 5 March also saw several service alterations in the area, viz. Edinburgh-Glasgow limited stop now every two hours, no longer continuing through to Anderston Cross and taking 100 minutes. Service 27, Edinburgh-Glasgow via Hamilton, terminated at Hamilton, services 140-3, 171, 172, 196-9 were withdrawn, service 144 was renumbered 199, and there were the following revised or new services:

29/30	Livingston	— Edinburgh
35A/B	Edinburgh	— Howden-Eastfield
148-51	Livingston	— Broxburn-Linlithgow-Grangemouth group
154	Broxburn	— Winchburgh-Grangemouth
200	Bathgate	— Livingston
201	Edinburgh	— Livingston-Bathgate
202	Bathgate	— Livingston-Broxburn
203-4	Edinburgh	— Broxburn-Livingston-Fauldhouse
205-6	Bathgate	— Loganlea-Livingston
207-8	Livingston New Town Circular, weekdays only	
209	Livingston	— Murieston, Monday-Friday shoppers' service

Another increase in fares came into effect on 11 March 1979, followed by another increase from 19 August, when the minimum fare became 10p and no reduction was offered on return fares. Tickets for seven days' unlimited travel in specified areas in the Borders were offered in the summer, viz. 'Reiver Rover' at £10, 'Waverley Wanderer' at £12.50. A joint effort sponsored by Borders Regional Council, Borders Health Board, Scottish Development Department and the Scottish Bus Group was the Borders Courier Service operated by Eastern Scottish with five new fourteen-seat buses based at Kelso, Peebles, Hawick and Galashiels, with one spare. These Monday to Friday services, all to Peel Hospital and carrying, as well as passengers, milk, medicines, stores, etc., commenced on 11 May and operated as follows: 1 — Peebles, Traquair, Innerleithen, Yarrow Valley, Selkirk, Galashiels, Peel Hospital; 2— Hawick, Ettrickbridge, Selkirk, Melrose, Peel Hospital; 3 — Galashiels, Kelso, Jedburgh, Lilliesleaf, Midlem, Selkirk, Peel Hospital; 4 — Coldstream, Swinton, Duns, Greenlaw, Hume, Earlston, Bemersyde, St Boswells, Galashiels, Peel Hospital. This last one followed that route only on Mondays and Fridays; on Tuesdays, Wednesdays and Thursdays it operated Coldingham, Eyemouth, Chirnside, Allanton, Duns, Greenlaw, Westruther, Lauder, Blainslie, Langshaw, Galashiels, Peel Hospital. Another interesting duty successfully undertaken in 1979 was the provision of a bus link between Berwick and Dunbar replacing daytime mainline trains between these points due to the collapse of Penmanshiel tunnel. This operated from March to August and called for an increasing number of vehicles as the summer traffic grew, when double-deckers had largely to be used. Nearly all Eastern Scottish depots provided vehicles and/or drivers, and some came from other group companies and United Automobile Co. at Berwick too. With often several hundred passengers from each train a large number of buses had always to be available and a van for passengers' luggage travelled with each convoy. A new simplified form of ABC timetable was introduced in November.

The next fares increase, of approximately 20%, took place on 3 February 1980. A new type of ticket machine, the 'Timtronic', was brought into use at Berwick depot in April. The ticket it issued showed the date, time, service and journey number, the stage from and to and also the appropriate fare which the machine calculated therefrom and which was also displayed on a panel on the machine. New uniforms in French navy blue with a blue shirt and S.B.G. tie were issued in the summer, these being standardised throughout the Scottish Bus Group. In April a bus was put on from Livingston to Mid Calder station connecting into the morning and midday trains to Birmingham. There was some revision and

Metroliner single-deck coach, M333, in Citylink livery.   A. J. Douglas

renumbering of services in the Glasgow area in June and around Airdrie in August, where further alterations were effected from 12 January 1981. A tourist service, the 'Border Harrier', was run for the Borders Regional Council for ten weeks from 1 July 1980, connecting Kelso, Abbotsford, Melrose, Selkirk, Bowhill, St Mary's Loch, Traquair and Peebles. A shoppers' express service from Melrose and Galashiels to Edinburgh on Wednesdays only commenced in August with a return flat fare of £2.50. An important development was the market analysis project which the Scottish Bus Group initiated throughout the country as 'Scotmap'. The Borders saw the first such exercise in Eastern Scottish territory in February, teams travelling over all routes and questioning passengers on their travel requirements; many households were questioned too. Eventually, when all the information was analysed, various desirable changes in the pattern of services became discernible and were subsequently implemented.

The Transport Act 1980 brought about a major change in the operation of long-distance coach services when from 6 October such services over more than thirty miles became no longer subject to licensing. The Eastern Scottish Edinburgh-London fare was now £11.50 single, £19.50 return, but a standby single fare of £7 was now offered, also economy returns at

£15.50 on certain days. Standby fares were now offered to Manchester and to Birmingham also. Competition from other operators on routes to London and elsewhere quickly developed, but in January 1981 Eastern Scottish abolished the standby fares and reduced the Edinburgh-London fare to £7.50, Edinburgh to Manchester to £8, Birmingham to £11, Hull to £14, and Bournemouth to £25, resulting in increased traffic for Eastern Scottish despite the competition. New coaches introduced early in 1981 were emblazoned on the sides with the saltire and 'Scottish' in much bigger letters, 'Eastern' being omitted except on the front. A new motorway service, every hour, between Edinburgh and Glasgow, service X14, commenced on 16 February 1981, taking 75 minutes, with a fare of £1.50 single and £2.50 return, students and o.a.p.s being carried for £1.50 return. This service proved very popular and was stepped up in late June. The coaches normally used carried overall advertising of the service.

Early in 1981 there were some changes to services in the Bathgate area and on 29 June a limited-stop morning journey from Fauldhouse to Edinburgh commenced. From 16 November the ordinary half-hourly Edinburgh-Glasgow via Bathgate service became hourly, with the others running instead from Edinburgh as far as Blackridge and thence to Harthill as service 17. There were further modifications in the Bathgate area too.

With the Scotmap service completed, resulting improvements were introduced, firstly in the Borders on 7 September 1981, including better town services in the area, followed by Edinburgh-East Lothian services on 1 March 1982. The latter included new rush-hour express or limited-stop journeys between Edinburgh and Haddington X08, Pencaitland X13, Seton Sands X29, and Wallyford X30. All households in the respective catchment areas were circularised. Limited-stop services all day from Edinburgh to Bonnyrigg and to Mayfield soon followed, together with improvements to other services in the Dalkeith area.

From 21 June 1982 the hourly Edinburgh-Glasgow express service was extended to Glasgow Airport with additional stops at the Zoo, Ingliston, Ratho, and Queen Street and Central railway stations, and Anderston Cross bus station in Glasgow, the fare for those travelling to the new terminus costing 50p more. This service was now run jointly with Western S.M.T. Co.

The use of conductors had now been reducing rapidly, and with the last of the rear-entrance buses withdrawn, one-man operation became universal from 5 December 1982. The last seven, three conductors and four conductresses, had worked from Linlithgow depot. 'Timtronic' ticket machines appeared in the Edinburgh area in September.

Metroliner six-wheel double-decker, MM147, leaving Glasgow for Edinburgh, Express.
A. J. Douglas.

1983 brought a short strike in February in protest at vandalism and attacks on crews of late evening buses. On 16 May a new express service was started from Galashiels to connect with mainline trains at Carlisle station and calling at Selkirk, Hawick and Langholm. The coaches used were lettered 'Scottish Borders Rail Link', flanked by the S.B.G. and B.R. logos. From 28 August Eastern Scottish cut their fare on the Edinburgh-Glasgow service X14 to £1.25 single and £2 return in response to a new Edinburgh-Glasgow service by Stagecoach of Perth. But a new pattern was emerging with the introduction from 1 October of Scottish Citylink services in which the other companies in the Scottish Bus Group took part, all using coaches painted blue and yellow boldly lettered 'Scottish Citylink'. The name of the owning company, e.g. Eastern Scottish, appeared only on the front and back. The Edinburgh-Glasgow route was included, as were routes to Perth, St Andrews, Aberdeen, Inverness, and English destinations. Despite the competition Scottish Citylink fared well, most passengers apparently preferring the established concern.

Locally there were route changes in Balerno village, and Lothian Region Transport participated in some Balerno peak-hour services which ran non-stop between Haymarket and Currie. Service 53A was withdrawn in favour of Lothian Region Transport and service 61 extended to Balerno.

However, in 1984 very far-reaching changes in the Scottish Bus Group organisation were in view, involving the hiving off into separate companies of parts of Scottish Omnibuses Ltd.'s area — almost like going back to 1926, so this would be an appropriate milestone at which to end this history. However, the new situation which came into effect legally on 1 March and operationally on 17 June 1985 requires brief mention to bring the story up to date. Scottish Omnibuses Ltd. and its subsidiaries now gave way to new separate companies. The relevant new company, Eastern Scottish Omnibuses Ltd., now operated in a much reduced area, only the Edinburgh, Musselburgh, Dalkeith, Livingston and Bathgate depots remaining under its jurisdiction. John Edmond remained general manager, and the livery of the vehicles was basically unchanged, though many became boldly emblazoned with such slogans as 'Best Bus Around': 205 single-deck and 162 double-deck buses remained in the fleet. The depots in the Borders, including Berwick and Dunbar, were transferred with their vehicles and staff to Lowland Scottish Omnibuses Ltd., and Linlithgow depot became a Midland Scottish Omnibuses Ltd. depot. Airdrie depot likewise became a Central Scottish Omnibuses Ltd. depot while Baillieston depot had been closed on 16 March, the vehicles going to Midland Scottish Omnibuses' Stepps depot. The Marine works of Eastern Scottish at Seafield Road in Edinburgh passed to a new company, S.B.G. Engineering Ltd., set up to handle the needs of all the companies in the group. The Citylink services, including services to London, were now operated by Scottish Citylink Coaches Ltd. though, as before, using coaches owned by Eastern Scottish and the other new companies and painted in Citylink livery.

5

The Rolling Stock After the First War

The vehicles in use up to the end of the First War period, except for the Lothians, have already been more conveniently described and numbers given, so far as is known, in the narrative of the period. Numbers of the Lothians, production of which continued until 1924, now follow, but as the numbers of a few of the earlier ones are uncertain, and since the S.M.T. numbers were the Edinburgh licence numbers, it may be helpful to explain first the Edinburgh licensing procedure. The vehicle owner was issued with a numbered document for each vehicle, which number was authorised to be painted on the vehicle he presented for inspection by the Hackney Carriage Inspector. Licences were renewed each year at 28 May, and for any additional vehicles the numbered licence documents were normally issued in numerical sequence, using up any blank numbers first, though by 1920 blocks of numbers were being retained for issue to the larger operators.

It should also be mentioned that prior to 1921 a registration number was not necessarily tied to a specific vehicle and a vehicle leaving a licensing authority's area had normally to be re-registered in its new area, while its old number would subsequently be reissued to another vehicle new to the old area. In 1921 chassis numbers had to be recorded against all registration numbers, new and existing, so that thereafter a vehicle's registration number did not normally change. Conditions at Fountainbridge seem to have been very hectic during the war, and it seems certain that a few of the earlier Lothian chassis exchanged registration numbers at that time. It has been mentioned earlier that several Lothians were sold as lorries and buses to other firms, and most of the former were subsequently bought back again to which reissued registration numbers seem to have been applied. Which the reissued numbers were cannot be definitely stated, but as there is a sequence of registration numbers nearly in step with 1921 chassis numbers up to No. 29, those registration numbers which do not fit in this sequence would appear to be the reissued ones. There are a number of alternatives to these reissued registration numbers, however, and also in the case of a few of the earlier registration numbers against licence numbers, e.g. it would be logical for S4400 not to be a reissued registration number, so fitting the licence No. 83 in sequence, but there is no chassis number available to fit S4400 at that period. Bearing in mind the foregoing factors and the sequence in which licence numbers were normally issued, the conjectural numbers, shown with a question mark, seem the most likely to be correct.

It will be noticed that the registration number S3597 is not in sequence, and the following seems the likely explanation. There is an official photograph of this bus as No. 55 with a new standard type of body though the wheels, and presumably the chassis, do not appear to be new. It may well be that this was the first of the standard type bodies produced, probably in 1914, when the Maudslay double-decker No. 55 may have been withdrawn, and put on an earlier chassis, namely chassis No. T5.4. It is possible that this 'new' bus was re-registered, receiving a reissued number. After the war, S3597 carried a charabanc body for a season, but in 1920, when again a bus, it caught fire at Newington station and is understood to have been completely destroyed. There is no evidence of its existence thereafter, nor does T5.4 appear in the 1921 chassis numbers.

S4543 had the first charabanc body, again about June 1914. Most of the Lothians carried bus bodies and charabanc bodies at various different times, some of them changing from the one to the other several times, but SF230, 253, 254, 274 and 330 were always charabancs and SF503 was always a bus. S3662 and S3703 had the low cab type of body, and after rebuilding to the standard pattern, the body of the former went to S4770, while that of the prototype S3057 was later on S4654. S3841 originally had one of the bodies with the roof level to the front, though it had acquired a standard body by 1925. It is not known which others originally had this type of body but S9102 or 3 had one about 1920, while S4963 and SG2106 carried them from at least 1925, and SF226 also had one in the winter of 1926-7. It may be noted that S4288 had disc wheels in its solid tyre days for a time, while S5550 ran with lorry type rear wheels for a short time during the war. S5496 had wood slat seats for a time. SG4580 and SG4581 were fitted with six-cylinder Minerva engines and on these, being longer, the body had to be mounted four inches further back with a short aluminium cowl between it and the radiator; the rear mudguards were therefore not concentric with the rear wheels. Pneumatic tyres were fitted to all the Lothians from 1923, and the clearance for the front wheels had to be raised to suit these, resulting in a curious effect in the case of a few bodies on which this was done before pneumatic-tyred wheels were fitted. In their later years several had the conductor's pull-cord bell replaced by a pneumatic or single-beat electric bell. Some were sent to Dundee at various times and others finished their days in the Galashiels list, while SF228 was operated as an Allen & Kennedy bus during 1928-9.

At the end of 1928 only four of the 88 Lothians in the company's fleet had been withdrawn, including S3597 destroyed by fire in 1920. The rest continued to work their normal routes alongside some of the Maudslays and Albions of 1926 with which they kept pace and which, although of more modern low-set appearance, did not offer noticeably superior comfort. Even in 1927 one was seen on an Edinburgh-Glasgow limited-stop journey. But their time was inevitably running out and in 1929 about 54 of them were withdrawn, leaving eleven buses, nearly all at Galashiels, to continue in use for a few more months, together with nineteen charabancs which served Edinburgh during the summer of 1930, most of them with new licence numbers in the 800s. This is surely a great tribute to these remarkable vehicles designed as long ago as 1913, the oldest of them being seventeen years old when withdrawn. Two, SF275 and SF504, were then converted to breakdown lorries for some further years' work, replacing two Thornycrofts, SG1434 and SG1724, previously used for this purpose. Several were also sold for use as lorries.

For the purpose of this work, numbers preceded by E are Edinburgh licence numbers, B are Bathgate fleet numbers, D are Dundee licence numbers, and G are Galashiels fleet numbers, though these prefixes were not of course actually used. Numbers with a ? are conjectural.

Registration No.	Chassis No. in 1921	Licence or Fleet No.		
S3057	T5.5	E95		
S3662	T5.2	E91		
S3703	T5.3	E94		
S3597		E92?	E55	
S3841		E93	E893	
S4288	T5.6	E98	D188	
S4287	T5.7	E78		
S4399	T5.8	E82	D187	
S4543	T5.9	E84		
S4617	T5.10	E85		
S4654	T5.12	E88	E889	
S4655	T5.11	E89	E891	
S4716	T5.13	E92?	E72	E872
S4748	T5.14	E96?	D?	
S4836	T5.15	E51	G131	
S4846	T5.16	E52	E852	
S4851	T5.18	E53		
S5224	T5.21	E54		
S5496	T5.22	E56		
S5550	T5.43	E57	G122	
S5697	T5.23	E58		
S5862	T5.24	E59		
S5916	T5.26	E60?	D?	E355
S6423	T5.33	E61		
S6729	T5.28	E62	D186	

Registration No.	Chassis No. in 1921	Licence or Fleet No.		
S6761	T5.27	E63		
S7063	T5.29	E66	D?	
S4068★		E67?	D?	E66
S4963†	T5.19	E69		
S4100★	T5.30	E72?	E92	
S4849★		E73		
S4770★	T5.20	E75	G133	
S4813†	T5.17	E76	E876	
S4400★	T5.37	E83		
S5595★	T5.1	E87?	E55	G120
S7618		E86		
S7715		E90		
S8461		E71		
S8533		E74	E874	
S8594		E77		
S8668		E79	E879	
S9102		E81?	D?	E64
S9103		E80	E840	
S9555		E102		
S9622		E103	E843	
S9707	T5.42	E104		
S9728	T5.51	E105	E845	
S9830		E106	E846	
S7322★		E107	D?	E97
SG792	T5.58	E108		
SG887	T5.57	E109		
SG888		E110	E850	
SG1039	T5.59	E111	E851	
SG1890	T5.56	E140?	E70	
SG2106	T5.61	E230?	D?	E354
SG2107		E231?	D?	E356
SG2128‡	T5.38	E65	G130	
SG2129	T5.63	E67	G134	
SG2319	T5.65	E232		
SG2755	T5.66	E233		
SG3387	T5.67	E107		
SG3756	T5.68	E99	G132	
SG4580	T5.69	E231	G135	
SG4581	T5.70	E234		
SG5639	T5.73	E101	GF121	
SG7201	74	E228		
SG7202	75	E229		
SG7203	76	E230		
SG7680	77	E227		
SG7681	78	E226	D121	
SG7738		E225		
SG7985		E224		
SG7991		E223		

Registration No.	Chassis No. in 1921	Licence or Fleet No.
SG8034		E222
SF226		E215
SF227	84	E216
SF228	85	E217
SF229	86	E218
SF230	87	E219
SF253	88	E242
SF254		E256
SF274	90	E257
SF275		E258
SF330	92	E259
SF365		E260
SF427	95	E351
SF503	97	E353
SF504	96	E352

* Probably former lorry re-registered with reissued registration number.
† Probably former S.M.T. Co.'s lorry, registration not changed.
‡ Probably former lorry re-registered. See note on page 15.
Three Lothians seem to have changed Edinburgh licence numbers in 1921 as shown.

The large batch of J type Thornycrofts purchased between 1920 and 1924 were ex-W.D. machines which the company rebuilt and lengthened by one foot. The charabanc bodies built for them and seating 27 were similar to those of both patterns on the Lothians but there were minor differences on some of them. Most of the earlier ones ran for a while without S.M.T. Co. lettering. In addition about six bodies were built by a Grimsby firm (possibly Lincoln Lorries) and another six or so by a Birmingham firm. There were a number of differences among these, relating to the height and rake of the sides and the windscreen mounting. The low-sided ones had no waist beading. Bus bodies were provided for a few of the Thornycrofts and these were similar to those on the Lothians and seated 28, though some were recorded in Dundee as seating 32, apparently including the seats in the driver's compartment. Several of the buses were arranged for forward control and provided with 32-seat bodies. These included the last nine on the list below and also others which carried numbers E96, 129 and 213, though when SG8290 and SF3001 became charabancs with pneumatic tyres in 1927 as E212 and 220 they were altered to normal control. It will be noted that two were registered in Dundee for the first new route started there. Many were fitted with pneumatic tyres about 1923, those known being marked *. There was a further Thornycroft charabanc, also later fitted with pneumatic tyres, S7075, E136, which may have been Dundee's No. 11 rebodied and re-

registered in Edinburgh late in 1920 with a reissued registration number. The last of the Thornycrofts disappeared about 1928.

Registration No.	Body			Licence Nos.		
SG1259	charabanc		E112			
SG1260	charabanc		E113			
SG1261	charabanc		E114			
SG1359	charabanc		E123?	D?	E87	
SG1360	charabanc/bus	*	E122			
SG1433	charabanc		E124			
SG1434	charabanc		E125			
SG1497	charabanc	*	E136?	D?	E214	
SG1538	charabanc		E115?			
SG1591	charabanc		E116			
SG1636	charabanc	*	E129?	D?	E357	
SG1637	charabanc	*	E130			
SG1664	charabanc		E117?			
SG1675	charabanc	*	E126			
SG1721	bus	*	E119			
SG1722	charabanc		E118?	D?		
SG1723	charabanc	*	E131			
SG1724	charabanc	*	E132			
SG1725	charabanc	*	E133			
SG1824	charabanc		E120			
SG1825	charabanc	*	E127			
SG1830	charabanc	*	E128			
SG1856	charabanc		E121			
SG1857	charabanc		E134			
SG1858	charabanc	*	E135			
SG1935	charabanc	*	E137			
SG1952	charabanc	*	E138			
SG1972	charabanc	*	E139			
SG2063	?		E64?	D48		
SG2284	bus	*	E68			
TS2737	bus		D46?			
TS2989	bus		D57	E60		
SG2895	bus		E234?	D?	E213?	D58
SG2960	bus/charabanc	*	E235	E337 when charabanc		
SG2961	bus		E236			
SG2994	bus	*	E237			
SG3247	charabanc	*	E140			
SG3302	bus		E129?	D?		
SG3303	charabanc		E118			
SG3454	charabanc	*	E123			
SG3526	charabanc	*	E81			
SG3689	charabanc		E100			
SG3923	bus		E96?	D53		
SG8033	bus		E221			
SG8181	bus		E220?	D52		

Registration No.	Body	Licence Nos.		
SG8212	bus	E219?	D46	
SG8237	bus	E218?	D56	
SG8243	bus	E217?	D?	E212
SG8290	bus/charabanc	E216?	D49	E212†
SG8714	bus	E215?	D51	
SF3001	bus/charabanc	E358	E220 when charabanc	
SF3662	bus	E361		

† after SG8243 withdrawn

The three charabancs acquired from Adam Young of Eskbank in 1921 were a Dennis SY1330? soon disposed of, and two Thornycrofts, of which SY816 which became E243 was an X type with a wooden roof. E244 was also a Thornycroft J type charabanc and was probably the other. Its registration number has not been traced. It is known that S.M.T. received a new Thornycroft J type chassis in late December 1919 on which they fitted an S.M.T. bus body and exhibited it at the Scottish Motor Show in January 1920 as a new bus for the G.N.S. Railway who received it at the end of that month. This vehicle was registered as SY901, which suggests that the chassis may have been ordered by S.M.T. for Adam Young and diverted to the G.N.S. Railway order. It is possible that S.M.T. supplied either SG1497 or SG1636 from their own fleet to Adam Young at that time instead of SY901. If this conjecture is correct, 244 would be either SG1497 or SG1636, both of which charabancs appear to have gone to Dundee, returning later as 214 and 357 respectively.

The numbers of the Lothians and Thornycrofts at Dundee prior to 1927 are not known (except for the three marked * in 1925), but appear likely to have been as shown in the table overleaf.

Next came the Fiats, all fourteen-seaters on pneumatic tyres. The charabancs, the first of them in 1921 and the last in 1926, were painted brown and bore no lettering. The first of the buses, SF1814-5, were licenced in March 1925 and some of the earlier charabancs later received bus bodies also. The first two buses, together with SF1984 and SG9704, were painted glossy dark grey all over. The other Fiat buses were painted green with black uppers and after about a year the grey ones were repainted in this style also. In some cases the normal green and cream was subsequently applied. The bus bodies had a flush hinged door near the front and an emergency door in the back, but twelve later ones had a recessed door at the front, two windows aside the emergency door in the back, and lacked the rounded corners of the usual bodywork. These twelve were the buses marked ‡. Some with the original type of body later had windows in the back aside the emergency door too: these are marked

†. SG4239 and SG5545 may have been acquired from some other operators; one of them may have been from Grahamslaw.

D	1920	1921	1922	1923	1924	1925	1926	1927
1	Thorny D&DMTS	→	→	→	→	→	→	lapsed
11	Thorny D&DMTS	lapsed						
13	Thorny SG1636	→	→	→	→	lapsed		
14	Thorny D&DMTS	→	→	→	→	→	→	lapsed
18	Thorny D&DMTS	→	→	→	→	→	→	lapsed
29	Thorny SG1359	Thorny SG2895	→	Lothian S5916	→	Thorny SG3302	→	lapsed
46	Thorny TS2737	→	→	→	→	Thorny SG8212	→	→
47	Thorny SG1497	→	→	Lothian S7063	→	→	→	
48	Lothian SG4068	→	→	Lothian SG2106	→	Thorny SG2063*	lapsed	
49		Lothian SG2107	→	→	→	Thorny SG8290*	lapsed	
50		Lothian S7322	Thorny SG1722	→	→	→	→	
51					Thorny SG8714	→	→	→
52					Thorny SG8243	Thorny SG8181	→	→
53							Thorny SG3923	→
56		Lothian S9102	→	→	Thorny SG8237	→	→	→
57		Thorny TS2989	→	20 seat	→	→	28 seat	lapsed
58		Lothian S4748	→	→	→	Thorny SG2895*	→	→

Registration No.	Body	Licence Nos.	
SG4067	charabanc	E238	
SG4068	charabanc	E239	
SG4131	charabanc	E240	
SG4239	charabanc	E?	
SG4832	charabanc/bus ‡	E241	
SG5545	charabanc/bus ‡	E270	
SG5640	charabanc	E244	
SG5818	charabanc	E245	
SG5819	charabanc	E246	
SG5820	charabanc/bus ‡	E247	
SG5896	charabanc	E248	
SG7793	charabanc/bus ‡	E250	
SG7794	charabanc	E249	
SG7832	charabanc	E253	
SG7833	charabanc/bus ‡	E252	
SG7834	charabanc/bus	E251	
SG7920	charabanc	E254	
SG8316	charabanc/bus ‡	E255	
SG9704	charabanc/bus †	E301	
SG9705	charabanc	E300	
SG9706	charabanc	E302	
SG9707	charabanc/bus †	E305	D82
SG9708	charabanc	E307	
SG9709	charabanc	E303	
SG9710	charabanc	E304	
SG9711	charabanc	E306	
SG9712	charabanc/bus †	E308	
SG9744	charabanc	E309	
SG9745	charabanc	E310	
SG9798	charabanc	E313	
SG9799	charabanc/bus	E312	
SG9800	charabanc	E311	
SG9877	charabanc	E316	
SG9878	charabanc	E314	
SG9879	charabanc	E315	
SG9918	charabanc	E317	
SG9919	charabanc	E318	
SG9920	charabanc	E319	
SG9921	charabanc	E320	
SG9978	charabanc	E321	
SG9979	charabanc/bus ‡	E322	
SG9980	charabanc	E323	
SF31	charabanc	E324	
SF32	charabanc	E325	
SF33	charabanc	E326	
SF34	charabanc	E327	
SF1814	bus †	E329	
SF1815	bus †	E328	D83

Registration No.	Body	Licence Nos.	
SF1984	bus †	E331	
SF2060	bus	E332	D81
SF2061	bus	E333	
SF2166	bus	E334	
SF2477	charabanc/bus ‡	E336	
SF2478	charabanc	E335	
SF2542	charabanc	E338	
SF2543	charabanc	E339	
SF2839	charabanc	E340	
SF2840	charabanc	E341	
SF2841	charabanc	E342	D75
SF2842	charabanc/bus ‡	E343	D118
SF2921	charabanc	E344	D76
SF2922	charabanc	E345	
SF2923	charabanc/bus ‡	E346	
SF2997	charabanc	E347	D77
SF2998	charabanc	E348	
SF2999	charabanc	E349	
SF3661	bus	E362	
SF3663	bus	E363	
SF3753	bus ‡	E364	
SF3754	bus	E365	
SF3755	bus ‡	E366	D119
SF3829	bus	E367	
SF4978	charabanc	E420	
SF4979	charabanc	E421	
SF4980	charabanc	E422	
SF4981	charabanc	E423	
SF4982	charabanc	E424	
SF5275	charabanc	E425	
SF5276	charabanc	E426	
SF5277	charabanc	E427	
SF5278	charabanc	E428	
SF5601	charabanc	E429	
SF5767	charabanc	E436	

Five other acquired Fiats were used in Edinburgh. Usually on the Bo'ness route SX2104, E350, was a twelve-seat bus with a small neat body though branded as fourteen seats and may have come from Henderson of Bo'ness. The other four were charabancs with non-standard bodies, the first two from the Borders fleet and the other two from unknown sources about 1926-7: LS1037 E434, LS1241 E435, ES3323 E330, ES3465 E369. The last of the Fiats disappeared about 1929.

With services developing rapidly in 1924-6, many additional vehicles were required and even a few more solid-tyred Thornycrofts appeared, as well as fourteen/fifteen seaters of other makes in addition to Fiat. These other small buses of 1925 were nine Beardmores and three Internationals as under. The Beardmores had fifteen-seat front entrance bodies with a folding door, and the fourteen-seat Internationals were similar but of heavier appearance. Both had an emergency door and two windows in the back. Painting was as for the Fiats. Both types were mostly used on the North Berwick route and lasted only till 1929.

Registration No.	Make	Licence No.
SF3797	Beardmore	E370
SF3798	Beardmore	E371
SF3799	Beardmore	E372
SF3800	Beardmore	E373
SF3823	Beardmore	E374
SF3824	Beardmore	E375
SF3838	International	E376
SF3856	Beardmore	E379
SF3857	Beardmore	E380
SF3859	International	E377
SF3860	International	E378
SF3861	Beardmore	E368

It should be mentioned here that during 1924-5 Lothian SG3756 and Thornycroft SG8243 had the lower panel painted green instead of cream, and about the same period a number of vehicles were painted a glossy dark grey all over. These were: Lothians S5550 and SG2107, Thornycrofts SG1637, SG1935 and TS2989, and, as already mentioned, Fiat buses SG9704, SF1814, SF1815 and SF1984.

There is no information about any vehicles acquired from Scott of Whitburn, but the Dean Motor Transport Co. handed over the following charabancs which were duly painted brown:

Registration No.	Make	Seats	Licence No.
?	Rochet-Schneider	14	E202
?	Rochet-Schneider	14	E337 *
WA5080	Crossley	14	E330 *
SG9365	Rochet-Schneider	20	E200
SF535	Rochet-Schneider	20	E291
SF536	Gotfredson	14	E293

* These were probably not the vehicles' original licence numbers.

The first three disappeared about 1926 but the Gotfredson survived as a runabout tender until about 1939.

Four vehicles were taken over from Henderson's Central Motor Services, Bo'ness, including two old A.E.Cs. which were not retained. The other two may have been Fiat SX2104 and perhaps a Guy SX2250.

The fourteen-seat Reo vehicles acquired from the R.T. Co. were:

Registration No.	Body	Licence or Fleet No.	
SG9035	bus	E195	
SG9253	bus	E262	
SG9613	charabanc	E196	G136
SG9730	charabanc	E197	
HS3568	charabanc	E198	G127
SF2279	charabanc	E263	G123
SF2280	charabanc	E264	G124
SF2628	charabanc	E266	G125

The two buses were repainted green with black uppers, and the charabancs became pale yellow. They were all withdrawn by 1930.

By 1925 production of Lothians had ceased and the company were looking for a substitute. An order was therefore placed for 60 Maudslay forward-control buses. Ten of the earlier ones had S.M.T. bodies similar to the Lothians. For the remainder a lighter type of body was built by Short Bros. and by Vickers. These latter differed from one another in the shape of the roof and other details. All had full front cabs and 32 seats. At that time there was a proposal that buses under $3\frac{3}{4}$ tons weight might be allowed to run up to the then general 20 mph speed limit. These Maudslays had only single rear tyres, and those with the Short Bros. and Vickers bodies just came within the $3\frac{3}{4}$ tons weight limit. The proposed change in the law did not materialise, however.

It is necessary at this point to refer to the numbering scheme which the company introduced in June 1931 following the cessation of local authority licensing and the Edinburgh fleet numbers hitherto used. The company's 1931 fleet list is given in full later, and as all the Maudslays were included in that list they need not be repeated here. Their earlier Edinburgh numbers will be found also in the 1931 list. Maudslay SF5771 was operated as an Allen & Kennedy vehicle in 1929.

Of the 50 vehicles acquired from Brook & Amos and Adam Purves at Galashiels, Nos. 2, 3 and 8 of the former and also the ex-Gala Motor Transport Co.'s two old chain-driven Caledons were scrapped immediately. The list, so far as is known, follows, Nos. 42-8 being the Adam Purves vehicles. Nos. 15 and 16 are believed to have been the former Aikman vehicles and Nos. 24-9 those of Henderson.

Registration No.	Make	Type		Seats	Fleet No.
NL3700	A.E.C.	bus	front ent.	26	G1
	Daimler	bus	front ent.	20	G2
XN3937?	Daimler	bus	front ent.	32	G3
LS1297	A.E.C.	bus	front ent.	32	G4?

Reg. No.	Make	Type	Seats	Fleet No.	
LS1160	Karrier	charabanc	20	G5	
LS1074	A.E.C.	bus rear ent.	32	G6	
S5810	A.E.C.	charabanc	30	G7	
CP1104	A.E.C.	charabanc	30	G8	
LS1241	Fiat	charabanc	14	G9?	E435
	A.E.C.	double-deck, open	52	G10	
XP?	Daimler	bus	20	G11	
LS1308	A.E.C.	charabanc	32	G12	
	Ford	bus	14	G13?	
	Ford	charabanc	14	G14?	
LS973	Unic	charabanc	14	G15	
	Vulcan	charabanc		G16?	
LS1353	Daimler	charabanc	26	G19	
XU4796	Daimler	charabanc	20	G21	
LS1409	Reo	bus front ent.	14	G22?	
LS1410	Reo	bus front ent.	14	G23	
SH1820	A.E.C.	charabanc		G24	
T7340	Daimler	charabanc	25	G27?	
T8596	Daimler	charabanc	26	G28	
GA8599	Leyland	charabanc		G29	
SP8425	Leyland	bus		G30?	
LS1526	Leyland	convertible	24	G31	
LS1527	Leyland	convertible	24	G32	
LS1528	Leyland	convertible	24	G33	
LS1537	Leyland	convertible	24	G34	
	Lancia	charabanc		G35	
LS1037	Fiat	charabanc	14	G42?	E434
TB1054	Leyland	charabanc	32	G43	
TA731	Leyland	charabanc	32	G44	
LS1163	Leyland	charabanc	14	G45	
T9855	Lancia	charabanc	20	G46	
VA2454	Lancia	charabanc	20	G47	
TA3199	Lancia	charabanc	20	G48	

The convertibles Nos. 31-4 were orthodox charabancs onto which a top consisting of a roof and back and sides, with individual doors and windows for the five rows of seats, could be fixed to the top of the charabanc body when required, so making it an enclosed vehicle.

There was also in the Brook & Amos fleet a small Crossley bus, a small Thornycroft charabanc, GB905, a second Lancia, an Albion, and another A.E.C. bus with double-entrance body, whose numbers are unknown. Most of Brook & Amos' vehicles were painted dark red, but No. 3 was yellow: of this bus it was said it 'spent most of its time at the bottom of hills it couldn't get up'. Brook & Amos had kept Nos. 1 and 10 on the Selkirk route and No. 6, known as 'Old Sheila', on the Melrose route.

Next there are the buses which were acquired from J. Tennant & Sons

and Hendry's Motor Service. Many of these remained in their own area
with local numbers and the list is not quite complete, as fourteen buses
were taken over from Tennant and it is believed eighteen from Hendry.
Some, however, were given Edinburgh licence numbers as shown:

Registration No.		Make	Seats	Fleet or Licence No.		
Ex-Tennant	SX1192	Halley	24			
	SX1354	Halley	24			
	SX1662	Halley	24	B39		
		Halley	24	B40		
	SX2135	Halley	24			
	SX2233	Halley	24	B38		
	SX2286	Dennis		E121		
	SX2297	Dennis		E120		
	SX2345	Halley	24			
	SX2358	Halley		E115		
	SX2384	Halley		E118	B36	
	SX2398	Albion	28	E96	E266	
	SX2402	Albion	28	E87	E300	
Ex-Hendry	VA1720	Leyland	40			
	VA1721	Leyland	38			
	VA3529	Leyland	32	B17	E210	
	VA3859	Leyland	32	B161		
	VA3875	Leyland	32	B19	E211	
	VA4471	Leyland	32	B1		
	VA4472	Leyland	32	B2		
	VA4473	Leyland	32	B3		
	VA4474	Leyland	32	B4		
	VA4613	Dennis	28	B169	E118	
	VA4614	Dennis	28	B170	E129	
	VA5103	Gilford	24	E117		
	VA5276	Albion	27	E113	E263	
	VA5385	Albion	27	E112	E262	E264
	VA5554	Gilford	24	E116		
	VA5603	Albion	26	E114	D122	

Tennant's Dennis's were of an older type than the Hendry ones and
were put on the Bo'ness route. Both types had front entrances. Of the
Halleys, SX2345 had a front entrance; the others had a double entrance
and are believed to have been built by Porteous of Linlithgow. Some,
including SX1354 and SX1662, later acquired S.M.T. bodies from the
Thornycrofts. SX2358 was of a different type, also with a double-entrance
body. It was a fast vehicle and was generally on the Whitburn route. The
Hendry Leylands were old rear-entrance buses, except VA1720-1 which
were forward-control SG7 models with double-entrance bodies, and none
of them lasted long. The Gilfords had front entrances. VA5103 was

operated as an Allen & Kennedy vehicle in 1927-9. The Albions were modern vehicles, normal control, with bodies of normal lines, except VA5603, which was a little different. Tennant's ones had front entrance, Hendry's had rear entrance.

Allen & Kennedy's fleet was a small one. Those in running order when taken over were two 20-seat, front-entrance Reos, SX2263 and SX2313, respectively E400 and E401. Also a modern 24-seat, front-entrance Albion, SX2406 E403. Another two not retained were an Ensign and a Crossley.

S.M.T.'s next new vehicles, late in 1926, came from the Albion factory, and unusually were normal-control buses. These had been destined for Midland Bus Services Ltd. who, for a consideration, released them to S.M.T. for the Edinburgh-Glasgow route, whose need for more buses was still pressing. They were of typical Albion appearance and details will be found in the 1931 list. Two more Albions followed, and these again, while being forward-control models, had ordinary half-cab bodies, thus departing from S.M.T. practice of full-fronted machines.

A large number of forward-control Albions with full-fronted bodies appeared in 1927. These were quite luxurious for their time, with armchair type leather seats. 1927 also saw a new type of vehicle for touring work. These were 26-seat Maudslays with side screens and a folding hood, but were not really charabancs as the seats were reached from a central aisle from a door at the front, there being also another door near the back. Details of all these are given in the 1931 list.

Further acquisitions to the Borders list in 1926-7 included the following, though the list is incomplete:

Reg. No.	Make	Type	Seats	Fleet No.		From
KS3148	Reo	bus	14	G51	G137?	Cairns & Welsh
KS3146	Reo	bus	14			Cairns & Welsh
KS2618	Reo	charabanc	14	G54		Cairns & Welsh
ES4958	Cottin-Desgoutes	charabanc	19			Cairns & Welsh
KS2044	Karrier	convertible	20			Cairns & Welsh
KS2978	Reo	charabanc				Cairns & Welsh
KS1433	Maudslay	charabanc	28			Selkirk Motor Co.
KS2937	Guy	charabanc	16	G67		Selkirk Motor Co.
LS1669	Chevrolet	bus, front ent.				Selkirk Motor Co.
LS1882	Chevrolet	bus, front ent.				Selkirk Motor Co.
LS1894	Chevrolet	bus, front ent.	14			new addition
LS1912	Chevrolet	charabanc	14	G72		new addition
LS1913	Chevrolet	charabanc	14	G73		new addition
LS1914	Chevrolet	charabanc	14	G74		new addition
LS1915	Chevrolet	charabanc	14	G75		new addition

Reg. No.	Make	Type	Seats	Fleet No.	From
DS701	Dennis	bus	20	G76	Little
KS3282	Reo	charabanc	20		Wheelan
KS2212	Guy				Mitchell
KS2214	Karrier	charabanc	20		Lyall
LS1948	Albion	coach			Hamilton
LS1949	Albion	coach			Hamilton
KS1694	De Dion	charabanc	20		Border Motor Tr.Co.
KS2578	Maudlsay	charabanc	20	G91	Border Motor Tr.Co.
KS2888	Karrier	bus, front ent.	25	G92	Border Motor Tr.Co.
KS3708	Karrier 6-wheeler	bus, front ent.	32	G93	Border Motor Tr.Co.
KS3033	Reo	charabanc	20	G94	Border Motor Tr.Co.
KS1142	Fiat	charabanc	20	G95	Border Motor Tr.Co.
DS1141	Reo				Richardson
DS1308	Chevrolet				Richardson
DS1047	Reo	bus, front ent.	14		Ramsay
DS1070	Reo	charabanc	20		Ramsay
DS1099	Reo	charabanc	14	G126	Ramsay
DS1301	Reo	bus, front ent.	20		Ramsay
	Vulcan	bus			Turnbull
KS2954	Leyland	charabanc	32		Turnbull
KS3105	Maudslay	bus, front ent.	24	E575	Turnbull
KS3470	Leyland	charabanc	25	E576	Turnbull
KS3700	Albion	coach	28	E574	Turnbull
KS3701	Maudslay	coach	28	E580	Turnbull
KS3763	Albion	f.h.c.bus, front ent.	32	E566	Turnbull
KS3820	Albion	n.c.bus, front ent.	26	E713	Turnbull
KS3821	Albion	n.c.bus, front ent.	26	E714	Turnbull
KS3460	Chevrolet	charabanc	14		Turnbull
KS3465	Reo	charabanc		G115	Turnbull
KS3490	Chevrolet	charabanc	14		Turnbull
KS3550	Chevrolet				Turnbull
SF6506	Chevrolet				Turnbull

Some of Turnbull's vehicles survived into the 1931 list as also did DS1301.

The 1928 additions included more full-fronted Albions and in these and all buses subsequently, top lights to the windows were omitted. The Maudslay buses of that year were similar but had a luggage rack on the roof. Waistbands were also omitted on both these and the Albions. The Star coaches were a smaller version of the 1927 Maudslays but the 1928 Maudslay coaches were slightly different, having more robust side-screens. There were also the Star buses with rather square bodies, there being only minor differences between the two bodybuilders' product. Details are given in the 1931 list.

There were also a few acquisitions in the Dundee district about this period as follows, the Albions surviving into the 1931 list:

Reg. No.	Make	Type	Seats	Licence No.		From
SR4498	Lancia		20	D59		McCallum & Graham
RS8305	Albion	f.h.c.bus, front ent.	32	D79		?
RS8306	Albion	f.h.c.bus, front ent.	32	D80		?
ES8558	Cottin-Desgoutes	charabanc	26	D123		Whyte
ES8942	Cottin-Desgoutes	charabanc	26	D122		Whyte
ES8884	Minerva	bus	26	D121	D189	Whyte
ES9948	Minerva	bus	26	D120		Whyte
ES8557	De Dion	bus, front ent.	20	D182		Gray
ES9716	Vulcan	bus	20	D181		Gray
ES9308	Albion	bus, front ent.	24	D180		Gray
GS41	Albion	bus, front ent.	29	D74		Gray

1929 saw another change as most of that year's purchases were Leylands, which appear to have been ordered through W. Alexander & Sons Ltd., though there were also some Maudslay buses which were generally similar to the 1928 lot, except for the last two which were of a flatter shape. The Titan TD1 double-deckers were the standard Leyland product, the first 27 having an open staircase, while the last ten were of the improved version with the platform and stair enclosed. Of the original lot, four, SC2923-4 and SC2938-9, respectively E673-4 and E688-9, were sold early in 1931 to the Glasgow General Omnibus & Motor Services Ltd., a subsidiary company, and thus did not reach the 1931 list. The Lions had the then standard rear-entrance Leyland body except for the first five, the bodies of which were, however, on generally similar lines, though with front entrance and of more robust appearance. These five were turned out in the silver-grey livery of Midland Bus Services Ltd., which later formed the nucleus of the Western S.M.T. Co., but were repainted in standard colours about the end of the year. Of the standard-bodied lot, those which became G21/8-50/2/8 had cutaway pattern entrances, but G21 and G51 subsequently exchanged bodies. The first two Tigers had standard Leyland front-entrance bodies, the remainder were coaches with a flat roof. Except for these, and the Maudslays, all the 1929 vehicles had destination screen boxes incorporated in the front of the roof, another novelty for S.M.T., though on the single-deckers the roller blinds were not fitted in them till some years later. Single-deckers now also had luggage racks on the roof. The numbers of all these new vehicles will be found in the 1931 list.

Four former Amos Proud Leylands with standard Leyland bodies came into the S.M.T. fleet in 1929, becoming G61-2 and H49-50 in the 1931 list. Fairbairn, in 1929, contributed GE4562, an Albion 29-seat front-entrance bus, 138 in the Borders list, which became A81 in the 1931 list, while A32-3 in the 1931 list of the then orthodox open-coach design had been ordered by that firm and spent their first summer as Edinburgh 355-6 in Fairbairn's deep blue livery. They were then about the last coaches to be painted in the pale yellow livery before the company's colour scheme was changed in May 1930 to blue for all types of vehicle.

Of the West Lothian Motor Services vehicles, the Albions, Daimlers and Dennis's were taken into S.M.T. stock. The latter were sent to the Borders as Nos. 139 and 140 and soon sold, though the prefix E was allocated for them in the new numbering scheme. The Albion which became A82 was of typical Albion lines, and the Daimlers which became D8-9 were rather similar. The others were somewhat different, the Daimler which became D12 being rather ungainly looking, with the window line of the driver's cab higher than the rest of the windows. Except for this one and D8, these vehicles remained in their former dark green livery but with S.M.T. Co. lettering for some time.

The Thornycrofts and Daimlers from Thomson's Tours were of orthodox open-coach pattern except for the last two Daimlers, which were closed coaches of low sleek lines. His Reo and Cottin-Desgoutes charabancs did not survive for the new list and were as follows: Reos SF1658 E381, SF2145 E383, SF2541 E385. The others were delicensed. The four buses from White's Motor Hiring Co. do not call for special notice, but a Maudslay 50-seat double-decker with open staircase and painted silver and green, which ran on trial service with S.M.T. for a short time in 1929, should be mentioned. This was VC1778 and carried the Edinburgh No. 128.

In 1930 the company made another innovation with an A.E.C. Regal MY3479 which originally carried the Strachan body with cutaway rear entrance, later to appear on B2. This had the Edinburgh No. 80, but in March 1931, SC9871 appeared with the said Strachan body and numbered 80, while MY3479 reappeared with its Cowieson body in June as B1, the new numbers having meantime come into use. SC9871, however, was of particular note in having an oil (diesel) engine, and it was not long before the company standardised on this type of power unit for buses. To return to 1930, however, there were also two lots of Leyland Tiger coaches for long-distance work. The Cowieson ones were of similar appearance to the previous year's ones but with destination screen boxes: the Burlingham ones were more low-set, and both were provided with specially comfortable seating. Another new make was a series of eight small

Chevrolet open coaches, while a more unusual one still, was an S.M.C., otherwise a six-cylinder Sunbeam, which had a 31-seat cutaway pattern, rear-entrance body by Taylor of Norwich. This was UK9189, receiving Edinburgh No. 79, and though the prefix M was allocated in the new list, the vehicle was disposed of before the renumbering.

Two other buses which ran on trial in the first few months of 1931 have to be mentioned. The first was a Tilling-Stevens with a 38-seat front-entrance body, MS9978, and this was followed by an Albion Valkyrie with a 32-seat front-entrance body, GG2513. Both, in turn, carried the Edinburgh No. 217.

An important change was made in May 1930 when a blue livery was adopted for all vehicles. Later there were many variations which will be mentioned in due course. Then, in 1932, the full spread-out lettering gave place to just a closely spaced 'S.M.T.'.

The Borders list so far as is known has been given on pages 142-3/5-6. Subsequent additions, mainly transfers from the Edinburgh fleet, may now be listed together for completeness:

Registration No.	Make	Borders No.	Former No.
S4400	Lothian	119	E83
S5595	Lothian	120	E55
SG5639	Lothian	121	E101
S5550	Lothian	122	E57
SF2279	Reo	123	E263
SF2280	Reo	124	E264
SF2628	Reo	125	E266
DS1099	Reo	126	
HS3568	Reo	127	E198
		128	
		129	
SG2128	Lothian	130	E65
S4836	Lothian	131	E51
SG3756	Lothian	132	E99
S4770	Lothian	133	E75
SG2129	Lothian	134	E67
SG4580	Lothian	135	E231
SG9613	Reo	136	E196
KS3148	Reo	137	G51
GE4562	Albion	138	
SX2775	Dennis	139	E769
SX2776	Dennis	140	E768

The numerical details of the vehicles included in the new 1931 list should now be given. This numbering scheme remained in use until 1956, and the list includes the additions until that date. A rather different arrangement was then followed which will be dealt with in due course. The basis of the new numbering scheme was that each make of chassis was numbered separately with a corresponding prefix letter, and the prefix letter was applied alphabetically to each make in the fleet when the list was drawn up. Leylands were further subdivided, and the letters then used were A up to P, omitting I and O. E, L and M dropped out at once and L was then used for a separate series for Stark's buses at Dunbar. The vehicles acquired from the several firms taken over about 1932 required the use of further letters and R, S, T, U, V and W came into use, together with a new E. Of these, S, T, U and V soon disappeared, to be used again, except U, for other new types afterwards acquired, followed by a new M and the use of O, also later, X. E was used for a third time during the war and BB for double-deck versions of B. In 1956 double-deck versions of other makes were dealt with similarly so that E became DD as D had then recently been re-used, and J became HH. Several of the second-hand vehicles, though listed, were never repainted in S.M.T. colours, while many more were never even included in the fleet list at all. In 1935, S was used to cover the few odd vehicles of various makes which were subsequently acquired and retained for service.

The fleet numbers were now shown on embossed metal plates fixed on the front of the driver's cab, though later, in some cases, transfers were used instead, mostly in the case of new vehicles. The garage to which the vehicle was attached was also shown below or alongside, in accordance with the following code:

A	New Street, Edinburgh		G	Dalkeith
B	Bathgate		H	Airdrie
C	Dundee area		I	Broxburn
D	Galashiels and Hawick		J	Berwick
E	Kelso		K	Peebles
F	Linlithgow		L	Carlisle

In 1937 Musselburgh was added as WA. L was dropped about this time, but revived in 1957 as a separate code for Hawick. In later years Musselburgh became W, Baxter's garage at Airdrie was V, the new Baillieston garage C, and Stark's garage at Dunbar S. Public Service Vehicle licence plates were of course carried on the back of the vehicle in the usual way, but as these numbers had no significance to the company, they need not be quoted.

It would be impracticable to describe in detail the many different types of bodywork represented over the next 25 years, and the conventional code will be used, with some amplification of the more important types given at the end of the list. In this code the seating capacity is given with a prefix, viz:

Single-deck bus	B
Single-deck coach, i.e. generally having a hinged or sliding door	C
Double-deck 'highbridge' type bus, i.e. with central gangways	H
Double-deck 'lowbridge' type bus, i.e. with sunken gangway upstairs	L

and followed by a suffix to indicate the position of the entrance, viz: Front F; Centre C; Rear R; Dual D.

A: Albion

No.	Reg. No.	New	Body	Builder	Former Nos.			Withdrawn
1	SC205	1927	B29R	Croall	E546			1933
2	SC206	1927	B29R	Croall	E547	D190		1933
3	SC219	1927	B29R	Croall	E548			1934
4	SC220	1927	B29R	Croall	E549			1934
5	SC261	1927	B29R	Croall	E552	D56	E649	1933
6	SC262	1927	B29R	Croall	E553			1933
7	SC263	1927	B29R	Croall	E557			1934
8	SC264	1927	B29R	Croall	E556			1934
9	SC265	1927	B29R	Croall	E555			1933
10	SC266	1927	B29R	Croall	E554			1934
11	SC267	1927	B29R	Croall	E551			1934
12	SC268	1927	B29R	Croall	E550	D46	E646	1934
13	SC568	1928	B29R	Croall	E559	D81		1933
14	SC569	1928	B29R	Croall	E558	D123		1933
15	SC570	1928	B29R	Croall	E560	D82	E547 E560	1933
16	SC2028	1928	B29R	Cowieson	E421	D193		1935
17	SC2029	1928	B29R	Cowieson	E428	D194		1935
18	SC2030	1928	B29R	Cowieson	E434	D185	D195	1935
19	SC2031	1928	B29R	Cowieson	E435			1934
20	SC2032	1928	B29R	Cowieson	E436			1934
21	SC2033	1928	B29R	Cowieson	E439			1934
22	SC2034	1928	B29R	Cowieson	E443	D183		1935
23	SC2035	1928	B29R	Cowieson	E444	D184		1935
24	SC2036	1928	B29R	Cowieson	E445	D185		1933
25	SC2037	1928	B29R	Cowieson	E446			1933
26	SC2038	1928	B29R	Cowieson	E447			1934
27	SC2039	1928	B29R	Cowieson	E448			1933
28	SC2040	1928	B29R	Cowieson	E449	D83		1935
29	SC2041	1928	B29R	Cowieson	E450	D89	D187	1935
30	SC2042	1928	B29R	Cowieson	E214	E445		1934
31	SC2043	1928	B29R	Cowieson	E537	D196		1935
32	SC4405	1929	C26F		E355			1938
33	SC4406	1929	C26F		E356			1938
34	SF7010	1926	B28F		E536			1933
35	SF7078	1926	B24R		E244	D18		1933
36	SF7079	1926	B24R		E537	D47		1933
37	SF7146	1926	B27R		E538			1933

A: Albion — *continued*

38	SF7147	1926	B24R	
39	SF7148	1926	B24R	
40	SF7149	1926	B28F	
41	SF7150	1926	B24R	
42	SF7151	1926	B29R	
43	SF7152	1926	B32R	
44	SF7453	1926	B32R	
45	SF9211	1927	B29R	Croall
46	SF9212	1927	B29R	Croall
47	SF9256	1927	B29R	Croall
48	SF9269	1927	B29R	Cowieson
49	SF9720	1927	B29R	Cowieson
50	SF9292	1927	B29R	Croall
51	SF9293	1927	B29R	Cowieson
52	SF9302	1927	B29R	Cowieson
53	SF9303	1927	B29R	Cowieson
54	SF9310	1927	B29R	Croall
55	SF9354	1927	B29R	Croall
56	SF9355	1927	B29R	Croall
57	SF9356	1927	B29R	Croall
58	SF9357	1927	B29R	Croall
59	SF9381	1927	B29R	Croall
60	SF9382	1927	B29R	Croall
61	SF9522	1927	B29R	Croall
62	SF9523	1927	B29R	Croall
63	SF9542	1927	B29R	Croall
64	SF9543	1927	B29R	Croall
65	SF9544	1927	B29R	Croall
66	SF9545	1927	B29R	Cowieson
67	SF9546	1927	B29R	Croall
68	SF9547	1927	B29R	Cowieson
69	SF9574	1927	B29R	Croall
70	SF9575	1927	B29R	Croall
71	SF9634	1927	B29R	Croall
72	SF9667	1927	B29R	Cowieson
73	SF9668	1927	B29R	Cowieson
74	SF9689	1927	B29R	Cowieson
75	SX2398	1926	B28F	
76	SX2402	1926	B28F	
77	SX2406	1926	B24F	Porteous
78	SX2784	1928	B26R	Strachan
79	SX2785	1928	B26R	Strachan
80	SX2826	1928	B26R	Strachan
81	GE4562	1929	B29F	
82	GE432	1928	B28F	
83	GS41	1926	B29F	
84	ES9308	1926	B24F	
85	KS3700	1926	C28F	

E539	D49		1933
E540	D50		1933
E541			1933
E542	D57		1933
E543			1933
E544			1933
E545			1933
E625	D53	E625	1932
E626	D53	E648	1932
E627			1934
E628			1933
E629	D78	E636	1934
E630	D48		1933
E631	D58	E537	1933
E632	D52		1933
E633	D54		1933
E634			1933
E635			1933
E636	D197		1933
E637			1934
E638			1934
E639	D45	E651	1934
E640			1934
E641	D45		1933
E642	D58		1933
D116			1933
D117			1933
E643	D55		1933
E644			1934
E645	D51		1933
E646	D198		1933
E647			1933
E648	D191		1933
E649	D199		1933
E650			1934
E651	D192		1933
E652			1934
E96	E266		1933
E87	E300		1933
E403			1933
E765	(W.L.M.S.)		1933
E764	(W.L.M.S.)		1933
E766	(W.L.M.S.)		1933
G138			1933
E767	(W.L.M.S.)		1933
D74			1933
D180			1933
E574			1932

A: Albion — *continued*

No.	Reg.	Year	Body	Builder	Ex	Date
86	KS3763	1926	B32F		E566	1934
87	KS3820	1927	B26F		E713	1934
88	KS3821	1927	B26F		E714	1934
89	RS8305	1927	B32F		D79	1933
90	RS8306	1927	B32F		D80	1933
91	VA5276	1925	B27R		E113 E263	1933
92	VA5385	1925	B27R		E112 E264	1933
93	VA5603	1926	B26R		E114 D122	1935
94	SC74	1927	B28F		Ex-Bowen	1933
95	SY3991	1929	B28F		Ex-Bowen	1933
96	FS1114	1931	B32F	Cowieson		1938
97	FS1115	1931	B32F	Cowieson		1938
98	FS1116	1931	B32F	Cowieson		1938
99	SX2302	1925	B24F		Ex-Masson	1934
100	SX2769	1928	B24F		Ex-Masson	1934
101	FS1762	1932	B32F	Alexander		1938
102	HH5230	1930	B30D		Ex-Hudson	1935
103	HH3318	1926	B20F		Ex-Hudson	1933
104	HH4185	1928	B25D		Ex-Hudson	1934
105	SY4169	1930	B28F	Mitchell	Ex-Sword	1935
106	FS6540	1933	B20F	Cowieson	Ex-Bell	1940
107	KS4336	1928	C26F	Mitchell	Ex-Graham	1938
108	KS4738	1929	C26F	Mitchell	Ex-Graham	1938
109	GS1189	1929	B26F		Ex-Lowson	1936
110	NL7458	1924	B20F		Ex-Lowson	1935
111	SY2692	1925	C20F	Roberts	Ex-Bowen	1936
112	SY3308	1928	C20F	Roberts	Ex-Bowen	1936
113	SY1855	1923	C14F	Alexander Mtrs.	Ex-Bowen	1935
114	US9608	1935	C32F	Duple	Ex-Dick	1948
115	SF4942	1925	C14F		Ex-Sword	1935
116	RR8219	1927	B32F		Ex-Browning	1936
117	GD9724	1928	B30R	Cowieson	Ex-Browning	1935
118	WS5569	1935	B34R	Cowieson		1948
119	VA7075	1927	B26F		Ex-Irvine	1941
120	VA9990	1930	B30F		Ex-Irvine	1941
121	US9605	1935	C26F	Burlingham	Ex-Irvine	1941
122	VD6298	1936	C32F		Ex-Irvine	1941
123	VD7969	1937	C32F		Ex-Irvine	1941
124	VD9383	1938	B39F		Ex-Irvine	1941

Notes: A92 bore the Edinburgh No. 262 for a time before correction to 264, the former number belonging to one of Bowen's vehicles. A93 was rebodied with a front-entrance body in 1933. A114 was an up-to-date coach with a well curved roof back and front. A32-3 were Vikings, A96-8 were Valkyries, A101/14/18 were Valiants, A106/21-3 were Victors, and A124 was a six-wheeler 'PW145'.

A: (Second); Austin CXD

1	JSF409	1952	C32F	Kenex	Sold to Highland 1952

A: (Third); Bristol

1	LSC61	1954	C38F	E.C.W.	1969-73
to	to				
30	LSC90	1954	C38F	E.C.W.	1969-73
31	NSG793	1956	C38F	E.C.W.	1969-73
to	to				
50	NSG812	1956	C38F	E.C.W.	1969-73

AA: Bristol Lodekka

1	NSG778	1956	H60R	E.C.W.	
to	to				see
15	NSG792	1956	H60R	E.C.W.	below

AA1, 2 and 3 (the latter being the former AA15 renumbered AA3 in 1964) were withdrawn at the end of 1975. The original AA3-14 were transferred to Highland Omnibuses in 1963 from where AA3, 4, 5, 9, 11 and 14 were to return again to Eastern Scottish in 1971-2 with the numbers AA576-81, being finally withdrawn between 1975 and 1977.

B: A.E.C.

1	MY3479	1930	C28F	Cowieson		1938
2	SC9871	1931	B30R	Strachan		1938
3	FS248	1931	C28F	Cowieson		1940-3
to	to					
13	FS258	1931	C28F	Cowieson		1940-3
14	SY4068	1929	B26F	Hall-Lewis	Ex-Bowen	1931
14	FS2251	1932	B34R	Alexander		1957-9*
to	to					
73	FS2310	1932	B34R	Alexander		1957-9
74	FS5561	1933	C28R	Burlingham		1940
to	to					
79	FS5566	1933	C28R	Burlingham		1940
80	KW9396	1930	C30R	Burlingham	Ex-County Motor Ser.	1937
81	FS8541	1934	C32R	Burlingham		1942
to	to					
92	FS8552	1934	C32R	Burlingham		1942
93	FS8553	1934	B34R	Burlingham		1940-60
to	to					
122	FS8582	1934	B34R	Burlingham		1940-60
123	FS8583	1934	B34R	Cowieson		1938
124	FS8584	1934	B34R	Cowieson		1940
125	FS8585	1934	B34R	Cowieson		1940
126	JR468	1933	C30R	Weyman	Ex-Orange Bros.	1941
—	TY9607	1932	C28R	Strachan	Ex-Orange Bros.	1935
—	TY7081	1930	C26F		Ex-Orange Bros.	1935

B: A.E.C. — *continued*

127	SY4512	1931	C24F	Duple	Ex-Dick	1945
128	SY3943	1929	C30F	Vickers	Ex-Dick	1937
129	WS636	1934	C26R	Burlingham	Ex-Herd	1940
130	WS4478	1935	B32F	Alexander		1958-64
to	to					
154	WS4502	1935	B32F	Alexander		1958-64
155	WS4503	1935	B34R	Cowieson		1960-2
to	to					
168	WS4516	1935	B34R	Cowieson		1960-2
169	WS4517	1936	B38F	Alexander		1961
170	VD1286	1932	B32F	Cowieson	Ex-Western S.M.T.	1945-7
to	to					
175	VD1291	1932	B32F	Cowieson	Ex-Western S.M.T.	1945-7
176	GX2742	1932	C32F	Duple	Ex-Browning	1940
177	GF5124	1930	C31F	London Lorries	Ex-Browning	1946
178	SX4031	1935	C32C	Burlingham	Ex-Browning	1943
179	BSC516	1938	B34R	Alexander		1958-64
to	to					
193	BSC530	1938	B34R	Alexander		1958-64
194	MV346	1931	C26R	Park Royal	Ex-Robertson	1940
194	ELY529	1938	B36F	Weyman	Ex-Caledonian	1961
195	CSF201	1939	B35F	Alexander		1954-64
to	to					
214	CSF220	1939	B395	Alexander		1954-64
215	DSC302	1940	B39F	Alexander		1954-64
to	to					
234	DSC321	1940	B39F	Alexander		1954-64
235	ESC429	1946	B35F	Duple		1960-4
to	to					
284	ESC478	1946	B35F	Duple		1960-4
285	FFS182	1947	B35F	Alexander		1961-5
to	to	to				
344	FFS241	1948	B35F	Alexander		1961-5
345	GSC233	1948	B35F	Burlingham		1963-5
to	to					
363	GSC251	1948	B35F	Burlingham		1963-5
364	GSC457	1949	C31F	Burlingham		1962
365	GSF684	1949	C35F	Burlingham		1964-6
to	to					
384	GSF703	1949	C35F	Burlingham		1964-6
385	GSF704	1949	B35F	Alexander		1964-6
to	to					
404	GSF723	1949	B35F	Alexander		1964-6
405	HWS907	1951	C30F	Alexander		1963-6
to	to					
424	HWS926	1951	C30F	Alexander		1963-6
425	LSC566	1954	B45F	Park Royal		1968-9
to	to					
430	LSC571	1954	B45F	Park Royal		1968-9

B: A.E.C. — *continued*

431	LWS875	1954	B45F	Park Royal	1970-2
to	to				
438	LWS882	1954	B45F	Park Royal	1970-2
439	HWS941	1951	B30F	Alexander	1963-6
to	to				
444	HWS946	1951	C30F	Alexander	1963-6
445	JSF145	1952	C40F	Alexander	1966
to	to				
454	JSF154	1952	C40F	Alexander	1966
455	KSC532	1953	C40F	Alexander	1963-6
to	to				
462	KSC539	1953	C30F	Alexander	1963-6
463	KSC540	1953	C38F	Alexander	1964-6
to	to				
479	KSC556	1953	C38F	Alexander	1964-6
480	LWS883	1955	B45F	Park Royal	1969-71
to	to				
496	LWS900	1955	B45F	Park Royal	1969-71
497	LWS901	1955	B41F	Park Royal	1969-72
to	to				
521	LWS925	1955	B41F	Park Royal	1969-72
522	NSG813	1956	B41F	Alexander	1969-73
to	to				
546	NSG837	1956	B41F	Alexander	1969-73
547	NSG543	1956	C30F	Alexander	1967

* Except B37 wrecked in 1934.

Notes: Post-war rebodying: B35F bodies with opening roof by Alexander were fitted to B15, 17, 23, 25, 29, 31, 32, 34, 35, 36, 38, 40, 43, 47, 52, 57, 59, 60, 61, 67, 68, 70, 93, 104, 108, 109, 110, 113, 117, 131-140, 142-150, 152, 154-169 in 1946-7-8, and to B197, 201, 203, 204 in 1953, and to B194 (ii) and B374 in 1955. Slightly different bodies by Burlingham were fitted to B14, 16, 18-22, 24, 27, 28, 33, 39, 41, 42, 44, 45, 46, 48-51, 53, 55, 56, 64, 65, 66, 69, 71, 72 in 1948, and again slightly different bodies by Croft to B30, 54, 58, 62, 63, 73 also in 1948. 37-seat Burlingham Seagull bodies were fitted to B141, 153, 179, 180, 182-185, 187, 188, 199, 207, 209, 226, 230 in 1952, and slightly different 35-seat bodies by Burlingham to B310-329 in 1953 and to B385-404 in 1954. B330-344 were lengthened and reconstructed as full-fronted 35-seat coaches in 1953 by Dickinson's of Dunbar. B26 acquired a coach body similar to those on B81-92 in 1946, but a B35F body by S.O.L. was fitted in 1952. Earlier, B157, 165 and 166 had been rebodied with bodies of similar but slightly different type to their original ones, and B175 got one of these too. B456 was fitted with a body similar to B547 in 1957. B310-404 were Regal IIIs, B405-424 and B439-479 were Regal IVs, B425-438 and B480-546 were Monocoaches, and B547 was the first Reliance for the fleet. It may be noted that fourteen

A.E.C. Regal IVs with 30-seat Alexander bodies, HWS927-940, went instead to Western S.M.T., their intended S.M.T. numbers B425-438 being later filled as shown in the list. Some premature withdrawals resulting from accidents should be mentioned, viz. B37 in 1934, B225 in 1943 and B223 in 1944. Of the second-hand vehicles, the first B14 was an A.D.C., B127, and the first B194 were Rangers of rather sleek lines with the window line slightly stepped down towards the rear. B129 was a Regent of straighter lines, while B128 was one of the original Reliances. B178 had an unusual body of pleasing lines.

BB: A.E.C.

1	DSG167	1942	L55R	Brush		1955
2	DSG168	1942	L55R	Brush		1955
3	FS5561	1944	L53R	Alexander		1955-7
to	to					
8	FS5566	1944	L53R	Alexander		1955-7
9	FS8541	1944	L53R	Alexander		1955-7
to	to					
20	FS8552	1944	L53R	Alexander		1955-7
21	FWS571	1948	L53R	Alexander		1969
22	ESC422	1948	L53R	Alexander		1965-9
to	to					
28	ESC428	1948	L53R	Alexander		1965-9
29	FFS150	1948	L53R	Alexander		1964-9
to	to					
60	FFS181	1948	L53R	Alexander		1964-9
61	GSF644	1949	L53R	Duple		1965-6
to	to					
80	GSF663	1949	L53R	Duple		1965-6
81	GSF664	1950	L53R	Burlingham		1965-7
to	to					
100	GSF683	1950	L53R	Burlingham		1965-7

Notes: The post-war ones were Regal IIIs. BB21 had to be re-registered from ESC421 owing to a licensing error. BB71 was destroyed in an accident in 1954 and reconstructed with an S.O.L. body, being re-registered LWS218.

C: Bedford

1	SC7511	1930	C14F	Alexander Mtrs.	E422	1934
to	to				to	
8	SC7518	1930	C14F	Alexander Mtrs.	E429	1934
9	SH3380	1929	B20F	Alexander Mtrs.	Ex-Gardner	1932
10	SH3902	1930	B14F		Ex-Gardner	1932
9	SC8310	1930	B14F		Ex-Nicol	1934
10	SX3203	1930	B14F	Waveney	Ex-Nicol	1934

C: Bedford — *continued*

11	FS5567	1933	C20F	Burlingham		1940
to	to					
16	FS5572	1933	C20F	Burlingham		1940
17	SX3479	1930	B14F	Porteous	Ex-McNair	1934
18	FS8586	1934	C20F	Burlingham		1940
to	to					
29	FS8597	1934	C20F	Burlingham		1940
30	FS8598	1934	C12F	S.M.T.		1941
31	FS8599	1934	C12F	S.M.T.		1941
32	FS8600	1934	C12F	S.M.T.		1941
33	FS8601	1934	C14F	S.M.T.		1940
to	to					
37	FS8605	1934	C14F	S.M.T.		1940
38	SY4220	1930	C11F	Alexander Mtrs.	Ex-Bowen	1936
39	FS349	1931	C15F		Ex-Herd	1937
40	FS2923	1932	C20F	Alexander Mtrs.	Ex-Herd	1937
41	SC7456	1930	C14F	Alexander Mtrs.	Ex-Herd	1935
42	WS4791	1935	C20R	Duple		1941
43	WS4792	1935	C26R	Duple		1941
44	WS4793	1935	C20R	Duple		1941
45	WS4794	1935	C24R	Burlingham		1941
46	WS8061	1936	C20F	Duple		1941
to	to					
65	WS8080	1936	C20F	Duple		1941
66	ASF334	1937	C20F	Duple		1953-4
to	to					
90	ASF358	1937	C20F	Duple		1953-4
91	ASF359	1937	C14F	Duple		1953-4
to	to					
95	ASF363	1937	C14F	Duple		1953-4
96	EFS151	1944	B32F	S.M.T.		1945-9
to	to					
155	EFS210	1944	B32F	S.M.T.		1945-9
156	FFS856	1947	C29F	S.M.T.		1962
to	to					
168	FFS868	1947	C29F	S.M.T.		1962
169	FFS869	1947	C25F	S.M.T.		1957-62
to	to					
187	FFS887	1947	C25F	S.M.T.		1957-62
188	JS7799	1948	C29F	S.M.T.		1960
189	JSF814	1952	C30F	Burlingham		1960-2
to	to					
208	JSF833	1952	C30F	Burlingham		1960-2

Notes: C188 was acquired from Mackenzie, Garve, in 1949 and originally numbered C206. Nos. C1-8, the second C9, and both C10s, as well as C17, 38 and 41, were Chevrolets, and the first C9 was a G.M.C. C156-175 received 24-seat Burlingham Seagull bodies in 1953, and C176-188 were reduced to 24 seats.

D: Daimler

1	SC2745	1928	B30R	Nrthrn. Counties	E434 (Whites)	1931
2	SC4191	1929	C26F	Cadogan	E386 (Thomson's Tours)	1935
3	SC4760	1929	C26F	Cadogan	E382 (Thomson's Tours)	1935
4	SC5118	1929	C26F	Buckingham	E578 (Thomson's Tours)	1934
5	SC5237	1929	C28F	Hoyal	E419 (Thomson's Tours)	1934
6	SC5300	1929	C26F	Hoyal	E380 (Thomson's Tours)	1934
7	SC5388	1929	C26F	Hoyal	E384 (Thomson's Tours)	1934
8	SC5392	1929	B32F	Hall Lewis	E738 (W.L.M.S.)	1933
9	SC5431	1929	B32F	Hall Lewis	E739 (W.L.M.S.)	1933
10	SX2945	1929	B32D	Strachan	E737 (W.L.M.S.)	1933
11	SX2946	1929	B32D	Strachan	E736 (W.L.M.S.)	1933
12	TS8168	1929	B31D	Nrthrn. Counties	E224 (W.L.M.S.)	1933
13	SY4142	1930	B32D	Nrthrn. Counties	Ex-Bowen	1933
14	TY7165	1930	B26F	Hall Lewis	Ex-Dewar	1935
15	SC4593	1929	C22F	Hoyal	Ex-Scott	1936
16	SC4594	1929	C22F	Hoyal	Ex-Scott	1936
17	SC4595	1929	C22F	Hoyal	Ex-Scott	1936
18	SC7556	1930	C24F	Hoyal	Ex-Scott	1939
19	SC7557	1930	C24F	Hoyal	Ex-Scott	1939
20	SY3940	1929	C28F		Ex-Bowen	1936
21	SY3640	1928	C28F		Ex-Dick	1935
22	WS1523	1934	C32F	Brush	Ex-Dick	1945
23	SY5035	1934	C32F	Brush	Ex-Dick	1943
24	SY4997	1934	C31F	English Electric	Ex-Dick	1943
25	SY4189	1930	C32F	Buckingham	Ex-Dick	1935
26	SC5237	1929	C28F	Hoyal	Ex-Sword	1935
27	SY5509	1935	C32F	Roberts	Ex-Bowen	1945
28	FS366	1931	C28F	Dickson	Ex-Westwood & Smith	1937
29	FS3389	1932	C30F	Cowieson	Ex-Westwood & Smith	1939
30	FS9314	1934	C32F	Harrington	Ex-Westwood & Smith	?
31	FS9776	1934	C29F	Westw'd & Smith	Ex-Westwood & Smith	?
32	WS3869	1935	C32F	Harrington	Ex-Westwood & Smith	?
33	SC7889	1930	C26F	Westw'd & Smith	Ex-Westwood & Smith	1936
	FS6007	1933	B32R		Ex-Irvine	1940

Notes: D1 and D21 were A.D.Cs. D15-20, 26 were of low sleek line. D22, 23, 24 were of straightforward neat appearance, the first two running for some time in Dick's red and white livery with S.M.T. lettering; the former had a Gardner 5-cylinder oil engine. D27 had a well curved roof and ran for a time in Bowen's livery. D4, 25, 30-33 were forward-control half-cab coaches with no nearside canopy. D30, 31, 32 were rather elaborate with a stepped-up window line, the last having a particularly raked driver's screen and slightly raked pillars.

D: (Second); Guy (Second)

1	LSC91	1954	B39F	S.O.L.		1962
to	to					
5	LSC95	1954	B39F	S.O.L.		1962

These were rebuilt from double-deckers E23-31, see below.

E: A.J.S.

1	SX3254	1931	B32F	Roberts	Ex-Rendall	1935
2	SC4807	1929	C20F		Ex-Herd	1936
3	SC7566	1930	C20F	Haywood	Ex-Herd	1936

E: (Second) Later DD; Guy (Second)

1	DSG176	1943	L55R	Nrthrn. Counties	1957
2	DSG177	1943	L55R	Nrthrn. Counties	1957
3	DSG178	1943	L55R	Brush	1960
4	DSG179	1943	L55R	Brush	1960
5	DWS352	1943	L55R	Nrthrn. Counties	1955
6	DWS353	1943	L55R	Nrthrn. Counties	1957
7	DWS354	1944	L55R	Massey	1954
8	DWS355	1944	L55R	Massey	1955
9	DWS843	1944	L55R	Nrthrn. Counties	1957
10	DWS844	1944	L55R	Nrthrn. Counties	1955
11	DWS845	1944	L55R	Roe	1955
12	DWS846	1944	L55R	Roe	1957
13	DWS921	1944	L55R	Roe	1957
14	DWS922	1944	L55R	Roe	1955
15	EFS350	1945	L55R	Weyman	1955-8
to	to				
22	EFS357	1945	L55R	Weyman	1955-8
23	HGC108	1945	H56R	Park Royal	1953
24	HGC113	1945	H56R	Park Royal	1953
25	HGC120	1945	H56R	Park Royal	1953
26	HGC122	1945	H56R	Park Royal	1953
27	GYL350	1945	H56R	Park Royal	1953
28	HGC123	1945	H56R	Park Royal	1953
29	HGC144	1945	H56R	Massey	1953
30	HGC145	1945	H56R	Massey	1953
31	HGC188	1945	H56R	Weyman	1953

Notes: E23-31 were ex-London Transport vehicles acquired in 1952, E30 having been briefly used by Alexander's before coming to S.M.T. E25-30 were painted light grey at first and then a pale shade of green. In 1954 they were rebuilt with new single-deck bodies, five of them becoming D1-5 above, and the other four going to Highland Omnibuses Ltd.

F: Gilford (First list)

1	SC160	1927	B26R		E547 (White's)	1931

F: Gilford (First list) — *continued*

2	SC250	1927	B26R			E558 (White's)		1931
3	SC838	1927	B26R			E559 (White's)		1931
4	FS1509	1931	B28R	Ex-Bowen's SC46 re-registered				

F: Gilford (Second list)

1	FS1509	1931	B26R		Previously F4		1934
2	SY3483	1928	B24F		Ex-Dunn		1934
3	SY3498	1928	B24F		Ex-Dunn		1934
4	SY3916	1929	B20F		Ex-Dunn		1932
5	SC4198	1929	B32R	Wycombe	Ex-Bowen		1936
6	UV5637	1929	C24F	Duple	Ex-Sword		1936

G: Leyland Lion

1	SC2941	1929	B31F	Midland Bus Ser.	E691	E136	1933
to	to				to	to	
5	SC2945	1929	B31F	Midland Bus Ser.	E695	E140	1933
6	SC3348	1929	B31R	Leyland	E94		1939
7	SC3349	1929	B31R	Leyland	E95		1939
8	SC3350	1929	B31R	Leyland	E96		1939
9	SC3353	1929	B31R	Leyland	E85		1943
10	SC3354	1929	B31R	Leyland	E86		1939
to	to				to		
17	SC3361	1929	B31R	Leyland	E93		1939
18	SC4301	1929	B31R	Leyland	E97		1939
to	to				to		
24	SC4307	1929	B31R	Leyland	E103		1939
25	SC4308	1929	B31R	Leyland	E104		1945
26	SC4309	1929	B31R	Leyland	E105		1939
to	to				to		
32	SC4315	1929	B31R	Leyland	E111		1939
33	SC4316	1929	B31R	Leyland	E112	D76	1939
34	SC4317	1929	B31R	Leyland	E113		1939
35	SC4318	1929	B31R	Leyland	E114		1939
36	SC4319	1929	B31R	Leyland	E115		1938
37	SC4320	1929	B31R	Leyland	E116		1939
to	to				to		
41	SC4324	1929	B31R	Leyland	E120		1939
42	SC4325	1929	B31R	Leyland	E123	D120	1939
43	SC4326	1929	B31R	Leyland	E122	D119	1948
44	SC4327	1929	B31R	Leyland	E121	D118	1939
45	SC4328	1929	B31R	Leyland	E124		1939
46	SC4329	1929	B31R	Leyland	E125		1939
47	SC4330	1929	B31R	Leyland	E126	D77	1939
48	SC4331	1929	B31R	Leyland	E127		1939
49	SC4332	1929	B31R	Leyland	E128	D121	1945
50	SC4333	1929	B31R	Leyland	E129		1939
51	SC4334	1929	B31R	Leyland	E130		1939
52	SC4335	1929	B31R	Leyland	E131		1945

G: Leyland Lion — *continued*

53	SC4336	1929	B31R	Leyland	E132		1939
54	SC4337	1929	B31R	Leyland	E134		1940
55	SC4338	1929	B31R	Leyland	E135		1939
56	SC4407	1929	B31R	Leyland	E84		1939
57	SC4408	1929	B31R	Leyland	E83		1939
58	SC4409	1929	B31R	Leyland	E82		1939
59	SC4410	1929	B31R	Leyland	E81	D75	1945
60	KS3470	1925	C25F		E576		1932
61	TY2423	1926	B31F	Leyland	E703		1933
62	TY3066	1927	B31F	Leyland	E701		1933
63	SY3419	1927	B30F	Leyland	Ex-Bowen		1933
64	VA4995	1925	B20F	Leyland	Ex-Bowen		1933
60	FS3212	1932	B32R	Alexander			1940
61	SY4441	1931	C28F	Roberts	Ex-Bowen		1940
62	TD5015	1926	B31F	Leyland	Ex-Lowson		1936
65	FH6413	1929	B31R	Leyland	Ex-Western S.M.T.		1939
66	VA9505	1929	B31R	Midland Bus Ser.	Ex-Western S.M.T.		1938
69	UC7191	1928	C34F		Ex-Browning		1935
70	SY3419	1927	B29R	Leyland	Ex-Browning		1935
71	HH1836	1923	C25F		Ex-Westwood & Smith		1936
67	SY3484	1928	B31R	Leyland	Ex-Coast Line		1937
to	to						
72	SY3489	1928	B31R	Leyland	Ex-Coast Line		1937
73	SY3659	1928	B31R	Leyland	Ex-Coast Line		1937
to	to						
76	SY3662	1928	B31R	Leyland	Ex-Coast Line		1937
77	SY4125	1930	B32F	Leyland	Ex-Coast Line		1939
78	SY4126	1930	B32F	Leyland	Ex-Coast Line		1939
79	SY4127	1930	B32F	Leyland	Ex-Coast Line		1939

Notes: The seemingly inconsistent re-use of numbers above 59 for later vehicles will be noticed. The first G60 and also G71 were older-type Leylands, while G64 was a Leveret with a body of somewhat dumpy appearance. G63, later to return as G70, also G62 (ii) and G67 (ii) to G76 had standard Leyland bodies, while G65, 66 were generally similar to G6-59. G65 had Gruss air-springs.

H: Leyland Tiger

1	SC3351	1929	B30F	Leyland	E210	E800	1954
2	SC3352	1929	B30F	Leyland	E211	E801	1949
3	SC4339	1929	C29F	Cowieson	E802		1954
to	60				to		
14	SC4350	1929	C29F	Cowieson	E813		1954
15	SC4361	1929	C29F	Cowieson	E814		1954
to	to				to		
30	SC4376	1929	C29F	Cowieson	E829		1954

H: Leyland Tiger — *continued*

31	SC7531	1930	C26F	Cowieson		E830	1938
to	to					to	
42	SC7542	1930	C26F	Cowieson		E841	1938
43	SC7991	1930	C27F	Burlingham		E842	1938
to	to					to	
48	SC7996	1930	C27F	Burlingham		E847	1938
49	TY3677	1928	B31R	Leyland		E709	1954
50	TY3678	1928	B31R	Leyland		E712	1954
51	FS5573	1933	B34R	Burlingham			1959-61
to	to						
84	FS5606	1933	B34R	Burlingham			1959-61
85	FS5607	1933	B34R	Metro.-Cammell			1959-60
to	to						
104	FS5626	1933	B34R	Metro.-Cammell			1959-60
105	KS6165	1933	C32R	Duple	Ex-Graham		1955
106	WS4518	1935	B32R	Cowieson		(H110 in 1955)	
to	to						
115	WS4527	1935	B34R	Cowieson			
116	GK431	1930	B28R	London Lorries	Ex-Western S.M.T.		1937
117	GK432	1930	B28R	London Lorries	Ex-Western S.M.T.		1937
118	GK433	1930	B28R	London Lorries	Ex-Western S.M.T.		1937
119	GK437	1930	B28R	London Lorries	Ex-Western S.M.T.		1937
120	VD1432	1932	B30F	Burlingham	Ex-Western S.M.T.		1947
121	AG8268	1932	B32F	Burlingham	Ex-Western S.M.T.		1954
122	AG8269	1932	B30F	Burlingham	Ex-Western S.M.T.		1940
123	AG8274	1932	B30F	Pickering	Ex-Western S.M.T.		1940
124	AG8276	1932	B30F	Pickering	Ex-Western S.M.T.		1950
125	AG8277	1932	B30F	Pickering	Ex-Western S.M.T.		1948
126	AG8280	1932	B30F	Pickering	Ex-Western S.M.T.		1940
127	AG8281	1932	B30F	Pickering	Ex-Western S.M.T.		1940
128	AG8282	1932	B30F	Pickering	Ex-Western S.M.T.		1940
129	AG8283	1932	B30F	Pickering	Ex-Western S.M.T.		1938
130	AG8285	1932	B30F	Pickering	Ex-Western S.M.T.		1940
131	AG8286	1932	B30F	Pickering	Ex-Western S.M.T.		1954
132	VA8459	1929	B32F	Midland Bus Ser.	Ex-Western S.M.T.		1937
133	VA8790	1929	B31F	Kelly	Ex-Western S.M.T.		1937
134	VA8793	1929	B31F	Kelly	Ex-Western S.M.T.		1937
135	VA8891	1929	B32R	Midland Bus Ser.	Ex-Western S.M.T.		1938
136	VA8952	1929	B30F	Kelly	Ex-Western S.M.T.		1937
137	VA8957	1929	B32R	Midland Bus Ser.	Ex-Western S.M.T.		1937
138	WS8081	1936	C22R	Burlingham			
to	to						
143	WS8086	1936	C22R	Burlingham			
144	SY5441	1935	B32R	Brush	Ex-Coast Line		1954
145	SY5442	1935	B32R	Brush	Ex-Coast Line		1955
146	SY5443	1935	B32R	Brush	Ex-Coast Line		1960
147	SY5444	1935	B32R	Brush	Ex-Coast Line		1955
148	SY5712	1936	B32R	Brush	Ex-Coast Line		1955

H: Leyland Tiger — *continued*

149	SY5713	1936	B32R	Brush	Ex-Coast Line	1955
150	SY5714	1936	B32R	Brush	Ex-Coast Line	1955
151	SY5715	1936	B32R	Brush	Ex-Coast Line	1955
152	ASF364	1937	B35R	Alexander		1940-55
to	to					
181	ASF393	1937	B35R	Alexander		1940-55
182	ASF394	1937	B35R	Alexander		1948-58
to	to					
196	ASF408	1937	B35F	Alexander		1948-58
197	ASF409	1937	C30F	Duple		1954
to	to					
204	ASF416	1937	C30F	Duple		1954
205	SY6020	1937	B32R	Brush		1954
206	SY6021	1937	B32R	Brush		1954
207	SY6022	1937	B32R	Brush		1954
208	SY6023	1937	B32R	Brush		1960
209	SY6024	1937	B32R	Brush		1960
210	CSF221	1939	B35R	Alexander		1950-5
to	to					
243	CSF254	1939	B35R	Alexander		1950-5
244	CWS165	1939	C30F	Alexander		1956
245	DSC281	1940	B39F	Alexander		1954-6
to	to					
263	DSC299	1940	B39F	Alexander		1954-6
264	DSC301	1940	B39F	Alexander		1954
265	MS9076	1929	B32F	Alexander	Ex-Irvine	1940

Notes: Rebodying: in 1937-8 new B34R bodies of the current pattern were provided on H1-10, 12-17, 19, 21-27, 29, 49, 50 while the others up to H48 were withdrawn. H110 got a different B35R body in 1944 but reverted to the original type later. Cowieson B34R bodies went to H105 and H175 in 1946-7. Except for H59 and H98 which had earlier been destroyed in fires, H51-104 were all rebodied in 1949, those up to H76 with C35F bodies by Burlingham, and H77 upwards with B35F bodies by Alexander. The latter were also put on H146, 208, 209 in 1954. H138-143 were converted to double-deckers and renumbered accordingly in 1942, and H106-109, 111, 112, 113, 115 and 161, 162, 163, 174 similarly in 1945. H114 had been burnt out in 1937. A Dorman-Ricardo oil engine was tried in H16. The buses transferred from the Western S.M.T. fleet were rather a mixed lot. The bodies of H132, 135, 137 were of Leyland appearance, the others were more rounded but H133, 134, 136 had flatter roofs. H116-119 had a large illuminated panel worded 'Western' mounted above the front of the roof and they ran in S.M.T. service for a month or so with these in place. H121 and H132 were in the Western white coach livery which they likewise retained for a time; the others were blue. The Coast Line buses had high-domed roofs and an unusually large destination screen box. H105 was a neat vehicle of straightforward lines.

J: Later HH; Leyland Titan

1	SC2921	1929 L51R	Leyland		E671	1948
2	SC2922	1929 L51R	Leyland		E672	1948
3	SC2925	1929 L51R	Leyland		E675	1947-8
to	to				to	
15	SC2937	1929 L51R	Leyland		E687	1947-8
16	SC2940	1929 L51R	Leyland		E690	1948
17	SC3341	1929 L51R	Leyland		E691	1947-8
to	to				to	
23	SC3347	1929 L51R	Leyland		E697	1947-8
24	SC5221	1929 L48R	Leyland		E698	1947-8
25	SC5222	1929 L48R	Leyland		E699	1947-8
26	SC5223	1929 L48R	Leyland		E700	1947-8
27	SC5224	1929 L48R	Leyland		E210	1947-8
to	to				to	
33	SC5230	1929 L48R	Leyland		E216	1947-8
34	BSC531	1938 L53R	Leyland			1954-6
to	to					
53	BSC550	1938 L53R	Leyland			1954-6
54	CSF255	1939 L53R	Leyland			1954-8
to	to					
59	CSF260	1939 L53R	Leyland			1954-8
60	WS8081	1942 L53R	Alexander			1955-8
to	to					
65	WS8086	1942 L53R	Alexander			1955-8
66	DSG169	1942 L53R	Leyland			1959
67	WS4518	1945 L53R	Alexander			1956-8
to	to					
70	WS4521	1945 L53R	Alexander			1956-8
71	WS4523	1945 L53R	Alexander			1957-8
72	WS4524	1945 L53R	Alexander			1957-8
73	WS4525	1945 L53R	Alexander			1957-8
74	WS4527	1945 L53R	Alexander			1957
75	ASF373	1945 L53R	Alexander			1957
76	ASF374	1945 L53R	Alexander			1957
77	ASF375	1945 L53R	Alexander			1957
78	ASF386	1945 L53R	Alexander			1958
79	CK4150	1929 H52R	Cowieson	Ex-Campbell		1948
80	GE7260	1930 H52R	Cowieson	Ex-Campbell		1948
81	GG908	1930 H52R	Cowieson	Ex-Campbell		1948
82	UF7422	1931 H52R	Short Bros.	Ex-Campbell		1946

Notes: J81 had the Glasgow Corporation arrangement of destination screen box.

K: Maudslay

1	SC1159	1928	B31R	Cowieson	E654		1936
2	SC1160	1928	B31R	Cowieson	E653		1935
3	SC1161	1928	B31R	Cowieson	E655		1935
to	to				to		
12	SC1170	1928	B31R	Cowieson	E664		1935
13	SC2044	1928	C26F	Hoyal	E539		1935
14	SC2045	1928	C26F	Hoyal	E540		1936
15	SC2046	1928	C26F	Hoyal	E542		1936
16	SC2047	1928	C26F	Hoyal	E550		1936
17	SC2048	1928	C26F	Hoyal	E552		1936
18	SC2049	1928	C26F	Hoyal	E626		1936
19	SC2050	1928	C26F	Hoyal	E629		1936
to	to				to		
23	SC2054	1928	C26F	Hoyal	E633		1936
24	SC2055	1928	C26F	Hoyal	E639		1936
25	SC2056	1928	C26F	Hoyal	E643		1936
26	SC2057	1928	C26F	Hoyal	E645		1936
27	SC2058	1928	C26F	Hoyal	E665		1935-6
to	to				to		
32	SC2063	1928	C26F	Hoyal	E670		1935-6
33	SC2064	1928	B31R	United	E220		1935
34	SC2065	1928	B31R	United	E221		1936
35	SC2066	1928	B31R	United	E235		1935-6
to	to				to		
41	SC2072	1928	B31R	United	E241		1935-6
42	SC2073	1928	B31R	United	E243		1935-6
43	SC2074	1928	B31R	United	E244		1935-6
44	SC2075	1928	B31R	United	E245		1935-6
45	SC2076	1928	B31R	United	E247		1936
46	SC2077	1928	B31R	United	E248		1936
47	SC2078	1928	B31R	United	E250		1935-6
to	to				to		
52	SC2083	1928	B31R	United	E255		1935-6
53	SC4377	1929	B32R	S.M.T.	E51		1936
to	to				to		
78	SC4402	1929	B32R	S.M.T.	E76		1936
79	SC4403	1929	B32R	Weyman	E77		1936
80	SC4404	1929	B32R	Weyman	E78		1936
81	SF3645	1925	B32R	S.M.T.	E359		1932
82	SF3646	1925	B32R	S.M.T.	E360		1931
83	SF4268	1925	B32R	S.M.T.	E201		1932
84	SF4269	1925	B32R	S.M.T.	E213	E249	1931
85	SF5599	1926	B32R	S.M.T.	E430		1931
86	SF5600	1926	B32R	S.M.T.	E431		1931
87	SF5678	1926	B32R	S.M.T.	E433		1931
88	SF5679	1926	B32R	S.M.T.	E432		1932
89	SF5680	1926	B32R	Short Bros.	E451		1932
90	SF5681	1926	B32R	Short Bros.	E452		1932

K: Maudslay — *continued*

91	SF5688	1926	B32R	Short Bros.	E453			1932
92	SF5689	1926	B32R	Short Bros.	E454			1932
93	SF5712	1926	B32R	Short Bros.	E459			1932
94	SF5713	1926	B32R	Short Bros.	E458			1932
95	SF5714	1926	B32R	Vickers	E476			1932
96	SF5754	1926	B32R	Short Bros.	E468			1932
97	SF5768	1926	B32R	Short Bros.	E457			1932
98	SF5769	1926	B32R	Short Bros.	E455			1932
99	SF5770	1926	B32R	S.M.T.	E438			1932
100	SF5771	1926	B32R	S.M.T.	E437			1932
101	SF5772	1926	B32R	Short Bros.	E456			1932
102	SF5773	1926	B32R	Short Bros.	E461			1932
103	SF5787	1926	B32R	Vickers	E477			1932
104	SF5809	1926	B32R	Vickers	E479			1932
105	SF5810	1926	B32R	Vickers	E478			1932
106	SF5811	1926	B32R	Short Bros.	E460			1932
107	SF5821	1926	B32R	Short Bros.	E465			1932
108	SF5822	1926	B32R	Vickers	E481			1932
109	SF5823	1926	B32R	Vickers	E480			1932
110	SF5911	1926	B32R	Short Bros.	E462			1932
111	SF5912	1926	B32R	Short Bros.	E464			1932
112	SF5913	1926	B32R	Short Bros.	E463			1932
113	SF5948	1926	B32R	Short Bros.	E470			1932
114	SF5949	1926	B32R	Short Bros.	E469			1932
115	SF5950	1926	B32R	Vickers	E484	D48	E484	1932
116	SF5951	1926	B32R	Vickers	E483	D54	E483	1932
117	SF5997	1926	B32R	Short Bros.	E467			1932
118	SF6017	1926	B32R	Vickers	E482			1932
119	SF6018	1926	B32R	Short Bros.	E466			1932
120	SF6044	1926	B32R	Vickers	E485	D55	E485	1932
121	SF6045	1926	B32R	Short Bros.	E472			1932
122	SF6046	1926	B32R	Short Bros.	E471			1932
123	SF6047	1926	B32R	Vickers	E486	D78	E486	1932
124	SF6048	1926	B32R	Vickers	E487			1932
125	SF6049	1926	B32R	Vickers	E488			1932
126	SF6050	1926	B32R	Vickers	E489			1932
127	SF6120	1926	B32R	Short Bros.	E474			1932
128	SF6121	1926	B32R	Short Bros.	E473			1932
129	SF6122	1926	B32R	Vickers	E492			1932
130	SF6123	1926	B32R	Short Bros.	E475			1932
131	SF6124	1926	B32R	Vickers	E493			1932
132	SF6125	1926	B32R	Vickers	E494			1932
133	SF6185	1926	B32R	Vickers	E491			1932
134	SF6186	1926	B32R	Vickers	E490			1932
135	SF6433	1926	B32R	Vickers	E495	D51	E495	1932
136	SF6434	1926	B32R	Vickers	E496			1932
137	SF6463	1926	B32R	Vickers	E497			1932
138	SF6492	1926	B32R	Vickers	E498			1932

G

K: Maudslay — *continued*

139	SF6557	1926	B32R	Vickers		E499	1932
140	SF6558	1926	B32R	Vickers		E500	1932
141	SF9155	1927	C26F	Short Bros.		E600	1935
142	SF9158	1927	C26F	Short Bros.		E601	1935
143	SF9182	1927	C26F	Short Bros.		E602	1935
144	SF9183	1927	C26F	Short Bros.		E603	1935
145	SF9221	1927	C26F	Short Bros.		E604	1935
146	SF9222	1927	C26F	Short Bros.		E605	1935
147	SF9235	1927	C26F	Short Bros.		E606	1935
148	SF9236	1927	C26F	Short Bros.		E609	1935
149	SF9237	1927	C26F	Short Bros.		E608	1935
150	SF9238	1927	C26F	Short Bros.		E607	1935
151	SF9275	1927	C26F	Short Bros.		E610	1935
152	SF9286	1927	C26F	Short Bros.		E611	1935
153	SF9287	1927	C26F	Short Bros.		E616	1935
154	SF9288	1927	C26F	Short Bros.		E615	1935
155	SF9289	1927	C26F	Short Bros.		E614	1935
156	SF9290	1927	C26F	Short Bros.		E613	1935
157	SF9291	1927	C26F	Short Bros.		E612	1935
158	SF9308	1927	C26F	Short Bros.		E617	1935
159	SF9309	1927	C26F	Short Bros.		E618	1935
160	SF9336	1927	C26F	Short Bros.		E619	1935
to	to					to	
164	SF9340	1927	C26F	Short Bros.		E623	1935
165	SF9942	1927	B30R	S.M.T.		E624	1936
166	KS2578	1924	C20F	Maudslay		G91	1931
167	KS3105	1926	B24F			E575	1931
168	KS3701	1927	C28F			E580	1933
169	TY9403	1932	C26F	Strachan		Ex-Orange Bros.	1938

L: Reo (First)

1	DS1301	1927	B20F		1931

Afterwards, the Leyland buses belonging to Stark's of Dunbar, which were painted in S.M.T. livery, were given numbers with the L prefix thus:

L: Leyland (Stark's)

1	SS2786	1928	Leyland Lion	B32F		E442	1941
2	SS2819	1928	Leyland Lion	B32R		E440	1934
3	SS3033	1929	Leyland Lion	B31R	Leyland	E441	1940
4	FV1098	1930	Leyland Badger	C24F	Leyland		1940
5	FV1099	1930	Leyland Badger	C24F	Leyland		1940
6	SS3161	1930	Leyland Tiger	B31R	Leyland	E443	1940
7	SS3472	1932	Leyland Tiger	B32R	Alexander		1953
8	SS4768	1937	Leyland Tiger	B35F	Alexander		1957
9	SS6440	1947	Leyland Tiger	B35F	Alexander		1963
10	SS6609	1947	Leyland Tiger	B35F	Alexander		1961
11	SS7525	1950	Leyland Tiger	B35F	Alexander		1967

Notes: L1 was rebodied with a B31R body by Forbes Brebner of Crieff in 1933 and L7 received a new B35R Alexander body in 1940. L6's body had a more sloping roof at the front than the usual bodies of the period. The Alexander bodies were the same as those supplied to S.M.T. vehicles at the same dates. L3 and L4 did not carry their numbers, nor were they lettered S.M.T.

The other Stark's buses painted in S.M.T. livery but not at that time carrying S.M.T. numbers were as follows:

SS4044	A.E.C. Q type	1934	C35F	Weyman		1943
CAG807	A.E.C. Regal	1948	C33F	Burlingham		1963
SS9615	A.E.C. Reliance	1955	B45F	Alexander	Later B39	
SS9616	A.E.C. Reliance	1955	B45F	Alexander	Later B40	

M: Morris (Second)

1	SY4242	1930	C20F	Morris	Ex-Bowen	1936
2	SY4511	1931	C20F	Eastwood & Kenning	Ex-Dick	1937
3	SY4248	1930	C20F		Ex-Dick	1935
4	SY4930	1932	B20F	London Lorries	Ex-Dick	1937
5	FS3397	1932	B30F	Park Royal	Ex-Browning	1938
6	XS2578	1930	C20F	Morris	Ex-Browning	1935

Notes: M2 and M3 retained Dick's red and white livery with S.M.T. lettering for a time, only the former eventually becoming blue. M5 was a Dictator, the others were Viceroys.

N: Star

1	SC2010	1928	C14F	Short Bros.	E301	1936
2	SC2011	1928	C14F	Short Bros.	E304	1936
3	SC2012	1928	C14F	Short Bros.	E305	1936
4	SC2013	1928	C14F	Short Bros.	E308	1936
5	SC2014	1928	C14F	Short Bros.	E309	1936
6	SC2015	1928	C14F	Short Bros.	E311	1936
7	SC2016	1928	C14F	Short Bros.	E312	1936
8	SC2017	1928	C14F	Short Bros.	E315	1936
9	SC2018	1928	C14F	Short Bros.	E317	1936
10	SC2019	1928	C14F	Short Bros.	E318	1936
11	SC2020	1928	C14F	Short Bros.	E320	1936
12	SC2021	1928	C14F	Short Bros.	E322	1936
13	SC2022	1928	C14F	Short Bros.	E328	1936
14	SC2023	1928	C14F	Short Bros.	E329	1936
15	SC2024	1928	C14F	Short Bros.	E330	1936
16	SC2025	1928	C14F	Short Bros.	E331	1936
17	SC2026	1928	C14F	Short Bros.	E332	1936
18	SC2027	1928	C14F	Short Bros.	E333	1936
19	SC2084	1928	B20F	Hall Lewis	E334	1934

N: Star — *continued*

20	SC2085	1928	B20F	Hall Lewis	E336	1934
21	SC2086	1928	B20F	Hall Lewis	E342	1934
22	SC2087	1928	B20F	Hall Lewis	E343	1934
23	SC2988	1928	B20F	Hall Lewis	E344	1936
24	SC2089	1928	B20F	Hall Lewis	E346	1934
25	SC2090	1928	B20F	Hoyal	E347	1934
26	SC2091	1928	B20F	Hoyal	E349	1934
27	SC2092	1928	B20F	Hoyal	E350	1934
28	SC2093	1928	B20F	Hoyal	E357	1936
29	SC2094	1928	B20F	Hoyal	E358	1934
30	SC2095	1928	B20F	Hall Lewis	E361	1934
31	SC2096	1928	B20F	Hoyal	E362	1932
32	SC2097	1928	B20F	Hoyal	E363	1936
33	SC2098	1928	B20F	Hoyal	E364	1934
34	SC2099	1928	B20F	Hoyal	E365	1936
35	SC2100	1928	B20F	Hoyal	E366	1936
36	SC2101	1928	B20F	Hoyal	E367	1934
37	SC2102	1928	B20F	Hoyal	E369	1934
38	SC2103	1928	B20F	Hoyal	E379	1934
39	SC100	1927	C19F		Ex-Herd	1935

Notes: The following were rebodied in 1932 with C18F bodies by Alexander Motors Ltd., Edinburgh: N23, 28, 32, 34, 35. N27 acquired a destination screen box on the front.

O: Leyland Lioness

1	SY3929	1929	C26F		Ex-Dick	1935
2	SY3388	1927	C27F	Leyland	Ex-Dick	1935
3	TD9220	1927	B26F	Leyland	Ex-Dick	1935
4	TY5609	1929	B26F	Leyland	Ex-Dick	1935
5	TE1140	1927	C24F	Hall Lewis	Ex-Browning	1935
6	GE1808	1928	C26F		Ex-Browning	1935

Note: O3 retained Dick's red and white livery with S.M.T. lettering while it lasted.

P: Thornycroft

1	SC1921	1928	C20F		E579 (Thomson's Tours)	1934
2	SC7076	1930	C20F		E387 (Thomson's Tours)	1934
3	DS1128	1925	B20F		Ex-Anderson	1934
4	SX2432	1926	B20F		Ex-Rendall	1934
5	SX2594	1927	B22F		Ex-Rendall	1934
6	SX2625	1927	B20F		Ex-Anderson	1934
7	SX2818	1928	B20F		Ex-Anderson	1934
8	SX3030	1930	B22F		Ex-Rendall	1934
9	SC1069	1928	C18F	Westw'd & Smith	Ex-Westwood & Smith	1936
10	SC1450	1928	C18F	Westw'd & Smith	Ex-Westwood & Smith	1936

P: Thornycroft — *continued*

11	SC3885	1929	C25F	Westw'd & Smith	Ex-Westwood & Smith	1936
12	SC3997	1929	C24	Westw'd & Smith	Ex-Westwood & Smith	1936
13	SC3998	1929	C24	Westw'd & Smith	Ex-Westwood & Smith	1936
14	FS5168	1933	C20F		Ex-Westwood & Smith	1936

Notes: P3 was a rather box-like affair, but most of the others were neat and orthodox. P11 had the later type of plated radiator, while P14 was a Speedy. P12 and P13 had a separate door to each row of seats.

R: Reo (Second)

1	GE7415	1930	B24F	Mitchell	Ex-Dunn	1934
2	SY4279	1930	B24F	Eaton	Ex-Dunn	1934
3	SY4251	1930	B20F		Ex-Dunn	1934
4	SY4246	1930	B20F		Ex-Dunn	1934
5	SY2808	1926	B24F		Ex-Dunn	1934
6	SB3093	1928	B20R		Ex-Lamond	1932
7	SC7412	1930	C15D	West'wd & Smith	Ex-Westwood & Smith	1936
8	SC9981	1931	C14D	West'wd & Smith	Ex-Westwood & Smith	1936
9	SC9982	1931	C14D	West'wd & Smith	Ex-Westwood & Smith	1936

Note: R1, 2, 8, 9 were more substantial looking models than the others.

S: Ford

1	SY3931	1929	B14F	Ex-Dunn	1932
2	SY4066	1930	B14F	Ex-Dunn	1932
3	SC6721	1930	B20F	Ex-Lamond	1932

S: (Second) Sundry Vehicles

1	SX2775	1928	Dennis	B14F		Ex-McNair	1934
2	FG6262	1926	Lancia	B20F		Ex-Lowson	1936
3	SX3747	1933	Dennis-Lancet	C30F	Dennis	Ex-Browning	1941
4	TS4937	1925	Lancia	C20		Ex-Robertson	1938
5	TS7825	1929	Lancia	C24		Ex-Robertson	1938
6	FS8	1931	Guy	C20F		Ex-Cruikshank	1939
7	SC7373	1930	Guy	C20F		Ex-Cruikshank	1939
4	VA9257	1929	Clyde	B26R		Ex-Irvine	1940
5	VD742	1931	Dennis Arrow	B32R		Ex-Irvine	1941
6 to 11	DSG170 to DSG175	1942 to 1943	Dennis-LancetII	B35R B35F	Strachan Strachan		1953 1953
1	LWS926	1955	S.M.T.	B32F	S.O.L.		1962
2	NSG298	1956	Albion Nimbus	B32F	Alexander		1956

Notes: The full width sloping front, tail, and bulbous roof of S3 made it a somewhat unusual vehicle. The Lancia S2 erroneously carried the number S1. The Albion Nimbus was returned to the makers after only three months.

T: Guy

1	NU4892	1928	B20F		Ex-Sword	1932
2	NU5776	1929	B20F		Ex-Sword	1932
3	SM4387	1924	C20F	Massey	Ex-Rendall	1934

T: (Second) Leyland Cheetah

1	WS8001	1936	B36R	Alexander		1944-6
to	to					
60	WS8060	1936	B36R	Alexander		1944-6
61	BSC501	1938	B35F	Alexander		1949
to	to					
75	BSC515	1938	B35F	Alexander		1949

U: De Dion Bouton

1	SY2816	1926	B20F		Ex-Dunn	1934
2	SF5052	1926	C14F		Ex-Scott	1934
3	SF5053	1926	C14F		Ex-Scott	1934

V: Morris

1	FS334	1931	C15F	Hoyal	Ex-Scott	1934
2	SC1479	1928	C15F	Hoyal	Ex-Scott	1934
3	SC1480	1928	C15F	Hoyal	Ex-Scott	1934

V: (Second) Leyland Cub

1	KS5732	1933	C20F	Cowieson	Ex-Graham	1940
2	SY4641	1932	C20R	Duple	Ex-Bowen	1940
3	SY4642	1932	C20R	Duple	Ex-Bowen	1940
4	SY4667	1932	C20R	Duple	Ex-Bowen	1940
5	FS6078	1933	C20F	Duple	Ex-Herd	1940

W: Commer

1	FS433	1931	C14F	Hoyal	Ex-Scott	1935
2	FS434	1931	C14F	Hoyal	Ex-Scott	1935
3	SY4442	1931	C19F	Roberts	Ex-Bowen	1936
4	SC4289	1929	C20F		Ex-Bowen	1937
5	WS3407	1935	C24F	Duple	Ex-Westwood & Smith	1940
6	YJ3666	1936	C26	Cadogan	Ex-Robertson	1941
7	YJ3667	1936	C26	Cadogan	Ex-Robertson	1941
8	YJ2241	1935	C20	Cadogan	Ex-Robertson	1941
9	YJ1424	1934	C20	Cadogan	Ex-Robertson	1941
10	YJ576	1933	C20	Cadogan	Ex-Robertson	1938
11	YJ4589	1937	C20	Cadogan	Ex-Robertson	1941
12	FS2868	1932	C20F	Waveney	Ex-Cruikshank	1940

13	FS9813	1934 C20F	Waveney	Ex-Cruikshank	1940
14	WS9743	1936 C26F	Waveney	Ex-Cruikshank	1941
15	AWS400	1937 C20F	Waveney	Ex-Cruikshank	1941
16	BSG915	1938 C20F	Waveney	Ex-Cruikshank	1941
17	VD1417	1932 C20		Ex-Irvine	1940

Notes: W6, 7, 14, 15, 16 had full-width front. W13 had a highly domed roof.

X: Bristol

1	SY4506	1931 B32F	Bristol	Ex-Coast Line	1939
2	SY4507	1931 B32F	Bristol	Ex-Coast Line	1939
3	SY4730	1932 B30D	Bristol	Ex-Coast Line	1939
4	SY4731	1932 B30D	Bristol	Ex-Coast Line	1939

Notes: X3, 4 had the more modern radiator.

Some thirty buses were acquired from Dewar, Beuken, McDowall, Brodie and Forbes in 1931, of which only one was retained as D14.

The following buses were sold to Alexander's with the Dundee area services in 1950: H2, 24, 153-160, 165, 166, 169, 170, 172, 176, 177, 178, 183, 213, 214, 215, 220-223, 225, 226, 227, 229-235, 239, 240, 242, 243, and T61-75.

To continue with some description of the new vehicles year by year: the 1931 purchases comprised only eleven A.E.C. Regals with Cowieson bodies similar to those on the previous year's Leylands, together with three Albion Valkyries and an Albion Valiant, all four with orthodox bodywork.

In 1932 there appeared a further lot of A.E.C. Regals with Alexander bodies for ordinary service. These had a cutaway rear entrance, an opening roof ahead of a solid-sided luggage rack, and large destination screen box with service numbers alongside. This front had a vertical face and was surmounted by a small panel lettered 'S.M.T.'. They had moquette upholstery and were very comfortable buses. They were fitted with oil engines later. As indicated in the list, five Stars were rebodied, their general lines resembling the foregoing except for the large destination and service number screens. A start had also been made in fitting coachwork over the backs of the Star and Maudslay coaches, thus shortening the folding hoods.

The 1933 buses resembled the previous year's ones but were Leyland Tigers, TS6s with oil engines and bodies by Burlingham and Metropolitan-Cammell. There were also six Bedford WLB coaches, and for the London service six A.E.C. Regals with oil engines and Burlingham bodies provided with toilets. Twelve more similar coaches followed in 1934 but in these the toilet was omitted. The 1934 service buses were also A.E.C. Regals but with sloping destination screens and other minor differences. These had four-cylinder oil engines. There was also another series of Bedford WLB coaches of varying sizes.

In 1935 there were Leyland Tigers again, resembling the previous ones and with the now standard oil engine, and also a solitary Albion with similar body and a Gardner six-cylinder oil engine. There was also a batch of A.E.C. Regals with what might now be described as dual-purpose bodies. A vertical-fronted combined destination, service number and S.M.T. panel was incorporated in the front of a well-domed roof into which a panel over the side windows was also set to display a bus travel slogan. The new fashion for a downswept moulding over the rear wheel was followed in these vehicles, and their livery was a darker blue with the waist and tail of a greenish blue colour. The lettering 'S.M.T.' was also much smaller and enclosed in a diamond device. This colour scheme and downswept tail moulding were applied to most acquired coaches in 1935 and also to existing coaches being repainted, though in the earlier examples the ordinary blue and white colours were used. In the interests of continuity it should be mentioned here that in 1936 the downswept tail moulding went out of favour except where taken-over vehicles already had it. From 1937 the greenish blue colour gave way to white again, and between then and 1939 several coaches reverted right back to straight waistband and ordinary blue and white livery, though in all cases the small 'S.M.T.' in the diamond device remained standard for coaches. The small 'S.M.T.' panels mounted above the roof were removed from most vehicles of all types around 1936.

The Bedford WTBs of 1936 had a more modern appearance with a sloping front and back and the last two windows set higher. Both these and the six London service Leyland Tigers were painted a very dark navy blue. The latter were not of very attractive appearance, but bore names on the back, viz., in order, 'Kenilworth', 'Ivanhoe', 'Bride of Lammermoor', 'Lady of the Lake', 'Rob Roy' and 'Heart of Midlothian'. For service buses sixty Leyland Cheetahs were ordered. Their Alexander bodies resembled, in general, the 1935 A.E.C. Regals but had a full front with well-raked windscreens and concealed radiator. The rear entrance was, as usual, of the cutaway pattern, and the ordinary blue livery was used.

The 1937 Bedford WTBs had a neater appearance with a uniform window line and a blue livery of a new shade which seemed to have a slightly grey tinge. This appeared on a few other coaches too on repainting in 1938-9. The rear entrance bodies of the 1937 Leyland Tigers were similar, apart from their fronts, to the previous year's Cheetahs, while the front-entrance ones of Alexander's Coronation design resembled the semi-coaches of 1935 but with a neater back and the omission of the slogan panel. The Duple bodied ones, however, were different, with a well-curved roof and generally pleasing lines. These last two types introduced a new coach livery to mark the Coronation in that year, namely pale yellow relieved with a red band sweeping down towards the back. This livery was subsequently applied to a few other coaches on repainting.

The 1938 A.E.C. Regals were generally similar to the previous service buses. The double-deckers, however, differed from the earlier ones in having flatter fronts. Some of the earlier ones were reconstructed about this time and most of these then lost their 'piano' front. In some cases the platform and stair were enclosed as well. Another lot of similar double-deckers came in 1939, together with more A.E.C. Regals of semi-coach pattern and in Coronation livery, and Leyland Tiger buses in ordinary blue. On these A.E.Cs. the roof luggage rack was omitted in favour of a boot inside at the back, and this became standard practice thereafter. Fortunately the 1940 order, A.E.C. and Leyland, all of the dual-purpose type and generally similar to the previous ones, were duly received. On these the pale yellow livery was modified by the relieving panel being blue instead of red.

It now became a matter of what could be got through the Ministry of Supply. First, early in 1942, were two A.E.C. Regent double-deckers with austerity lines which ran their first few months in grey paint. These were followed by a Leyland Titan which differed only in detail. The former London service coaches, H138-143, also appeared as double-deckers with bodies similar to the aforementioned and renumbered J60-65. Then the earlier London service A.E.Cs. were similarly converted to double-deckers in 1944, B74-79, 81-92 becoming BB3-20, while further Leyland Tigers were similarly dealt with in 1945, viz. H106-109, 111, 112, 113, 115 and H161, 162, 163, 174 becoming respectively J67-78. These 1944 and 1945 conversions were turned out in grey and retained this colour till after the war. Meantime some Guy Arabs with 6LW engines and double-deck austerity bodies by various builders, and hence detail differences, were added over the years 1943-4-5. Of these, E15, 16, 17 had external roof ribs and these and also E5, 6, 9, 10 had utility wooden seats. E3-10 and E15, 16, 17 wore grey livery, retaining it till after the war in most cases, while E11-14 were in a dark blue relieved only by white on the lower saloon window pillars. E9, 10 had this livery also for a time later. Restrictions had been eased by the time E18-22 arrived and these had a more shapely roof at the back. The whole lot, and also BB1, 2, were reconstructed with minor improvements in the early fifties.

For single-deckers there were 60 of the standard utility Bedford OWBs in 1944-5 which served only till sufficient new buses could be obtained after the war. A few were eventually repainted in the ordinary blue livery, but all had been withdrawn by the end of 1949. The only other wartime single-deckers were six Dennis-Lancet IIs with austerity-shape bodies which were also in grey till after the war. It is thought that H120 was the only pre-war vehicle to be painted grey during the war.

The first new vehicles after the war were the Duple-bodied A.E.C. Regals of 1946-7, with a curved roof of pleasing lines and front screen set in a raked and curved shape panel. Those with Alexander bodies which followed in 1947-8 were of straighter lines and had more orthodox screen boxes. Still more with Burlingham bus bodies were added in 1948, these differing in having a more domed roof with a panel above the side windows and a deeper screen box. Many bodies of these Alexander and Burlingham types were also provided to rebody the pre-war A.E.Cs. and Leyland Tigers as detailed in the list, while the few supplied by Croft's had a flatter roof. All the foregoing with the exception of the Burlingham bodies were in the pale yellow livery with red 'flashes' and blue roof, and this livery was applied also to some of the pre-war Bedfords in 1946.

B364 was a somewhat ugly coach in pale yellow with green mouldings, though its appearance was improved a little afterwards. It was, however, the first in the fleet of 8ft. width and the forerunner of the graceful and well-known Seagull model of Burlingham's. As shown in the list, many A.E.Cs., both pre-war and post-war, subsequently received Seagull coach bodies. Meantime there were also the Burlingham semi-coaches of 1949 with a curved roof and door mouldings to match, used both for new A.E.Cs. and rebodying pre-war Leylands. The earlier post-war Bedfords and C188 had the standard Duple Vista design of body but most of these subsequently received Burlingham Seagull bodies as had the later ones when new. The Seagull bodies of different seating capacities showed other minor differences and the 37-seaters had solid cornice panels.

Pre-war vehicles not rebodied were reconstructed with, in most cases, minor modifications, though some were lengthened to 30ft. The 1948 double-deckers were a semi-utility design of plain angular line but the 1949 and 1950 series, which were 8ft. wide, were of much improved appearance with a more raked front, and the latter had curved frames for the end windows.

The bodies on the Mark IV A.E.Cs. were very comfortable though somewhat box-like in appearance, as were the Monocoaches with their high-domed roof. The separate lots of the former had various detail differences. Both these types and all subsequent new vehicles were to the recently authorised 8ft. width. B405-424, 439-444, 455-462 and B547 were equipped with toilets for the London service. The Bristol LS6G coaches and Lodekkas were the standard product, but it should be mentioned that the coaches, including the 1958 MW6Gs, were later reseated for 40 — or in a few cases 41 — passengers and fitted with destination screen boxes in the front of the roof, many receiving green bus livery.

In June 1949 the colour scheme reverted to green with a cream roof and with pillars and flashes of a darker shade of green. Vehicles with a straight waistband had these painted cream too, as was the panel above the lower saloon of double-deckers. Thereafter, until 1956, all vehicles were turned out in this livery, except for the Bristol coaches, and B364 and B547, for which the pale yellow or cream colour with green pillars and mouldings were retained. B463-479 were also in this livery but had a large, curved green panel on the lower part of the sides. Burlingham Seagull bodies were painted similarly. The other Mark IV A.E.Cs. also received the normal cream livery later on, though some of them and the Bristols eventually received the green bus livery. Most of the 1940 bodies were reconstructed with either a narrow, straight waist panel painted white, or no panelling, in which case the S.M.T. and diamond device was in aluminium flanked by a moulding. A few other bodies were treated similarly.

It will be appreciated that a great number of variations in detail and in painting had appeared on individual vehicles over these years, which it would be tedious to record even if space could be found. There were also odd vehicles of various makes which ran on trial service for short periods.

One vehicle of this period requires special mention. The company desired an economical lightweight bus and, as in 1913, set about building it themselves. The resulting vehicle, in 1955, numbered S1, was an all-Scottish production with an Albion engine. Several novel features were incorporated such as rubber suspension. 24ft. long by 7ft. 9in. wide and of integral construction, its appearance was rather box-like though somewhat improved later. Nevertheless, carrying 32 passengers for its 3½ tons weight, it gave a good account of itself. It might have been called a Lothian but remained anonymous and lasted only until 1962. No further examples were built.

S.M.T. fleet numbering became rather complex after 1956. New vehicles were thereafter usually numbered in one series following B547, with the appropriate prefix letter, though there were exceptions. A new series of numbers on the same basis was started in 1964, when the old series had reached 964, yet Nos. 965-999 in the old series were subsequently used up in 1973. Early in 1965 Eastern Scottish began to prefix the fleet numbers of coaches thus: Coach with toilet X, Coach without toilet Y, Dual-purpose vehicle Z. Inevitably many prefixes were changed as the vehicles got older, and these prefixes have therefore been ignored. The use of metal plates for fleet numbers duly disappeared in favour of small characters transferred on the front and back of the vehicles.

Before continuing with Eastern Scottish's annual purchases of new vehicles, it will be convenient to mention those taken over with other firms and usually numbered into blanks in the Eastern Scottish list. First in January 1958 the acquisition of Lowland Motorways Ltd. brought the following additions:

B44	JJF604	A.E.C. Regal	C35F	Plaxton	1962
B45	JJF605	A.E.C. Regal	C35F	Plaxton	1962
B46	GGA524	A.E.C. Regal III	C33F	Duple	1962
B47	GGG875	A.E.C. Regal III	C33F	Duple	1962
B48	HGE796	A.E.C. Regal III	C33F	Burlingham	1962
B49	HGE797	A.E.C. Regal III	C33F	Burlingham	1962
B50	JGD978	A.E.C. Regal IV	C35C	Burlingham	1966
BB1	JXC181	A.E.C. RT	H56R	Cravens	1963
BB2	JXC224	A.E.C. RT	H56R	Cravens	1964
BB3	JXC220	A.E.C. RT	H56R	Cravens	1964
BB4	KGK743	A.E.C. RT	H56R	Cravens	1963
BB5	KGK760	A.E.C. RT	H56R	Cravens	1963
BB6	KGK768	A.E.C. RT	H56R	Cravens	1963
EE1	ASD492	Daimler CWA6	L55R	Brush	1960
EE2	ASD495	Daimler CWA6	L55R	Brush	1959
H105	JGD667	Leyland PSU1	C35C	Burlingham	1966
H106	LYS943	Leyland PSUC1	C41F	Alexander	1960
H107	FCS451	Leyland PSUC1	C41F	Alexander	1960
HH1	FEV181	Leyland TD5	L55R	E.C.W.	1958
HH2	GAT61	Leyland TD5	H54R	E.C.W.	1962
HH3	GAT62	Leyland TD5	H54R	E.C.W.	1962
HH4	CS7024	Leyland TD5	H56R	Leyland	1960
HH5	LVA484	Leyland PD2/20	L55R	Northern Counties	1967
HH6	LYS757	Leyland PD2/12	L53R	Leyland	1973
HH7	LYS758	Leyland PD2/12	L53R	Leyland	1970
HH8	JY6759	Leyland TD4	L48R	Weymann	1959
HH9	JY6766	Leyland TD4	L48R	Weymann	1960
HH10	BDR255	Leyland TD5	L48R	Weymann	1960
HH11	CDR352	Leyland TD7	L55R	Roe	1960
HH12	CDR353	Leyland TD7	L55R	Roe	1958
HH13	CDR357	Leyland TD7	L55R	Roe	1959
HH14	VS3066	Leyland TD4	L53R	Leyland	1959

HH15	VS3067	Leyland TD4	L53R	Leyland		1960
HH16	VS3636	Leyland TD5	H54R	Leyland		1960
HH17	VS3640	Leyland TD5	H54R	Leyland		1960
SS3	DGB470	Albion CX19	H56R	Pickering		1958

Many of the Lowland Motorways vehicles had been obtained second-hand, for example BB1-6 from London Transport, and HH2, 3 from East Yorkshire Motor Services Ltd., with their distinctive 'Beverley Bar' domed roofs. A few of the double-deckers were subsequently thoroughly overhauled with new destination screens, waistbands, etc. B50 was renumbered B36 in 1964.

In December 1962, Baxter's Bus Services Ltd. were taken over and the following vehicles joined the Eastern Scottish fleet:

B12	KVA750	A.E.C. Reliance	B44F	Crossley	1969
B13	LVA623	A.E.C. Reliance	B45F	Park Royal	1969
B14	LVA624	A.E.C. Reliance	C41F	Park Royal	1970
B15	LVD218	A.E.C. Reliance	C41F	Alexander	1971
B16	LVD219	A.E.C. Reliance	B45F	Alexander	1970
B17	NVA142	A.E.C. Reliance	B45F	Alexander	1969
B18	EVJ807	A.E.C. Regal	B35F	Massey	1965
B19	OVD108	A.E.C. Reliance	C41F	Burlingham	1970
B20	OVD109	A.E.C. Reliance	B45F	Burlingham	1970
B21	RVA110	A.E.C. Reliance	C41F	Burlingham	1970
B22	RVA111	A.E.C. Reliance	B45F	Burlingham	1971
B23	RVA112	A.E.C. Reliance	C41F	Alexander	1973
B24	SVD114	A.E.C. Reliance	B45F	Burlingham	1972
B25	UVA115	A.E.C. Reliance	C41F	Burlingham	1974
B26	UVA116	A.E.C. Reliance	C41F	Burlingham	1972
B27	WVA40	A.E.C. Reliance	C41F	Duple	1975
B28	WVD117	A.E.C. Reliance	B45F	Alexander	1975
B29	WVD118	A.E.C. Reliance	B45F	Alexander	1975
B30	119AVA	A.E.C. Reliance	C41F	Alexander	1975
B31	120AVA	A.E.C. Reliance	C41F	Alexander	1977
B32	141AVA	A.E.C. Reliance	C41F	Burlingham	1973
B33	42CVD	A.E.C. Reliance	C41F	Plaxton	1977
B34	122CVD	A.E.C. Reliance	B45F	Alexander	1977
BB18	78BVD	A.E.C. Bridgemaster	H72F	Park Royal	1973
BB19	PVD567	A.E.C. Regent V	L55R	Massey	1974
BB20	PVD568	A.E.C. Regent V	L55R	Massey	1974
C21	TVA649	Bedford SB1	C37F	Burlingham	1971
H1	HVA883	Leyland PSU1	B44F	Leyland	1968
H2	NTJ985	Leyland PSU1	B44F	Leyland	1967
H3	SVD113	Leyland PSUC1	C41F	Alexander	1963
HH24	HVD59	Leyland PD2/10	L55R	Leyland	1968
HH25	HVD60	Leyland PD2/10	L55R	Leyland	1968
HH26	KVA657	Leyland PD2/10	L55R	Massey	1969
HH27	KVA658	Leyland PD2/10	L55R	Massey	1969

HH28	KVD286	Leyland PD2/10	L55R	Massey	1970
HH29	FVD224	Leyland PD2/10	L53R	Leyland	1969
HH30	FVD225	Leyland PD2/10	L53R	Leyland	1968
HH31	NVD861	Leyland PD2/10	L55R	Massey	1973
HH32	NVD862	Leyland PD2/10	L55R	Massey	1972
HH33	NVD863	Leyland PD2/10	L55R	Massey	1973
HH34	OVA864	Leyland PD2/12	L55R	Massey	1970
HH35	OVA865	Leyland PD2/12	L55R	Massey	1971
HH36	OVA866	Leyland PD2/12	L55R	Massey	1971
HH37	RVD469	Leyland PD2/40	L55R	Massey	1972
HH38	TVA70	Leyland PD2/41	L55R	Massey	1972
HH39	TVA71	Leyland PD2/41	L55R	Massey	1975
HH40	TVD72	Leyland PD2/41	L55R	Massey	1974
HH41	TVD73	Leyland PD2/41	L55R	Massey	1975
HH42	VVD74	Leyland PD2/37	L56R	Massey	1973
HH43	WVA75	Leyland PD2/37	L56R	Massey	1975
HH44	XVA276	Leyland PD2/37	L56R	Massey	1975
HH45	YVD77	Leyland PD2/37	L56R	Massey	1973

Most of Baxter's vehicles were of the bodybuilders' standard pattern and continued in service for several more years. Certain buses on order but not delivered until later are dealt with following the main series of Eastern Scottish numbers.

All of Stark's buses at Dunbar, some of which were numbered in the L series, were renumbered into the Eastern Scottish list in 1964 thus:

B39	SS9615	A.E.C. Reliance	B45F	Alexander	1972
B40	SS9616	A.E.C. Reliance	B45F	Alexander	1972
C22	SS7486	Bedford OB	C29F	Duple	1966
F1	GSS804	Ford Thames Trader	C41F	Duple	1964
F2	FSS929	Ford Thames Trader	C41F	Duple	1964
F3	430YTD	Ford Thames Trader	C41F	Duple	1964
F4	GSS452	Ford Thames Trader	C41F	Duple	1964
H3	SS7525	Leyland PS1	C35F	Alexander	1967
H4	SS8015	Leyland PSU1	C39F	Burlingham	1967
H5	EWG240	Leyland PSUC1	B45F	Alexander	1967
H6	DSS21	Leyland PSUC1	C41F	Alexander	1975
H7	ESS127	Leyland PSUC1	C41F	Alexander	1975
H8	ESS989	Leyland PSUC1	C41F	Alexander	1975
T1	ESS487	Trojan	C13F	Trojan	1967

F2, 3, 4 and T1 had very rounded fronts; F1 was of a neater more modern appearance, and bodywork of the others was similar to their Eastern Scottish equivalents.

Some vehicles transferred from other companies in the group from time to time have also to be included, viz:

AA4	GCS238	Bristol LD6G	H60R	E.C.W.	Ex-Western S.M.T.	1971	1971
AA5	GCS245	Bristol LD6G	H60R	E.C.W.	Ex-Western S.M.T.	1971	
AA6	GCS246	Bristol LD6G	H60R	E.C.W.	Ex-Western S.M.T.	1971	1971
AA7	GCS247	Bristol LD6G	H60R	E.C.W.	Ex-Western S.M.T.	1971	1971
AA8	GCS248	Bristol LD6G	H60R	E.C.W.	Ex-Western S.M.T.	1971	1974
AA9	GCS249	Bristol LD6G	H60R	E.C.W.	Ex-Western S.M.T.	1971	1976
B35	KWG569	A.E.C. Reliance	B41F	Alexander	Ex-Alexander	1963	1974
B41	AWG636	A.E.C. Regal I	B35F	Alexander	Ex-Alexander	1966	1966
B42	AWG643	A.E.C. Regal I	B35F	Alexander	Ex-Alexander	1966	1966
B43	AWG644	A.E.C. Regal I	B35F	Alexander	Ex-Alexander	1966	1966
B44	AWG645	A.E.C. Regal I	B35F	Alexander	Ex-Alexander	1966	1966
B45	AWG646	A.E.C. Regal I	B35F	Alexander	Ex-Alexander	1966	1966
B46	DSA115	A.E.C. Regal I	B35F	Brush	Ex-Alexander	1966	1966
B100	FMS977	A.E.C. Monocoach	B45F	Park Royal	Ex-Alexander	1960	1970
B101	FMS983	A.E.C. Monocoach	B45F	Park Royal	Ex-Alexander	1960	1971
H10	BWG316	Leyland PS1	C35F	Alexander	Ex-Alexander 1968	ret'rn'd 1968	
H11	BWG516	Leyland PS1	C35F	Alexander	Ex-Alexander 1968	ret'rn'd 1968	
H12	AWG537	Leyland PS1	C35F	Alexander	Ex-Alexander 1968	ret'rn'd 1968	
H13	AWG541	Leyland PS1	C35F	Alexander	Ex-Alexander 1968	ret'rn'd 1968	
HH10	BVD925	Leyland PD1	L53R	Northern Counties	Ex-Central S.M.T.	1961	1964
HH11	BVD926	Leyland PD1	L53R	Northern Counties	Ex-Central S.M.T.	1961	1964
HH12	BVD927	Leyland PD1	L53R	Northern Counties	Ex-Central S.M.T.	1961	1964
HH13	BVD928	Leyland PD1	L53R	Northern Counties	Ex-Central S.M.T.	1961	1964
HH14	BVD929	Leyland PD1	L53R	Northern Counties	Ex-Central S.M.T.	1961	1964
HH15	BVD930	Leyland PD1	L53R	Leyland	Ex-Central S.M.T.	1961	1964
HH16	BVD931	Leyland PD1	L53R	Leyland	Ex-Central S.M.T.	1961	1964
HH17	BVD932	Leyland PD1	L53R	Leyland	Ex-Central S.M.T.	1961	1964
HH18	BVD933	Leyland PD1	L53R	Leyland	Ex-Central S.M.T.	1961	1964
HH19	BVD934	Leyland PD1	L53R	Leyland	Ex-Central S.M.T.	1961	1964
HH20	BVD935	Leyland PD1	L53R	Leyland	Ex-Central S.M.T.	1961	1964
HH21	BVD936	Leyland PD1	L53R	Leyland	Ex-Central S.M.T.	1961	1964
HH22	BVD937	Leyland PD1	L53R	Leyland	Ex-Central S.M.T.	1961	1964
HH23	BVD938	Leyland PD1	L53R	Leyland	Ex-Central S.M.T.	1961	1964
HH46	BCS337	Leyland PD1	L53R	Leyland	Ex-Western S.M.T.	1965	1966
HH47	BCS339	Leyland PD1	L53R	Leyland	Ex-Western S.M.T.	1965	1966
HH48	CAG130	Leyland PD1	L53R	Northern Counties	Ex-Western S.M.T.	1965	1969
HH49	CAG132	Leyland PD1	L53R	Northern Counties	Ex-Western S.M.T.	1965	1967

AA4-7 and HH23 were never used in service but AA5 was converted to an open-top bus for use on special occasions. It replaced in this capacity DSG169, formerly HH66, and its predecessor CSF258, formerly J57. B100, 101 were renumbered B37, 38 in 1964. DSG169 has since been restored to closed-top condition and is preserved in pre-1949 blue S.M.T. livery.

In dealing now with the ordinary additions to the fleet since 1956 it will be noticed that with the exception of one bus and three lots of coaches, the one series of numbers from 548 was continued for all types with only the prefix as before indicating the make of vehicle. First the exceptions:

S2   RSC427. An Albion Aberdonian B41F Alexander body new in 1957 and transferred
          to Alexander's shortly thereafter
B1-11 WSF201-210 and YSF242. A.E.C. Reliance C34F Burlingham bodies new in
          1960; they were painted in maroon and cream and carried names on the
          back, viz 'Sir Walter Scott', 'Ivanhoe', 'Rob Roy', 'Guy Mannering',
          'Lady of the Lake', 'Marmion', 'Lord of the Isles', 'Kenilworth',
          'Waverley', 'Redgauntlet' and 'Heart of Midlothian'. About 1968 they
          were repainted in the normal green and cream livery, except for B11
          which, however, exchanged names with B3 at that time, the latter
          reverting to maroon and cream again. Green and cream were later
          applied to these two as well and all were withdrawn at the end of 1972.
C1-20 YWS850-869. Bedford VAS1 Duple Bella Vista C24F bodies new in 1962 and
          withdrawn in 1969-70. C6 appeared in the maroon and cream livery in
          1968.
K1-12 DFS1C-DFS12C. Albion viking VK43L C34F Alexander Y type bodies with
          wide windows new in 1965 and transferred to Alexander (Northern)
          and Highland Omnibuses in 1972.

The main series of numbers now follows:

HH548	OWS548					
to	to					
HH567	OWS567	1957	Leyland PD2/20	L56R	Park Royal	1969-75
		1957	Leyland PD2/20	L56R	Park Royal	1969-75
B568	OWS568	1957	A.E.C. Monocoach	B41F	Alexander	1968-73
to	to					
B581	OWS581	1957	A.E.C. Monocoach	B41F	Alexander	1968-73
AA582	OWS582	1957	Bristol LD6G	H60R	E.C.W.	1973-8
to	to					
AA621	OWS621	1957	Bristol LD6G	H60R	E.C.W.	1973-8
A622	RSC622	1958	Bristol MW6G	C38F	E.C.W.	1974-6
to	to					
A641	RSC641	1958	Bristol MW6G	C38F	E.C.W.	1974-6
AA642	RSC642	1958	Bristol LD6G	H60R	E.C.W.	1974-8
to	to					
AA657	RSC657	1958	Bristol LD6G	H60R	E.C.W.	1974-8
B658	RSC658	1958	A.E.C. Reliance	B41F	Park Royal	1973-6
to	to					
B669	RSC669	1958	A.E.C. Reliance	B41F	Park Royal	1973-6
B670	SWS670	1959	A.E.C. Reliance	C38F	Alexander	1973-5
to	to					
B689	SWS689	1959	A.E.C. Reliance	C38F	Alexander	1973-5
B690	SWS690	1959	A.E.C. Reliance	C41F	Park Royal	1969-75
to	to					
B718	SWS718	1959	A.E.C. Reliance	C41F	Park Royal	1969-75
AA719	SWS719	1959	Bristol LD6G	H60R	E.C.W.	1975-8
to	to					
AA749	SWS749	1959	Bristol LD6G	H60R	E.C.W.	1975-8
AA750	USC750	1960	Bristol LD6G	H60R	E.C.W.	1975-9
to	to					
AA774	USC774	1960	Bristol LD6G	H60R	E.C.W.	1975-9

B775	USC775	1960	A.E.C. Reliance	C41F	Alexander		1969-75
to	to						
B809	USC809	1960	A.E.C. Reliance	C41F	Alexander		1969-75
B810	WSC810	1961	A.E.C. Reliance	C41F	Alexander		1975-7
to	to						
B834	WSC834	1961	A.E.C. Reliance	C41F	Alexander		1975-7
AA845	WSC845	1961	Bristol LD6G	H60R	E.C.W.		1977-80
to	to						
AA869	WSC869	1961	Bristol LD6G	H60R	E.C.W.		1977-80
AA870	YWS870	1962	Bristol FLF6G	H70F	E.C.W.	(1)	1977-80
to	to						
AA894	YWS894	1962	Bristol FLF6G	H70F	E.C.W.		1977-80
B895	YWS895	1962	A.E.C. Reliance, 30ft.	C41F	Alexander	(8)	1977-8
to	to						
B909	YWS909	1962	A.E.C. Reliance, 30ft.	C41F	Alexander		1977-8
B910	YWS910	1962	A.E.C. Reliance, 36ft.	C38F	Alexander Y type	(3)	1975
B911	8911SF	1963	A.E.C. Reliance, 30ft.	C38F	Alexander Y type	(3)	1975-8
to	to						
B916	8916SF	1963	A.E.C. Reliance, 30ft.	C38F	Alexander Y type		1975-8
B917	8917SF	1963	A.E.C. Reliance, 36ft.	C49F	Alexander Y type	(3)	1978
to	to						
B922	8922SF	1963	A.E.C. Reliance, 36ft.	C49F	Alexander Y type		1978
B923	8923SF	1963	A.E.C. Reliance, 30ft.	C41F	Alexander Y type	(9)	1975-8
to	to						
B942	8942SF	1963	A.E.C. Reliance, 30ft.	C41F	Alexander Y type		1975-8
AA943	8943SF	1963	Bristol FSG6	H60R	E.C.W.		1978-9
to	to						
AA960	8960SF	1963	Bristol FSG6	H60R	E.C.W.		1978-9
DD961	9961SF	1963	Daimler Fleetline	H73F	Alexander		1979
BB962	9962SF	1963	A.E.C. Bridgemaster	H70F	Park Royal	(2)	
BB963	9963SF	1963	A.E.C. Renown	H74F	Park Royal	(2)	
B964	121CVD	1963	A.E.C. Reliance, 30ft.	C41F	Alexander		1978
DD80	DVA680C	1965	Daimler Fleetline	H75F	Alexander		1980

At this stage, in 1964, with the numbers again approaching four figures, another new start was made commencing at eleven, as follows:

AA11	AFS11B	1964	Bristol FS6G	H60R	E.C.W.			1979-80
to	to							
AA21	AFS21B	1964	Bristol FS6G	H60R	E.C.W.			1979-80
AA22	CSG22C	1965	Bristol FLF6G	H70F	E.C.W.			1977-80
to	to							
AA49	CSG49C	1965	Bristol FLF6G	H70F	E.C.W.			1977-80
B50	AFS50B	1964	A.E.C. Reliance, 36ft.	C40F	Alexander Y type (3)	(10)	1978-9
to	to							
B60	AFS60B	1964	A.E.C. Reliance, 36ft.	C40F	Alexander Y type			1978-9
B61	AFS61B	1964	A.E.C. Reliance, 36ft.	C45F	Alexander Y type			1976-80
to	to							
B65	AFS65B	1964	A.E.C. Reliance, 36ft.	C45F	Alexander Y type			1976-80

B66	AFS66B	1964	A.E.C. Reliance, 36ft.	C49F	Alexander Y type (3)	(11)	1978-9
to	to						
B77	AFS77B	1964	A.E.C. Reliance, 36ft.	C49F	Alexander Y type		1978-9
B78	AFS78B	1964	A.E.C. Reliance, 36ft.	B53F	Alexander Y type		1978-80
to	to						
B92	AFS92B	1964	A.E.C. Reliance, 36ft.	B53F	Alexander Y type		1978-80
B93	AFS93B	1964	A.E.C. Reliance, 30ft.	C41F	Alexander Y type	(3)	1978-9
to	to						
B99	AFS99B	1964	A.E.C. Reliance, 30ft.	C41F	Alexander Y type		1978-9
B100	AFS100B	1964	A.E.C. Reliance, 30ft.	C38F	Alexander Y type	(3)	1978-9
to	to						
B105	AFS105B	1964	A.E.C. Reliance, 30ft.	C38F	Alexander Y type		1978-9
B106	EWS106D	1966	A.E.C. Reliance 590	C49F	Alexander Y type (3)	(4)	1977-9
to	to						
B161	EWS161D	1966	A.E.C. Reliance 590	C49F	Alexander Y type		1977-9
A162	EWS162D	1966	Bristol RELH6G	C38F	Alexander Y type (3)	(5)	1980
to	to						
A194	EWS194D	1966	Bristol RELH6G	C38F	Alexander Y type		1980
A195	EWS195D	1966	Bristol RELG6G	C45F	Alexander Y type	(3)	1980-1
to	to						
A206	EWS206D	1966	Bristol RELH6G	C45F	Alexander Y type		1980-1
A207	GSG207D	1966	Bristol FLF6G	H76F	E.C.W.		1980-1
to	to						
AA231	GSG231D	1966	Bristol FLF6G	H76F	E.C.W.		1980-1
C232	HSF232E	1967	Bedford VAM5	B45F	Alexander Y type		1979
to	to						
C251	HSF251E	1967	Bedford VAM5	B45F	Alexander Y type		1979
C252	LFS252E	1968	Bedford VAM70	C41F	Willowbrook		1979-80
to	to						
C271	LFS271E	1968	Bedford VAM70	C41F	Willowbrook		1979-80
A272	LFS272F	1969	Bristol REMH6G	C42F	Alexander M type	(12)	1979
to	to						
A279	LFS279F	1969	Bristol REMH6G	C42F	Alexander M type		1979
AA280	LFS280F	1968	Bristol VRTLL6G	H83F	E.C.W.		1973
to	to						
AA304	LFS304F	1968	Bristol VRTLL6G	H83F	E.C.W.		1973
AA305	0SF305G	1969	Bristol VRTSL6G	H77F	E.C.W.		1973
to	to						
AA314	0SF314G	1969	Bristol VRTSL6G	H77F	E.C.W.		1973

It should be mentioned here that the foregoing VRT type did not find favour with Eastern Scottish and so, in 1973, AA280-314 were exchanged for 34 FLF6G Lodekkas from a number of different subsidiaries of the National Bus Company in England. The buses received in exchange had H70F E.C.W. bodies and were added onto the old series of numbers as follows:

AA965-972	KPM85E to KPM92E
AA973-974	LBL847E, LBL848E

AA975-979	KVF476E to KVF480E						
AA980-986	KPW481E to KPW487E						
AA987-989	LAH488E to LAH490E						
AA990-991	KDL144F, KDL145F						
AA992-993	ONG349F, ONG350F						
AA994	ONG353F						
AA995-998	RHN948F to RHN951F						
AA999	SHN252F						

All were withdrawn 1979-82, but AA971 became a second open-top bus for use on special occasions.

Continuing the new list:

A315	OSF315G	1970	Bristol LH6P	C38F	Alexander Y type	(3)	1980
to	to						
A332	OSF332G	1970	Bristol LH6P	C38F	Alexander Y type		1980
A333	SFS333H	1970	Bristol LH6P	C38F	Alexander Y type	(3)	1980
to	to						
A348	SFS348H	1970	Bristol LH6P	C38F	Alexander Y type		1980
A349	SFS349H	1970	Bristol REMH6G	C42F	Alexander M type		1980-2
to	to						
A373	SFS373H	1970	Bristol REMH6G	C42F	Alexander M type		1980-2
A374	SWG678H	1970	Bristol LH6P	C41F	Alexander Y type	(3)	1980
H375	HSG564N	1975	Leyland PSU5/4R	C42F	Alexander M type	(13)	1975
H376	HSG565N	1975	Leyland PSU5/4R	C42F	Alexander M type	(13)	1975
H377	HSG566N	1975	Leyland PSU5/4R	C42F	Alexander M type	(13)	1975
H378	VCS378	1963	Leyland PSU3/3R	C38F	Alexander Y type	(3)	1978-9
to	to						
H390	VCS390	1963	Leyland PSU3/3R	C38F	Alexander Y type		1978-9
H391	XCS903	1964	Leyland PSU3/3R	C38F	Alexander Y type	(3)	1979
H392	XCS904	1964	Leyland PSU3/3R	C38F	Alexander Y type	(3)	1979
H393	XCS905	1964	Leyland PSU3/3R	C38F	Alexander Y type	(3)	1979
H394	PWS394H	1969	Leyland PSU3/3R	C49F	Alexander Y type	(3)	1981-3
to	to						
H399	PWS399H	1969	Leyland PSU3/3R	C49F	Alexander Y type		1981-3
DD400	USF400J	1971	Daimler CRG6	H75F	E.C.W.	(16)	From 1984
to	to						
DD419	USF419J	1971	Daimler CRG6	H75F	E.C.W.		
H420	YSC420K	1972	Leyland PSU3/3R	C45F	Alexander Y type	(3)	1982-3
to	to						
H435	YSC435K	1972	Leyland PSU3/3R	C45F	Alexander Y type		1982-3
H436	YSC436K	1972	Leyland PSU3/3R	C49F	Alexander Y type	(3)	1982-3
to	to						
H449	YSC449K	1972	Leyland PSU3/3R	C49F	Alexander Y type		1982-3
C450	USF450J	1971	Bedford YRQ	C45F	Alexander Y type	(3)	1981
to	to						
C460	USF460J	1971	Bedford YRQ	C45F	Alexander Y type		1981
C461	BFS461L	1972	Bedford YRQ	C45F	Alexander Y type	(3)	1981-2
to	to						
C475	BFS475L	1972	Bedford YRQ	C45F	Alexander Y type		1981-2

H476 to H490	BFS476L to BFS490L	1973	Leyland PSU3/3R	C49F	Alexander Y type			1982-3
		1973	Leyland PSU3/3R	C49F	Alexander Y type			1982-3
DD491 to DD510	BSG491L to BSG510L	1973	Daimler CRG6	H75F	E.C.W.			
		1973	Daimler CRG6	H75F	E.C.W.			
C511 to C520	BSG511L to BSG520L	1973	Bedford YRQ	C45F	Alexander Y type		(3)	1981-4
		1973	Bedford YRQ	C45F	Alexander Y type			1981-4
H521 to H528	BSG521L to BSG528L	1973	Leyland PSU3/3R	C45F	Alexander Y type		(6)	1984
		1973	Leyland PSU3/3R	C45F	Alexander Y type			1984
H529 to H543	BSG529L to BSG543L	1973	Leyland PSU3/3R	C49F	Alexander Y type		(3)	1984
		1973	Leyland PSU3/3R	C49F	Alexander Y type			1984
H544 to H553	OSG544M to OSG553M	1974	Leyland PSU3/3R	C49F	Alexander Y type		(14)	1975
		1974	Leyland PSU3/3R	C49F	Alexander Y type			1975
H554 to H563	PFS554M to PFS563M	1974	Leyland PSU3/3R	B53F	Alexander Y type		(15)	1975
		1974	Leyland PSU3/3R	B53F	Alexander Y type			1975
C564 to C570	RFS564M to RFS570M	1974	Bedford YRQ	C38F	Alexander Y type (3)		(7)	1982-3
		1974	Bedford YRQ	C38F	Alexander Y type			1982-3
C571	SFS571N	1974	Bedford YRQ	C38F	Alexander Y type (3)		(7)	1982
C572	SFS403N	1974	Bedford YRQ	C38F	Alexander Y type (3)		(7)	1983
C573	SFS404N	1974	Bedford YRQ	C38F	Alexander Y type (3)		(7)	1983
C574 to C578	SFS574N to SFS578N	1974	Bedford YRQ	C38F	Alexander Y type (3)		(7)	1982
		1974	Bedford YRQ	C38F	Alexander Y type			1982

Notes:　(1)　AA871 transferred to Alexander, Fife, in 1974.

(2)　Transferred to Highland Omnibuses Ltd. in 1973.

(3)　Wide windows.

(4)　Several were sold to Highland Omnibuses and Alexander in 1969-73.

(5)　A185 withdrawn in 1974 and A168, 169 sold to Alexander, Fife, in 1977.

(6)　Altered to B53F in 1980.

(7)　Altered to B45F in 1980.

(8)　B897 withdrawn in 1974.

(9)　B931 withdrawn in 1971.

(10)　B52 withdrawn in 1970.

(11)　B69 withdrawn in 1971.

(12)　A273 withdrawn in 1972.

(13) Transferred to Alexander, Northern, and Fife in 1975.
(14) Transferred to Alexander, Midland, in 1975.
(15) Transferred to Central S.M.T. in 1975.
(16) DD406 burnt out 1973, new H75F E.C.W. body 1974.

At this stage the following descriptions may usefully be given: the Leyland PD2/20s had the then still usual half-cab and the so-called tin-front, and were used mainly for replacement of the Glasgow tramcars on the Airdrie route. The Monocoaches, Lodekkas and Bristols were similar to their earlier counterparts, but the Lodekkas of 1962 and 1965 were forward-entrance models with seating increased to 70. Rear-entrance ones from 1960 were fitted with doors enclosing the platform. The Reliances resembled the Monocoaches with only minor differences between the two bodybuilders up to 1962 when B910 appeared as the first of the 36ft.-long models with Alexander Y type body and wide windows, though not all subsequent ones were of that length, and although the Y type body became a standard, again not all had wide windows. B910-916 were equipped with toilets. B698 was an unlucky bus: after a crash in 1963 it was rebodied with an Alexander Y type body, only to be wrecked again in 1964; repaired, it ran again and was withdrawn in 1973.

DD961 and BB962 were ordered by Baxter's but not delivered until 1963. The latter had been registered as 480DVA but this number was cancelled. The former was burnt out in 1965 and, although rebodied by Alexander's in 1966, the temporary lack of it resulted in the diversion of a similar bus from the Western S.M.T. order of 1965 to the Baxter fleet which had by then reverted to their old local blue livery; this new bus was given the number DD80, corresponding to its Baxter local number. BB963 was received instead of a second Bridgemaster that Baxter's had ordered. B964 was also a Baxter's bus of 1962 but stored unused until 1963.

From 1956, new coaches, apart from the exceptions already specifically recorded, were painted cream with green mouldings. The green used for buses was changed in 1965 to a slightly darker shade which became known as Lothian green, and bus roofs were now painted dark green instead of cream. However, there were instances of one lot of new vehicles being green and another lot of similar vehicles cream, according to their seating capacity. There were minor variations in style on some vehicles, and many coaches received a broad green band on the bottom of the body as a livery for dual-purpose vehicles. As they got older, some coaches were further demoted to the green bus livery. It has earlier been mentioned that some noticeable variations of the green colour scheme were tried on a few vehicles in the early sixties but these experiments lasted only a few months.

Bristols were favoured again in 1966, some — A162-194 — being equipped with toilets, and still larger Lodekkas with 76 seats. B50-60 were reseated for 45 in 1966. The 1967 deliveries were Bedford VAM5s followed in 1968 by Bedford VAM70s. 1968 also saw the largest capacity double-deckers, rear-engined Bristol VRTs with as many as 83 seats, though the 1969 ones were shorter and had only 77 seats. 1969 also saw the first of the twelve-metre Bristol motorway type coaches on which Alexander's massive-looking M type bodies with high-set raked windows and provided with toilets were painted in a distinctive livery of yellow and black, for the London service. The 1970 deliveries were all Bristols, some with the M type bodies and some with the more usual Y type. Of the latter, A315-332 were reseated for 45 passengers in 1975. Another one, A374, was transferred from Highland Omnibuses in 1971; it had originally been an Alexander Midland vehicle. Sixteen Leyland Leopards, H378-393, with Y type bodies equipped with toilets, were acquired from Western S.M.T. in May 1969, and six new ones, H394-399, without toilets and seating 49, were delivered in December. The toilets were very soon removed from the ex-Western S.M.T. ones and their seating increased to 49.

Following the introduction of the M type coaches for the London service, the toilets were removed from B910-916 and A175-194 in 1969-.72, when the seating was also increased to 49 on the Bristols and on B913, 914, and to 45 on the others.

After many years, Daimlers reappeared in 1971 in the form of the Fleetline double-decker, seating 75. There were also Bedfords again, but now the YRQ model. Henceforth, up to 1974, all new additions to the fleet were of these two makes or Leyland Leopards, all single-deckers having Y type bodies. Early in 1975 three Leyland Leopards with M type bodies were added and took three unused numbers, H375, 376, 377, but were sold off within a few months.

As already recorded, a basically white livery was applied to the London motorway service coaches from 1976, and a new standardised form of fleetname for all vehicles in 1978.

The prototype of an entirely new make appeared in 1974, S661, a Seddon Pennine VII with Alexander Y type body. In due course many Seddons followed, both buses and coaches, with Alexander Y type or T type bodies, the latter having a stepped-down roof over the entrance and higher windows slightly raked in at the top. Another new type appeared in 1977, the Leyland National, and then in 1978, the Volvo Ailsa double-decker. These need no description here.

To help meet a shortage of vehicles, 20 buses dating from 1971 were transferred from Central S.M.T. in 1975, followed by twelve old 1962 vehicles bought from Lothian Region Transport in 1977. The latter were all withdrawn at the end of 1978, and the former in 1983. These all took the numbers of the Bristol VRTs disposed of in 1973, viz:

DD281	TGM201J	Daimler Fleetline	H77R	E.C.W.	Ex-Central
to	to				
DD300	TGM220J	Daimler Fleetline	H77R	E.C.W.	Ex-Central
HH301	YWS601	Leyland PD2A/30	H66R	Alexander	Ex-L.R.T.
HH302	YWS602	Leyland PD2A/30	H66R	Alexander	Ex-L.R.T.
HH303	YWS603	Leyland PD2A/30	H66R	Alexander	Ex-L.R.T.
HH304	YWS606	Leyland PD2A/30	H66R	Alexander	Ex-L.R.T.
HH305	YWS607	Leyland PD2A/30	H66R	Alexander	Ex-L.R.T.
HH306	YWS608	Leyland PD2A/30	H66R	Alexander	Ex-L.R.T.
HH307	YWS610	Leyland PD2A/30	H66R	Alexander	Ex-L.R.T.
HH308	YWS611	Leyland PD2A/30	H66R	Alexander	Ex-L.R.T.
HH309	YWS612	Leyland PD2A/30	H66R	Alexander	Ex-L.R.T.
HH310	YWS613	Leyland PD2A/30	H66R	Alexander	Ex-L.R.T.
HH311	YWS617	Leyland PD2A/30	H66R	Alexander	Ex-L.R.T.
HH312	YWS638	Leyland PD2A/30	H66R	Alexander	Ex-L.R.T.

Meantime the numbers for new vehicles had continued upwards from 662, the gap 579-660 not being filled until 1979, as follows:

N579	RFS579V	1980	Leyland National 2	B52F	National	
to	to					
N590	RFS590V	1980	Leyland National 2	B52F	National	
S591	RSX591V	1979	Seddon Pennine VII	B53F	Alexander Y type	
to	to					
S594	RSX594V	1979	Seddon Pennine VII	B53F	Alexander Y type	
S595	SSX595V	1980	Seddon Pennine VII	B53F	Alexander Y type	
to	to					
S630	SSX630V	1980	Seddon Pennine VII	B53F	Alexander Y type	
S631	YSG631W	1980	Seddon Pennine VII	B53F	Alexander Y type	
to	to					
S660	YSG660W	1980	Seddon Pennine VII	B53F	Alexander Y type	
S661	OFS661M	1974	Seddon Pennine VII	C49F	Alexander Y type	
S662	KSX662N	1975	Seddon Pennine VII	B49F	Alexander Y type	
to	to					
S671	KSX671N	1975	Seddon Pennine VII	B49F	Alexander Y type	
S672	KSX672N	1976	Seddon Pennine VII	C45F	Alexander Y type	C49F in 1984
to	to					
S681	KSX681N	1976	Seddon Pennine VII	C45F	Alexander Y type	C49F in 1984
S682	KSX682N	1976	Seddon Pennine VII	B49F	Alexander T type	
to	to					
S691	KSX691N	1976	Seddon Pennine VII	B49F	Alexander Y type	

DD692	KSX692N	1975	Daimler Fleetline	H75F	E.C.W.	
to	to					
DD716	KSX716N	1975	Daimler Fleetline	H75F	E.C.W.	
C717	LSG717P	1975	Bedford YRQ	C38F	Alexander Y type	From 1983
to	to					
C721	LSG721P	1975	Bedford YRQ	C38F	Alexander Y type	
C722	LSG722P	1975	Bedford YRQ	B45F	Alexander Y type	From 1983
to	to					
C726	LSG726P	1975	Bedford YRQ	B45F	Alexander Y type	
C727	MSF727P	1975	Bedford YRT	B49F	Alexander Y type	1984
to	to					
C736	MSF736P	1975	Bedford YRT	B49F	Alexander Y type	1984
C737	MSF737P	1975	Bedford YRT	B53F	Alexander Y type	1982-4
to	to					
C746	MSF746P	1975	Bedford YRT	B53F	Alexander Y type	1982-4
S747	MSF747P	1976	Seddon Pennine VII	C42F	Alexander M type (Toilet)	
to	to					
S752	MSF752P	1976	Seddon Pennine VII	C42F	Alexander M type (Toilet)	
S753	VSX753R	1976	Seddon Pennine VII	C45F	Alexander Y type	
to	to					
S762	VSX762R	1976	Seddon Pennine VII	C45F	Alexander Y type	
N763	BSF763S	1977	Leyland National 2	B52F	National	
to	to					
N772	BSF772S	1977	Leyland National 2	B52F	National	
VV773	CSG773S	1978	Volvo Ailsa	H79F	Alexander	
to	to					
VV782	CSG782S	1978	Volvo Ailsa	H79F	Alexander	
S783	CSG783S	1978	Seddon Pennine VII	C45F	Plaxton Supreme	
to	to					
S794	CSG794S	1978	Seddon Pennine VII	C45F	Plaxton Supreme	
S795	DFS795S	1978	Seddon Pennine VII	C49	Plaxton Supreme	
to	to					
S811	DFS811S	1978	Seddon Pennine VII	C49	Plaxton Supreme	
S812	CFS812S	1978	Seddon Pennine VII	B53F	Alexander Y type	
to	to					
S831	CFS831S	1978	Seddon Pennine VII	B53F	Alexander Y type	
S832	ESC832S	1978	Seddon Pennine VII	B53F	Alexander Y type	
to	to					
S851	ESC851S	1978	Seddon Pennine VII	B53F	Alexander Y type	
DD852	GSC852T	1978	Daimler Fleetline	H75F	E.C.W.	
to	to					
DD861	GSC861T	1978	Daimler Fleetline	H75F	E.C.W.	
N862	GSX862T	1978	Leyland National 2	B52F	National	
to	to					
N871	GSX871T	1978	Leyland National 2	B52F	National	
S872	GSX872T	1978	Seddon Pennine VII	C49F	Alexander T type	
to	to					
S901	GSX901T	1978	Seddon Pennine VII	C49F	Alexander T type	

S902	JSF902T	1978-9	Seddon Pennine VII	C49F	Alexander T type	
to	to					
S931	JSF931T	1978-9	Seddon Pennine VII	C49F	Alexander T type	
S932	LSC932T	1979	Seddon Pennine VII	B53F	Alexander Y type	
to	to					
S941	LSC941T	1979	Seddon Pennine VII	B53F	Alexander Y type	
S942	LSC942T	1979	Seddon Pennine VII	C49F	Plaxton Supreme	
to	to					
S956	LSC956T	1979	Seddon Pennine VII	C49F	Plaxton Supreme	
S957	NSX957T	1979	Seddon Pennine VII	C49F	Plaxton Supreme	
to	to					
S960	NSX960T	1979	Seddon Pennine VII	C49F	Plaxton Supreme	
S961	OSF961V	1979	Seddon Pennine VII	C49F	Plaxton Supreme	
to	to					
S966	OSF966V	1979	Seddon Pennine VII	C49F	Plaxton Supreme	
S967	USX967V	1980	Seddon Pennine VII	C49F	Plaxton Supreme	
to	to					
S971	USX971V	1980	Seddon Pennine VII	C49F	Plaxton Supreme	
S972	DSC972W	1981	Seddon Pennine VII	C49F	Plaxton Supreme	
to	to					
S976	DSC976W	1981	Seddon Pennine VII	C49F	Plaxton Supreme	
S977	JFS977X	1982	Seddon Pennine VII	B53F	Alexander Y type	
to	to					
S986	JFS986X	1982	Seddon Pennine VII	B53F	Alexander Y type	

By this time a new start had become necessary, and this was arranged on a basis of 1-50 for special vehicles, 51-300 for double-deckers, and 301 upwards for single-deckers. First in the new series were the midi-buses for the Border Courier service, replaced after two years by larger ones. The new model Leyland Tiger arrived in 1981 with Duple Dominant III bodies incorporating a toilet, and the Leyland Olympian double-decker in 1982, followed by the Metroliner in various forms in 1984. The new list now follows:

C1	HSU1T	1979	Bedford CFL	B13F	Reebur	1981
to	to					
C6	HSU6T	1979	Bedford CFL	B13F	Reebur	1981
C7	FFS7X	1981	Bedford VAS5	C17F	Reebur	
to	to					
C10	FFS10X	1981	Bedford VAS5	C17F	Reebur	
DD51	OSG51V	1979	Daimler Fleetline	H75F	E.C.W.	
to	to					(DD56 wrecked 1983)
DD75	OSG75V	1979	Daimler Fleetline	H75F	E.C.W.	
VV76	HSF76X	1981-2	Volvo Ailsa	H79F	Alexander	
to	to					
VV95	HSF95X	1981-2	Volvo Ailsa	H79F	Alexander	
HH96	ULS96X	1982	Leyland Olympian	H77F	E.C.W.	
to	to					
HH115	ULS115X	1982	Leyland Olympian	H77F	E.C.W.	

HH116 to HH135	ALS116Y to ALS135Y	1983 1983	Leyland Olympian Leyland Olympian	H77F H77F	Alexander Alexander
LL136 to LL143	A136BSC to A143BSC	1984 1984	Leyland Olympian Leyland Olympian	H77F H77F	Alexander Alexander
LL144	B144GSC	1984	Leyland Olympian	H63F	Alexander
LL145	B145GSC	1984	Leyland Olympian	H63F	Alexander
MM146	A146BSC	1984	M.C.W. Metroliner	H69D	M.C.W.
MM147	A147BSC	1984	M.C.W. Metroliner	H69D	M.C.W.
MM148	A148BSC	1984	M.C.W. Metroliner	H69D	M.C.W.
VV149 to VV158	B149GSC to B158GSC	1984 1984	Volvo Ailsa Volvo Ailsa	H81F H81F	Alexander Alexander
LL159 to LL168	B159KSC to B168KSC	1985 1985	Leyland Olympian Leyland Olympian	H77F H77F	Alexander Alexander
VV169 to VV173	B169KSC to B173KSC	1985 1985	Volvo Citybus Volvo Citybus	H84F H84F	Alexander Alexander
N301 to N310	YFS301W to YFS310W	1981 1981	Leyland National 2 Leyland National 2	B52F B52F	National National
H311 to H316	PSF311Y to PSF316Y	1982 1982	Leyland Tiger Leyland Tiger	C49F C49F	Alexander T type Alexander T type
H317 to H321	TFS317Y to TFS321Y	1983 1983	Leyland Tiger Leyland Tiger	C49F C49F	Plaxton Paramount Plaxton Paramount
L322 to L329	A322BSC to A329BSC	1984 1984	Leyland Tiger Leyland Tiger	C49F C49F	Alexander T.E. type Alexander T.E. type
L330	A330BSC	1984	Leyland Tiger	C49F	Plaxton Paramount
L331	A331BSC	1984	Leyland Tiger	C49F	Plaxton Paramount
L332	A332BSC	1984	Leyland Tiger	C49F	Plaxton Paramount
M333	A333BSC	1984	M.C.W. Metroliner	C48F	M.C.W.
M334	A334BSC	1984	M.C.W. Metroliner	C48F	M.C.W. wrecked 1985
L335 to L342	B335RLS to B342RLS	1985 1985	Leyland Tiger Leyland Tiger	C49F C49F	Plaxton Paramount Plaxton Paramount
H544 to H551	BSG544W to BSG551W	1981 1981	Leyland Tiger Leyland Tiger	C46F C46F	Duple Dominant III Duple Dominant III
H552 to H557	MSC552X to MSC557X	1981 1981	Leyland Tiger Leyland Tiger	C46F C46F	Duple Goldliner Duple Goldliner
H558 to H561	PSF558Y to PSF561Y	1982 1982	Leyland Tiger Leyland Tiger	C46F C46F	Duple Goldliner Duple Goldliner

L562	A562BSX	1984	Leyland Royal Tiger C46F	Roe-Doyen
L563	A563BSX	1984	Leyland Royal Tiger C40F	Roe-Doyen
L564	B564LSC	1985	Leyland Royal Tiger C46F	Duple Caribbean
to	to			
L569	B569LSC	1985	Leyland Royal Tiger C46F	Duple Caribbean

MM146, 147, 148, M333, 334, H544-561, L562-569 had toilet facilities. The H and HH prefixes were changed to L and LL in 1984.

An unusual coach acquired from Western S.M.T. early in 1985 should be included. This was a Seddon Pennine VII with C24F Alexander T type body, the rear half accommodating wheelchairs which gained access from a centre entrance equipped with a lifting device. It was registered MSJ389P and numbered DS389.

The normal bus livery had been improved in 1984 with lower-deck window pillars being painted cream.

The buses and coaches left in the reduced Eastern Scottish Omnibuses Ltd. fleet at June 1985 were: DD51-5, 60-70, 72-5, VV76-95, LL100-15, 117-9, 122-9, 132-42, 144-5, MM146-8, VV149-58, LL160-3, VV169-73, L311-2, 328-32, M333-4, L335-42, DS389, DD402, 405, 408, 414, 491-7, 499, 501, 503-10, L544, 550-69, S591-7, 611-3, 616-30, 635-8, 640-50, 654-9, 661, 663, 668-70, 672-3, 675, 677, 683-7, 690-1, DD692-702, 704-12, 714, 716, S747-53, 755, 759-60, VV773-82, S785-90, 793-4, 797-801, 805, 808-9, 812-9, 832, 834-9, 845, 850, DD852-3, 855-6, 859-61, S872, 876-87, 893, 896-8, 900-4, 909-11, 915, 922-3, 925-6, 931-3, 938-9, 942-4, 947-9, 951, 953-5, 958-62, 965-8, 970, 972-3, 979-82. Coaches painted in Citylink livery were: LL144-5, MM146-8, M333-4, L544-69, S747-9, S785-7.

Postscript

From its tentative first steps in 1906, the infant S.M.T. grew to a point where its influence could really be felt throughout Scotland. Its early ventures were as speculative as many that failed, but S.M.T. had dedicated and innovative management right from the start. They recognised the potential for the motor bus and played an important part in improving the vehicles to the point where the all-powerful electric tramways and steam railways had a serious challenger.

With better buses in the 1920s and 1930s, it seemed that little could stop S.M.T., and the spectacular expansion of the period was achieved by a combination of natural growth and shrewd acquisition.

The injection of railway capital allowed S.M.T. to consolidate its position with the creation of a group of companies covering much of Scotland, under the firm control of William Thomson, who kept his options open by developing an important private car sales and service organisation in parallel with the bus business.

Without the quality of management staff over the years, S.M.T. could have been ripe for acquisition by others with transport interests, but when the company sold out to the British Transport Commission in 1949, it was on S.M.T.'s terms.

Today's Eastern Scottish company is still recognisably built on the strong base of S.M.T. Its immediate operating area contracted in 1985 when S.B.G. (Scottish Bus Group) restructured, but with a sizeable network of services in Edinburgh and the Lothians, its resources are spread more rationally, allowing the company to concentrate on the markets it knows best. Its influence, though, spreads far beyond this area, a consequence both of history and continued involvement in S.B.G.'s long-distance Citylink services.

With the rest of the bus industry, Eastern Scottish is facing the uncertainties of deregulation, but its list of commercially registered services suggests that it is adopting a positive attitude towards the new legislation, and is grasping the opportunities presented.

Few British bus companies can trace their direct ancestry over 80 years, but as S.M.T., Eastern Scottish was born into an unregulated world and thrived and grew in this environment. The regulation of the 1930s brought some order into the industry, and allowed S.M.T. to consolidate its position as Scotland's principal bus operator. Now we return to a deregulated situation, with Eastern Scottish, leaner and fitter, ready to accept the challenge of the new environment.

History suggests that it will take things in its stride.

Index